Coping with Stress

ALSO BY PAUL R. ROBBINS
AND FROM MCFARLAND

---

*Anger, Aggression and Violence: An Interdisciplinary Approach* (2000)

*Adolescent Suicide* (1998)

*Romantic Relationships: A Psychologist Answers Frequently Asked Questions* (1996)

*Understanding Depression* (1993)

*The Psychology of Dreams* (1988; paperback 2005)

# Coping with Stress

## *Commonsense Strategies*

PAUL R. ROBBINS

McFarland & Company, Inc., Publishers
*Jefferson, North Carolina, and London*

Extracts from "Cadet Training: An Ethnographic Study of Stress and Coping," by Melanie A. Gold, D.O., from *Military Medicine: International Journal of ASMUS,* Vol. 165, Vol. 2, pp. 147–152, ©Military Medicine. Reprinted by permission.
Excerpts from "A Factor Analysis of Coping Behavior," by Paul R. Robbins and Roland Tanck, from *The Journal of Clinical Psychology,* 1978, Vol. 34, pp. 379–380, reprinted by permission of John Wiley & Sons.

LIBRARY OF CONGRESS CATALOGUING-IN-PUBLICATION DATA

Robbins, Paul R. (Paul Richard)
Coping with stress : commonsense strategies / Paul R. Robbins.
p. cm.
Includes bibliographical references and index.

**ISBN-13: 978-0-7864-2875-5** (∞)
(softcover : 50# alkaline paper)

1. Stress (Psychology) I. Title
BF575.S75R578 2007
155.9'042 — dc22 2006101238

British Library cataloguing data are available



Manufactured in the United States of America

*McFarland & Company, Inc., Publishers*
*Box 611, Jefferson, North Carolina 28640*
*www.mcfarlandpub.com*

To my good friends
John Muhlenberg, Marjory Larson, and Gay Neale

# *Acknowledgments*

The author wishes to express his deep appreciation to Sharon Hauge for her many contributions to the book. He would also like to thank Herschel Shosteck, Claudia Curry, Shirley Wilson and Lynn Nelson for their helpful comments. Grateful acknowledgment is also made to the following for permission to reprint excerpts from their copyrighted materials: *Military Medicine*, international journal of AMSUS, for excerpts from the paper by Melanie A. Gold and Stanford B. Friedman, "Cadet Basic Training: An Ethnographic Study of Stress and Coping," which appeared in *Military Medicine*, Volume 165, 2, pages 147–152; and John Wiley and Sons for excerpts from the paper by Paul R. Robbins and Roland H. Tanck, "A Factor Analysis of Coping Behaviors," which appeared in *The Journal of Clinical Psychology*, 1978, Volume 34, 2, pages 379–380.

# *Table of Contents*

# *Introduction*

The experience of stress is part of our human condition, a legacy of our biological inheritance. There are textbook definitions of stress which I could offer, but I'm sure we all recognize stress when we experience it. It is a feeling of extra alertness, energy, anxiety, and at its upper reaches pronounced physical symptoms such as a pounding heart and difficulties in breathing. Think of stage fright or panic attacks. Such acute stress can be very uncomfortable.

From an evolutionary point of view, stress was clearly adaptive. Our ancestors found a world filled with perils and the capacity to react quickly with the mind focused and the body fully mobilized to deal with these dangers had survival value. While most of the perils faced by our ancestors have long disappeared, the experience of stress can still be adaptive. Think of the athlete primed to run a race. The rush of adrenaline provides an edge. Or think of soldiers in combat or police and firefighters responding to an emergency. They need to be ready and in a real sense more than ready.

However, in our everyday lives in today's world, such events are clearly exceptions, not the rule. Still, we react with stress to a variety of situations which are far from life-threatening. We often feel stress in situations which are part of our ordinary routines and experiences in the classroom, on the job and in our relationships. And sometimes stress is not a transitory event; it is chronic. We can become tense, on edge over days, weeks, or even longer. The problem is that such chronic stress is not likely to be adaptive — far from it. Chronic stress can play a role in the development of a wide variety of physical problems ranging in seriousness from occasional headaches and upset stomachs to cardiovascular disease. High levels of stress tend to precede the emotional malaise of depression. Too much stress can make people irritable and difficult to get along with, injuring their relationships. Too much stress can impair one's performance on the job and in general can adversely affect one's quality of life.

With the recognition of the deleterious effects of too much stress, it is not surprising that there is widespread interest in finding ways of helping people to cope more effectively with stress. Extensive research has been undertaken on the problem and the research findings have led to the development of practical programs to deal with stress. Many companies and organizations have recognized that an overly stressed employee is not likely to be a productive employee and have instituted stress management programs.

The widespread interest in coping with stress has also shown itself in a succession of articles in the popular press. To cite a recent example, the November 2005 issue of *Consumer Reports* includes an article entitled "RX: Reduce Stress." These articles attest to the need for useful, reliable and readable information about coping with stress. This book attempts to address this need. It provides a wide-ranging look at what we know about coping with stress, what seems to be effective and what is not.

As is true for my other books on psychological topics published by McFarland & Company, the ideas advanced in this book are heavily based on research. This includes a number of my own studies on coping with stress as well as the work of many other investigators, some, like myself, psychologists, and some working in other disciplines. While I have tried to minimize the use of technical language in describing this research, I have always believed that a book on psychological topics without documentation lacks credibility. Because the research literature on coping with stress is voluminous, I have had to be selective in what I have reported. My bias has been to include more recent articles and those which seem to me particularly interesting.

This book has a point of view that I would like to make explicit. I believe that there is no magic bullet for coping with stress. There is no tried and true technique which is likely to work for everybody. Nor is there a one-size-fits-all technique which can be used for all stress-provoking situations. Rather, there are a variety of techniques that can be effective for reducing stress. I believe that if the individual chooses from this array of stress reducing techniques those which are both comfortable to use and seem helpful, he or she should gain a better sense of control over situations which are stress-provoking, and in so doing may reduce the level of stress experienced.

The book begins with a discussion of the nature of stress, looking at the effects of stress in our daily lives, considering some of the ways researchers study stress, and examining how our bodies react to stressful events. The focus then turns to the ways psychologists think about coping behaviors — how they conceptualize coping, measure it and study it. Specific techniques for coping with stress are considered, beginning with strategies for coping with stress that are generally ineffective. I believe that the way to start is to know how not to dig yourself into a deeper hole. Next, some of the strategies that are more likely to be effective in coping with stress are explored. Following that are techniques for improving some basic interpersonal skills: tuning into what other people are saying and feeling and conflict resolution. Polishing these skills can help to avoid and defuse interpersonal stress. Also considered are defensive maneuvers to deal with stress that may take place with little or no awareness. Finally, for those considering professional help, there is some basic information about drugs, psychotherapy and alternative medicine approaches.

# 1

## *Some Basics About Stress*

I have never known anyone who has not experienced stress. It is part of the human condition, hardwired into our biology. Sometimes, stress can be acute. Picture in your mind a soldier about to enter combat, a firefighter fighting a blaze, a doctor trying to resuscitate a patient in the emergency room. Sometimes, stress is prolonged, even chronic. Think of a daughter taking care of her mother afflicted with Alzheimer's disease, a father dealing with a drug-addicted son, a man or woman working day after day with a difficult, unpleasant co-worker, a couple going through a divorce, or simply the piling on of lots of little things, daily hassles that have a cumulative effect of pushing one towards one's emotional limits.

Dictionary definitions of stress may use psychological terms such as being under a mental or emotional strain or they may highlight the body's reaction to situations involving pain or hazard. Both the psychological state and the body's reaction are important components of the feeling we call stress.

The experience of stress can be a complex of feelings. Fear when stress is acute, and anxiety, irritability, and resentment when it is chronic. A vague discomfort and frequent bouts of worrying are the background noises of chronic stress. And when people find themselves in situations that in the past have often aroused stress, there may be a heightened sense of being apprehensive, on guard.

For many people, the emotions of stress are unpleasant and unwelcome. As we shall see, stress predisposes one to develop physical symptoms. And, stress can make a trial of sleep.

I don't know of any other word in the English language which has quite the same meaning as stress. Feeling under a strain or experiencing tension may be as close as anything. Feeling anxious or jittery are clearly related states, but one can have these feelings without any clear reason. Sometimes, people who experience the emotional turbulence of panic attacks can't point to anything specific which triggered them. When one is feeling stress, however, one can usually quickly point out one or perhaps a number of reasons for feeling this way. These reasons we point to — the situations that cause stress — are called stressors.

Researchers sometimes draw a distinction between stress situations that are physical in nature (e.g., jumping from an airplane in a parachute) and those which are social in nature (e.g., asking someone out on a date when you feel you might be turned down). The distinction, however, can get blurred, for the parachute jumper might have a group of buddies urging him to jump. The individual might feel very frightened at the prospect of jumping into space, but jumps anyway because he doesn't want to lose face. For most of us living in contemporary America, the stressors we encounter tend to be social — or to be more precise, social-psychological. Such stressors may arise in almost any significant area of our lives. Three of the more ubiquitous sources of stress in our culture are the school, the job, and our relationships.

School is a good place to start. Some children suffer from such a severe case of school phobia that their parents can hardly drag them to school. Stress among college students is widespread. My colleague, Roland Tanck, and I once carried out a study of stress reported by college students.[1] We asked the students to fill out a diary every night over a 10 day period. In the diary we asked the students to respond to some specific questions. One of the questions was, "Did you feel under any pressure or stress today relating to your school work?" We found that during the ten day period 95 percent of the students reported that they felt pressure stemming from their school work. On the average they felt such pressure on half of the days in which they completed the diaries.

In the diary we also asked the students to respond to a more general question: "Did you feel tense or anxious today?" and, *if yes*, "What do you think was causing these feelings?" Here are some typical responses.

"Term paper due tomorrow."

"School work pressures."

"Anxiety about the upcoming test."

"School, a friend of mine and I had a disagreement, my job, it was generally a down day."

"The exam."

"Knowing how much school work I have to do and feeling angry with myself for not having done anything over the weekend."

"I wish I knew so I could stop it."

In reading through the responses to this question in hundreds of diaries, we found some references to interpersonal conflicts, often with boyfriends, girlfriends or roommates, and occasional references to one's job or family, but as might be expected in a sample of university students, the lion's share of reported tension was generated by pressures stemming from school work and particularly by upcoming exams. Anxiety is often anticipatory in nature and for many of the students it seemed to reach a peak as the day of the exam approached. For many students, actually beginning the test, just getting started answering the questions can be a relief, but for some, the stress during the exam itself can become so intense that they freeze, paying more attention to their own thoughts and distress than to answering the questions. When stress reaches such high levels, one's ability to perform can become a casualty.

A recent study of sixth and ninth graders carried out in Sweden found that the youngsters who reported feeling higher levels of stress before taking a test of reading and arithmetical skills did less well on the test.[2] Those who entered the testing situation with a mind-set of worry and self-doubt showed higher levels of the stress hormone cortisol during the exam. The youngsters who felt that they were in control of the situation did not show a comparable rise in cortisol levels. There is an important idea here that we shall come back to again — that when we have developed ways to cope with stress that give us a sense of control, we can lessen the impact of stressors when they arise.

Most of us can appreciate the tension students may feel about taking examinations because we have been there ourselves. The anticipation of an examination or even the memory of exams in the past can work their way into our unconscious. Have you ever dreamed about being late for an exam? Or somehow not being able to find the classroom? Or even the building? Such dreams are common enough. Or how about having a dream of taking an exam and being baffled by a question? You look at the clock; it is moving ever onward. And for a moment you may experience a moment of acute anxiety.

Let's turn to stress on the job. While many jobs are rewarding and satisfying, there is no denying that stress is commonplace in the workplace.

Job-related stress has been the subject of articles in both scientific journals and popular magazines. In May 1999, the banner headline of the American Psychological Association's publication *The Monitor* stated that stress in the workplace was reaching the critical point.[3] The lead article went on to state that American workers were working harder and longer and leaving people more at risk than ever to develop psychological problems. Recent studies have confirmed this assertion. Not only do large numbers of people continue to experience stress in the workplace, this stress is associated with both poorer physical and mental health. For example, researchers carrying out a survey on over 9000 people working in a wide variety of occupations in Quebec, Canada, found that such work related conditions as physical and psychological demands, irregular schedules, and workplace harassment were linked to psychological distress.[4] In discussing their findings, the researchers used the term *pathogenic* to describe workplace conditions that fostered such distress. Along the same lines, British researchers conducting a long-range study of the health of white-collar civil service workers reported strong associations between self reports of job insecurity and poorer physical and mental health.[5] Can a job make you sick? The answer is apparently yes.

Dan Jamieson is a case in point. The conflicts he has experienced about his job have aroused so much stress that he feels queasy as Monday morning approaches. On Sunday nights, he can hardly sleep. Dan, a tall lanky man now in his 50s, has been teaching for almost 30 years. Dan is an idealistic person who chose a life of service. He has always found it extremely gratifying to see his students learning, growing, and developing the skills needed for successful careers. He is fond of talking about his students who have gone on to medical schools and become doctors. But, in Dan's opinion, teaching school is not what it used to be. In his school, many of the students are insufficiently prepared, show little interest in learning, and only seem to be passing time. He has found it difficult to reach the students and to motivate them to learn. To compound the problem, academic standards in his school have eroded. The school's administrators have been under pressure from the state to maintain graduation rates and seem more concerned with keeping up the statistics than whether the students are learning. There is a not too subtle pressure to simply pass students on — what we call social promotion — and this has put Dan in direct conflict with the administrators and the implicit policies of the school. Dan feels a constant tug between what he feels is right and what he is being pressured to do. He has become increasingly uncomfortable and unhappy with his job and often dreads the thought of going to work.

The sources of stress on the job are many and varied. They include the demands of the job itself, the relationships of the employees with their supervisors, the relationships of the employees themselves, and the physical and psychological characteristics of the work environment. Problems and conflicts can arise in any of these areas resulting in stress for the employee.

Every job has its demand requirements. Things that have to be done, often more than one task at a time, and sometimes under the pressure of deadlines. For many people, multitasking under time pressure can be very stressful. Think of a hectic office in which phone calls are coming in right and left, a crowded restaurant in which the chefs have to turn out one meal after another to sometimes impatient customers, or even more stressful an air traffic controller trying to guide pilots in and out of airports, keeping a safe distance between them, with no room for making a mistake. Or consider a job on the other extreme, the grind of working on an assembly line, doing the same monotonous task day in and day out. Consider yourself among the fortunate if you find the work you are doing interesting and you can do it at a comfortable pace.

The state of the nation's economy, the competitive pressures from globalization, and rapid changes in technology can all have a direct impact on the security of one's job. The business cycle with its expansion and contraction and attendant layoffs and a fairly rapid movement of workers from one job to another forces continuing adjustments among workers. With increasing frequency, American workers must adapt to new situations, new co-workers, new technologies, and new communities in which to live. And as we shall see, research shows that major changes in life, whether unemployment or relocation, can engender stress for both the worker and the family.

The relationships in the workplace are a major source of both satisfaction and stress. The people you work with can become close friends and confidants that you enjoy seeing every day. People can also be difficult. Most of us can think of co-workers whom we really liked and perhaps a few who we wished worked elsewhere.

For many Americans, the workplace is structured in a way that fosters competition. Large organizations are typically set up in a pyramid structure with a few high-paying positions at the top of the pyramid and many lower paying positions as one approaches the bottom. The people at the bottom want to move up; the people at the top want to hang on. In such a structure, some interpersonal conflict seems almost inevitable. Movement up this ladder may be based on merit, personal aggressiveness, networking, and sometimes measures which step over the line of normative workplace behavior. A patient of mine described the atmosphere of her work place as "semi-paranoid," a place where watching one's backside was necessary for survival. She used the term "sharking" to describe some of the questionable maneuvers co-workers employed to gain a competitive advantage.

Perhaps it is the competitive struggle to get ahead or merely hang on to one's job, perhaps it is stress levels generated in other aspects of life, but whatever the cause, there is a considerable verbal abuse of employees on the job. Writing in the *Monitor on Psychology*, Jennifer Daw noted a survey of over 1000 American employees which suggested that the workplace can become an acrimonious environment.[6] Nearly half of the respondents reported that yelling and verbal abuse were common in their workplaces. Statistics collected for the year 1996 indicated that more than 18,000 nonfatal assaults were reported in the workplace.

Even when one's place of work is essentially free of such pathological elements, there are usually stressors aplenty facing many employees. The day may begin very early with the need to deposit young children at daycare centers to be followed by commuting through rush-hour traffic. At the office, there may be deadlines to meet, meetings to attend, eyestrain from staring at a computer monitor for hours on end, worries about evaluation, and then another rush hour commute to return home to deal with family responsibilities. And what if something goes wrong along the way? Where is there time to fix things?

For many people, jobs are a generally pleasant, meaningful way to spend the day. For others, jobs can be a headache, only it takes more than an aspirin to fix things.

Our third area of discussion, interpersonal relations, has been a source of stress, at one time or another, for almost everyone.

Interpersonal stresses which occur within the family and within dating and marital relationships can be the most wrenching of all. For these individuals are the people that mean most to us, and to have things grow tense, even sour, in such relationships can create a mix of very uncomfortable feelings. Tensions among intimates have been grist for the mill for poets and novelists and how many songs have been written about cheating hearts, lonely hearts, and broken hearts?

I have worked in therapy with many single people whose tension-filled relationships have brought them to the point of despair. Stress in the marital relationship can even be more fundamentally distressing, for this can tear into the fabric of the life one has built. Sharing a home, life, and bed with a partner when the relationship has gone sour is at best joyless. More often, it is punctuated by acrimony. If the situation is allowed to fester, both partners may build up a mental file cabinet filled with grievances. These accumulating resentments may spill over into heated, full scale clashes. One may escape, albeit briefly, from difficulties on the job or at school, but it is difficult to escape for long from a tension-filled marriage. And giving up on one's marriage often means the shattering of one's dreams.

The pervasive effects of marital discord on everyday functioning were neatly demonstrated in a study carried out by a research team led by Rosalind Barnett at Brandeis University.[7] Middle-aged adults were assessed by a self-reporting psychological instrument for the number of marital concerns they were experiencing. Then, during a working day the subjects were monitored for self reported stress, blood pressure, and the stress hormone cortisol. The men and women studied who reported more marital concerns experienced more stress during the day, had higher blood pressure, and a flattened cortisol slope over the day. These findings suggest that domestic strains have an impact beyond the tension filled interactions at home and may have a lingering effect on the other activities of daily life.

My own research carried out with Arnold Meyersburg and Roland Tanck have shown that the psychological experience of interpersonal stress often combines a mix of emotions which include anxiety, frustration, and feeling rebuffed, plus healthy doses of anger, expressed and unexpressed.[8] Have you ever been in a situation where you believe you have been treated unfairly and at times feel aggrieved, yet at the same time the person who aroused these negative feelings is someone who is very important to you — your spouse, a girlfriend or boyfriend, a parent or even your child? This mix of emotions is a common everyday experience. At times, you may feel like screaming at the person who caused you this distress, yet you know deep down this is not what you want. What you really want is a restoration of peace, harmony, and love.

One of the components of interpersonal stress that is particularly difficult to deal with is anger. When you feel that others are giving you a difficult time or treating you unfairly, when you feel rejected repeatedly, feelings of anger are likely to emerge and build up. Not only are chronic feelings of anger very uncomfortable, such feelings can distract you from focusing on the tasks that are part of your daily routines.

## *The Study of Stress*

Researchers approach the study of stress in two fundamental ways. The first is to question people about the stress they have experienced in their lives. The second is to carry out experiments. In the first approach, this often means conducting interviews with and giving psychological tests to people who have experienced a recent event which is generally recognized as stressful, such as being present during a natural disaster or a man-made trauma such as a terrorist attack. Another variant of this approach is to study patients who have been diagnosed with various types of stress disorders.

The interview has always been an important tool for learning about the details of an event or events experienced. This has been true in such diverse endeavors as police work, social science research, and clinical work with patients. In interviews seeking to learn about a person's experience with stress, the researcher might elect to focus on current stressful events or he or she could be interested in learning about past events, particularly if the focus of the study is on reactions to natural or man-made disasters. In a study in which data gathering resources are limited, the researcher might have to rely on a single interview. In addition to asking questions about the events and about the person's immediate and longer-term reactions, specific questions would probably be included inquiring about both physiological and psychological symptoms of stress. When psychological tests are given, they are usually self administered.

Occasionally, researchers have gone beyond the use of these conventional methods and have taken a longer and more thorough look at what is going on. A case in point would be a study carried out on West Point cadets in which the researchers actually lived with the cadets over a period of time, observing them, talking with them, and even participating with them in selected field activities such as road marching and physical training. This method of data gathering, called participant-observation, was borrowed from anthropology. While participant observation takes a great deal of time and energy, it provides a detailed, first-hand view of a phenomenon which can be invaluable, particularly in the early stages of research on a topic. The researchers in the West Point study, Melanie Gold and Stanford Friedman, noted that among the chief sources of stress for the cadets were time-management pressures, sleep deprivation, conflicts between the emphasis on teamwork and competitive grading, and inexperience in a leadership role.

Being there, listening and observing enabled the researchers at West Point to obtain a real grasp of the stressors that were part and parcel of cadet training. You can see the richness of the data obtained from participant-observation in these examples of comments recorded from upper-class cadets.

"The stress is put on you to perform by the cadre and your classmates because you don't want to make a mistake and because you are ignorant of what is expected or what actions are right or wrong. You fear making a mistake and you fear the consequences."[9]

"The new cadets only know the schedule for the day's activities one day in advance unless their cadre chooses to tell them. This is part of the stress ... at West Point, you never know what activity or experience will happen more than a day in advance."

"It is a shock, a culture shock, when you come out of high school and you were everything, and then you come here [West Point] and, as a plebe, you are nothing."

"The worst stress I ever had was trying to prepare for a course that I was failing. I stayed up 36 hours straight trying to prepare."

Interestingly, an account of life in West Point 160 years ago suggests that many of the stressors these researchers noted were evident then as well.[10] Fashioning a young person into an officer has been and remains a pressure-filled business.

One of the indicators that researchers have used as a measure of stress is the experience of major changes in the individual's life. By major life changes, we mean such events as leaving home for the first time, getting married or divorced, having children, changing jobs, moving from one place to another, and retiring. When a person makes a major life change, there may be gains or losses involved. In time, the gains may outweigh the losses, but there will be a period of adjustment which can be quite stressful. A common example would be the couple in their late

60s who lived in a cold, northern city and decided to move to Florida. All the familiar aspects of their lives are suddenly gone — friends, family, church — and now, while they are warmer in the winter, they don't know a soul. The stress caused by the change should eventually fade, but for a time it is an unpleasant reality. And, of course, there are some major changes which are simply negative, through and through, like the death of a loved one. Such losses can be agonizing and difficult to come to terms with.

In using major life changes as an index of stress, it is usually assumed that the more of these major changes the person goes through, the higher level of stress is experienced.

The second basic approach to studying stress is to induce stress experimentally. This approach raises obvious ethical problems. Creating stress can be inconsistent with the ethical imperative for researchers of doing no harm. The solution to this dilemma has often been to use mild stressors, such as immersing the hand of the subject in very cold water, exposing the subject to loud noise, or asking the subject to do mental arithmetic under time pressure. I remember when I was in graduate school, I participated in an experiment in which people were given mild electric shocks to study the effects of punishment on the perception of ambiguous figures. When I tried the shocks on myself, I could see why it was so difficult to recruit people.

It is possible to intensify the stress levels in experiments by informing the subjects that the procedure they are about to try is really a test of an important personal characteristic such as mental acuity or intelligence and further that they are in competition with others in performing the test and are being closely evaluated. If such deception is used to increase the threat level, it is absolutely mandatory that the subjects are quickly debriefed about the true nature of the experiment.

Even a mild stressor can have an effect, although I suspect it is likely to be transitory. A group of investigators working in Germany played road traffic noise through loudspeakers while a group of men were trying to participate in a seminar. About half of the men exposed to the constant noise experienced both psychological stress and physiological reactions.[11] Noise-sensitive subjects reacted the most. Think of the delivery truck and taxicab drivers who make their living by daily driving in the noisy, congested streets of our great cities. If some of these drivers get irritable, it is small wonder.

Such solutions to the dilemma of putting subjects under real stress yet being above board and ethical about it are far from ideal. Mild stressors, while effective, may have too small an impact to fully study the effects of stress and deception isn't a happy choice. One alternative which I like is to study people who have chosen to venture into authentically stressful situations. While there is a problem here in that such subjects are probably not representative of the general population in important ways, using such subjects makes it possible to conduct controlled experiments which are both realistic and raise fewer ethical problems. Here is an example of such a study. The researchers, led by James Meyerhoff of the Walter Reed Army Institute of Research, recruited police trainees who were about to graduate from the Federal Law Enforcement Training Center.[12] All of the subjects were volunteers. They took part in a live, simulated hostage situation in which they were involved in exchanging gunfire at close range using nonlethal ammunition (simunitions). The subjects were provided minimal cover and had to make very rapid decisions. The details of the staged situation provided in the report, which was published in the *Annals of The New York Academy of Sciences*, are sketchy but it sounds like something one might see on a prime-time television crime show.

The trainees reacted physiologically with increased heart rate and blood pressure and elevated levels of the stress hormone cortisol. The performance of the subjects under such stress was far from ideal. Despite extensive training, many of the recruits did not react well under pressure. Most telling was the statistic that 19 percent of the subjects (nearly one in five) shot the hostage. What I found particularly interesting (as well as counterintuitive) was that the subjects with the most pronounced physiological stress reactions performed better. I would have expected very strong reactions to be associated with poor performance, but it wasn't.

Another approach in stress experiments is to tailor the stressor to the individual subjects. An illustration of this approach was a study of the physiological reactions of couples under stress.[13] Recently married couples (volunteers for the study) were asked to discuss two or three types of marital conflicts that were judged by the researchers to be most reflective of their own marriage and to try to resolve them. While the spouses talked about these sensitive issues, they were videotaped and their behaviors toward one another were subsequently evaluated by analysts using an objective coding system. Before, during, and after the interviews, blood samples were drawn from both spouses to allow measurements of the levels of the stress hormones cortisol, epinephrine, and norepinephrine. Perhaps the most interesting finding was that when a wife was coded as acting negatively toward her husband (i.e., being critical, disagreeing, interrupting), and he subsequently withdrew, the woman experienced a rise in the level of stress hormones. It was as if the closeness that she valued in the marriage had suddenly gone, and she reacted internally.

## *Stress and the Body*

We have alluded briefly to some of the body's reactions when the individual is exposed to stressors. Now, let's look at these reactions in more detail.

Many of us received our introduction to the body's reaction to stress-provoking situations with the "fight or flight" paradigm annunciated by Walter Cannon.[14] When we perceive emergency or threatening situations, the body quickly mobilizes to increase the chances of effectively dealing with the situation. The heart pumps blood faster, blood pressure increases, the airways dilate, the digestive processes are put on the back burner, the pupils dilate, and the person becomes more vigilant. As we have suggested, any number of situations can elicit such responses. Hans Selye, the godfather of stress research, was the theorist who labeled such situations as stressors; he thought of the body's reaction as stress.[15] However, today, we usually think of stress not only as the body's reaction to stressors, but the subjective experience as well.

Through the work of Selye and the many researchers who have followed in his footsteps, the body's mechanisms of responding to stressors are now better understood. Utilizing a series of hormonal secretions, one chain of events takes place involving what is called the HPA axis. H stands for the hypothalamus, a small area deep within the brain that receives input from virtually all areas of the central nervous system. The hypothalamus releases a hormone called CRH that stimulates P (the pituitary gland), which is located in a bony cavity in the base of the skull. The pituitary gland, in turn, secretes a hormone, ACTH, which regulates the actions of A (the adrenal cortex), the outer part of the adrenal glands, which are located in the chest cavity next to the kidneys. The adrenal cortex then secretes a hormone, cortisol, into the bloodstream. Cortisol has been called the stress hormone.

Cortisol has a multiplicity of physiological effects. It plays a role in the regulation of blood pressure and the way the body uses its carbohydrates, proteins, and fats — its sources of energy. When cortisol is secreted, the brain receives more glucose for energy and fat cells are released into the muscles. The body has primed itself to better support action.

Cortisol levels can be assessed through analysis of blood samples or alternatively through collection of saliva samples. The use of saliva makes it easier to take repeated measurements of cortisol during an experiment. Measurements of cortisol give researchers an important physiological measure of stress levels to complement self report psychological measures. In the absence of stressors, cortisol levels are by no means static. Cortisol levels normally fluctuate during the day with highest levels around daybreak and lowest levels around midnight.

The secretion of cortisol in response to stressors has been demonstrated in many experiments such as the one we just described involving police trainees. As such, cortisol levels have often been used as an indicator of stress.

Selye believed that the HPA axis could be activated by all types of stressors, but a recent analysis of a large body of research indicates that stressors are by no means equal in their capability of stimulating the release of cortisol. UCLA psychologists Sally Dickerson and Margaret Kemeny examined over 200 laboratory studies in which various stressors (e.g., exposure to noise, public speaking, doing mental arithmetic) were examined for their effects on cortisol levels.[16] The researchers were able to assess what the overall trend was for the studies using a statistical technique called meta-analysis.[17] While the analysis confirmed that, in general, psychological stressors increased cortisol levels, stressors differed appreciably in their effects on cortisol. Perhaps most important, the researchers identified two characteristics of stressors that were associated with higher cortisol levels. The first characteristic was a situation where the stressor was likely to evoke a perception that the subject was being socially evaluated. If the experimental procedure could threaten a person's status in the eyes of others, that others could think less well of the person, this situation heightened the impact on cortisol levels. Having to give a speech with the perception that you are being evaluated or having to do mental arithmetic while someone was scoring your performance, these are the kinds of stressors that boosted cortisol levels in the laboratory.

One can easily extrapolate from these laboratory experiments to situations in the real world. How about giving a report in a meeting at work to your peers and supervisors or being called on at school to answer a difficult math problem, or trying to turn out a terrific meal for a large dinner party when you are under time pressure?

The other factor that the researchers identified as associated with higher cortisol levels was an uncontrollable outcome. Think of a person who is waiting for the results of a biopsy for a suspicious growth. He or she can do nothing to affect the results — whether the growth is benign or malignant. For the typical interpersonal stress situations of everyday life, people may feel varying degrees of control. When one believes that a conversation is going badly and is getting out of control, such as a heated argument between spouses, the results of the meta-analysis suggest that cortisol levels are likely to rise.

When stress arousing situations come to an end, cortisol levels usually return to normal levels. The process, however, is not instantaneous. Dickerson and Kemeny's analysis suggests that returning to normal may take forty minutes or so. Cortisol elevations brought on by socially evaluated, uncontrollable stressors are likely to persist longer than stressors without these characteristics.

In addition to the secretion of cortisol via the HPA axis, the body also secretes other substances in response to stressors. These substances are called catacholamines and include epinephrine and norepinephrine. Epinephrine is better known as adrenaline. The secretion of these hormones is the work of what is called the SAM system. In this system, signals coming from the hypothalamus via the sympathetic nervous system innervates the adrenal medulla (the inner portion of the adrenal gland) which secretes these chemicals into the bloodstream preparing the body for Cannon's fight or flight response. People often refer to the feeling that accompanies this action as a surge or rush of adrenaline.

While the basic neuroendrocine response to stressors is the same for males and females, the secretion of cortisol and catecholamines into the bloodstream in females may be less likely to evidence a fight or flight reaction. A group of psychologists at the University of California at Los Angeles, led by Shelley Taylor, has noted that for a variety of reasons — biological, social, and evolutionary — women are less likely to either fight or flee, and more likely to tend and befriend.[18] Under stress, they may give care to their children and look for support, particularly from other women. These ideas are an important qualification to thinking about stress reactions simply as a fight or flight stance.

## *Stress and the Brain*

We have long known that some parts of the brain such as the hypothalamus play a critical role in mediating our response to stressors. Now, with the aid of new technologies such as brain imaging techniques, scientists are learning more and more about how various structures in the brain are involved in our response to stressors. Two of the brain imaging techniques that have been frequently used in these studies are functional magnetic resonance imaging (fMRI) and positron emission tomography (PET). FMRI is an adaptation of the familiar MRI that is routinely used to image structures in the body that have been damaged by injuries or disease. FMRI is an non-invasive procedure that uses radio waves to image brain activity. As the use of PET may be unfamiliar, I will try to convey a sense of what takes place.

Imagine you have volunteered to be a research subject in an experiment which uses PET. The setting is a research laboratory in a medical center. It is a pleasant enough, but antiseptic room. You're lying on a comfortable couch. Your head is positioned inside a large, doughnut-shaped device. You are asked to keep your head very still. The researcher, let's say she is a young woman dressed in a laboratory coat, stands next to the couch. She tells you to visualize a pleasant scene in your mind, perhaps a man and a woman standing next to each other on the beach. Later she might ask you to visualize an unpleasant, stress arousing scene like victims being taken away from an automobile wreck

While you are following these instructions, you receive a short infusion of a chemical. You know the chemical now moving within your bloodstream contains a radioactive substance. The idea troubles you at first, but the lead investigator of the study has assured you that the dose would be minimal, similar to what you might receive from an x-ray

The young lady in the white coat continues to give you instructions to visualize scenes as the infusion of the chemical continues. Overhead, the doughnut-shaped device has been monitoring what is happening in your brain. To be more precise, what is happening in a certain narrow area of your brain which is of special interest to the research team.

Some time later, you will be thanked and debriefed and later still, the researchers will process the data. They will need the aid of computers, for the data is complex. Eventually, the researchers will come up with numbers, which they can subject to conventional statistical analysis. And, they can also stare at almost surreal images of the brain, colored this hue or that to represent brain activity or lack of activity.

To backtrack for a moment, the radioactive chemical used in the procedure releases elemental particles called positrons. When these particles collide with electrons, gamma rays are emitted from the subject's body where they are detected by the PET scanner that partially encloses the subject's head. And as we indicated, computers analyze these data, transforming them into visualizations of the functioning of the brain.

PET presents the researchers with various options to measure brain activity. The researchers might be interested in measuring oxygen metabolism, sugar metabolism, or cerebral blood flow. The measure of cerebral blood flow perhaps lends itself best to intuitive understanding. Stated simply, where blood flow increases in a part of the brain, that part of the brain is more active. When blood flow lessens, the activity level of that part of the brain decreases. Using regional blood flow measured by PET, it is possible to carry out some interesting experiments that tell the researcher which brain structures are involved in our responses to stressors.

Typically, research subjects are asked to mentally respond to different types of stimulation while undergoing PET. Here is an example. A research team, led by Lisa Shin, working in the psychiatric neuroscience program at the Massachusetts General Hospital, obtained PET data from women who had been sexually abused as children.[19] Before the brain imaging was carried out, the women provided the researchers with written descriptions of two neutral memories and two of their most stressful sexual abuse memories. During the scans the women closed their eyes, and then recalled and imagined these neutral and traumatic memories as vividly as possible. Remembering the sexual abuse incident was clearly stressful; there were rises in both heart rate and blood pressure, particularly among the women who had been diagnosed as suffering from post-traumatic stress disorder. One of these women experienced a flashback during the experiment, feeling that she was reliving the event again and had little awareness of her present surroundings. Clearly, using research subjects with severe problems presents some risk, although the negative effects are likely to be transitory and self-limiting.

PET revealed that compared to the reaction from neutral memories, imagining the sexual abuse memories was associated with increased regional blood flow in the orbitofrontal cortex and anterior temporal poles. Women who had been diagnosed with post-traumatic stress disorder showed the greatest increase in cerebral blood flow.

While much remains to be learned about the details, the prefrontal cortex appears to be one of the areas of the brain that is involved in processing emotions and this includes stress. Interestingly, research suggests that the two sides of the prefrontal cortex may be differently involved in this processing. Reviewing research on this problem in the *Psychological Bulletin*, Richard Davidson and his colleagues noted that, "We know that the prefrontal cortex is associated with emotional processing and there appears to be asymmetries in how the prefrontal cortex functions. Sectors of the left prefrontal cortex seem more associated with positive emotions while sectors in the right prefrontal cortex seen more associated with negative emotions."[20]

Deep within the brain there is another structure, this one small and almond shaped, which is clearly involved in acute stress reactions. This structure is called the amygdala. In a review article on cognitive neuroscience, Thomas Albright and his colleagues suggested that the amygdala may play a critical role in the expression of emotions.[21] They view the amygdala as intervening between the brain stem and hypothalamus (structures which are concerned with the bodily manifestations of emotion such as the pounding heart) and the newer areas of the brain such as the prefrontal cortices which are concerned with conscious feeling. Electrical stimulation of the amygdala in human subjects produces feelings of fear. Damage to the amygdala in animals produces tameness. Experimental psychologists have long known how to condition fear in an animal; they may play a tone, and then administer an electric shock. In time, fear will be elicited by the tone. We now know that a part of the amygdala is required for the memory of this pairing and the resulting conditioned fear.

People who have suffered discrete lesions of the amygdala have difficulty recognizing facial signs of fear in others, but seem to be able to recognize other emotions. Brain imaging studies of patients with anxiety disorders indicate that when these patients are exposed to stimuli that provoke anxiety reactions, the amygdala is activated. People with social phobias, for example, show amygdala activity when viewing pictures of human faces. It has been suggested that the amygdala plays an important role in our initial learning about threats and in the expression of fear. Interestingly, the administration of cocaine with its resulting high may significantly deactivate the amygdala. And damage to the structure may weaken our ability to recognize new situations that we should fear.[22]

PET and fMRI studies of brain activity have been made of combat veterans suffering from post-traumatic stress disorder.[23] During the scans, the veterans are exposed to fear arousing stimuli. Some researchers have reported exaggerated amygdala responses during this exposure. Considerable work is now going on with both animal and human subjects to better understand the role of this important structure in mediating stress.

## *Stress and the Immune System*

While the actions of the HPA and SAM systems are the most visible ways in which the body reacts to stressors, there are additional, more subtle ways as well. One of the paths in which stress impacts the body is its effects on the immune system. A host of pathogens — bacteria, viruses, parasites, and fungi can infect the body and it is the task of the immune system to identify such harmful organisms and eliminate them. The immune system consists of a variety of specialized cells that originate in the bone marrow and remain sequestered in organs such as the spleen until released into the bloodstream. A badly compromised immune system, such as occurs with AIDS, can lead to the development of opportunistic infections. There is evidence that chronic stress is associated with decreases in immune functioning. The consequences of such immunosuppression for the health of the individual are not entirely clear.

It is very interesting that the immune system's response to acute stress appears quite different from its response to chronic stress. Far from being suppressed in its response to acute stress, the immune system becomes activated. In laboratory studies, the response of the immune system to acute experimental stressors such as public speaking or doing mental arithmetic is to increase immune activity, particularly natural immunity, the first line of defense against infection. In a paper entitled "Psychological stresses and the human immune system: A meta-analytic study of 30 years of inquiry," Suzanne Segerstrom and Gregory

Miller noted, "The most robust effect of this kind of experience was a marked increase in the number of natural killer cells ... and large granular lymphocytes in peripheral blood."[24] These authors view the response of the immune system to acute stress as an adaptive response; the immune system is acting as if the individual were facing a threat that might involve injury and subsequent infection. From an evolutionary perspective, this would certainly have been adaptive for our distant ancestors who frequently faced physical threats. The noninvasive laboratory stressors used in today's experiments are not likely to cause either injury or infection, but the immune system is still programmed to react. Segerstrom and Miller noted that the immune system's response to acute stress seemed "consistent with the view that acute stressors caused immune cells to redistribute into the compartments in which they will be most effective."[25] When these authors went on to discuss the contrasting response to chronic stress, they noted that "the most chronic stressors were associated with the most global immunosuppression, as they were associated with reliable decreases in almost all functional immune measures examined. Increasing stressor duration, therefore, resulted in a change from potentially adaptive changes to potentially detrimental changes, initially in cellular immunity and then in immune function more broadly."[26]

While the reaction of the immune system to acute stressors may be viewed from an evolutionary perspective as an adaptive mechanism, the reaction of the immune system to chronic stress suggests the image of an army demobilizing after a war. Segerstrom and Miller noted that chronic stressors "have a negative effect on almost all functional measures of the immune system. Both natural and specific immunity were negatively affected."[27]

A demonstration of the possible effects of chronic stress on the immune system comes from a study of the people who lived near the Three Mile Island nuclear power plant, which sustained a serious nuclear accident in 1979.[28] A team led by Andrew Baum reported that the people in the community experienced high levels of stress for some time following the accident. Radioactive gas and water remained trapped in the containment building and the people not only worried about their safety but also had to think about possible effects on their health. Long after the accident, the residents evidenced lower levels of immune functioning than a matched control group of people living in another area.

Other examples of investigations which suggest a link between chronic stress and lowered immune system functioning include research which studied women who had lost their jobs and a study of the effects of caring for relatives who had Alzheimer's disease.[29] The first study, carried out in Sweden, found that after nine months of unemployment, the women showed evidence of reduced immune response. In the second study, the stress of caring for a family member with Alzheimer's disease was also associated with lowered immune response.[30] In reviewing the studies in *The Psychological Bulletin,* Ann O'Leary suggested that "prolonged stress may result in prolonged immunosuppression."[31]

A short exposure to a stress situation is not likely to cause any real problems for the immune system. The immune system is too robust for that and has too many built in redundancies. But, long term stress could pose a problem and this could be particularly true for elderly people whose immune systems may have lost some of their resiliency. And, where it is clearly important to keep the immune system functioning at top levels, as is true for AIDS patients, it seems prudent to do whatever one can to keep patients' stress levels down.

There are other, more circuitous links between stress and the health of the body. People experiencing chronic stress may sleep poorly, eat carelessly, perhaps drink too much, and generally not take very good care of themselves. Indifferent health habits may be mirrored in not seeking timely medical care when needed. Problems may develop with their health which were preventable.

## *Stress and Illness*

Stress is often associated with disease. However, it is not always easy to disentangle what is cause and what is effect. There is little doubt that chronic stress can play a role, sometimes an important role in bringing on certain diseases. However, it is also true that having a disease which is painful, disabling or disfiguring can be a chronic source of stress. Losing one's ability to do the normal things one has been doing in life can be very distressing, very difficult to come to terms with. With this caveat that the relation between stress and disease can be multisided, let us look at some of the research evidence that links stress to illness.

The research evidence suggests that high levels of stress increase the chances of a person becoming ill. This includes both physical illness and emotional illness such as depression. Indeed, stress sometimes acts as a trigger for emotional and mental illnesses. Stress can play a role in both garden-variety physical complaints such as headaches and gastrointestinal complaints as well as in some major diseases such as cardiovascular disease.

Let's consider the relation of stress and the garden variety physical symptoms most of us experience. A study carried out by Arnold Meyersburg, Roland Tanck, and myself using our diary technique provides a good illustration of the association.[32] Every night for a period of 10 days university students responded to a group of questions which allowed us to derive a score for interpersonal stress. Some examples of items in the measure were, "Did you feel trapped in an uncomfortable situation that you wanted to get out of?" "Did you feel rebuffed or hurt by someone today?" and, "Did you feel angry or annoyed today?" The students also responded to a short checklist of physical complaints. We found a clear relation between the level of interpersonal stress reported for the 10 days and the number of physical complaints reported. A variety of symptoms in our checklist, headaches, dizziness, weakness, colds and back pain, were associated with interpersonal stress. It would seem that the association of stress with reports of physical complaints was widespread.

In our study, on the days when physical symptoms were reported, interpersonal stress was also reported at high levels. We thought that it might be possible that high stress levels would also precede the days in which symptoms were reported, but that was not the case. Several years later, we replicated the study and once again found that the measure of interpersonal stress was related to the report of physical symptoms.[33]

The experience of stress, of course, may not be confined to the day of the unpleasant event. Thinking about an impending situation that is feared or dreaded is often itself distressing, and can create a chronic state of stress. When a person is anticipating an upcoming event which has serious implications, when the situation seems to be uncontrollable, and when that period of anticipation is prolonged — these scenarios create the ideal environment for the development of physical symptoms. A carefully carried out study in the mid–1970s provides a nice demonstration of this.[34] The investigators, a team of physicians and sociologists led by Stanislaus Kasl, collected data from male blue-collar workers employed in two manufacturing plants — one produced paint, the other display fixtures. Both plants were scheduled to permanently shut down which would result in job loss for all of the employees. During the weeks preceding the plant closedowns, the workers filled out a daily health diary. The researchers found that the number of days in which the employees reported that they felt less well than usual was higher than reported by a control group of comparable workers who were not facing the threat of losing their jobs.

The conclusions from our study and the study carried out by Kasl and his colleagues were based on the self reports of patients about the physical complaints they were experiencing. Sheldon Cohen and a group of researchers at the University of Pittsburgh Medical Center studied the impact of stress on disease in a way which I find very convincing.[35] Cohen's team first interviewed their subjects (volunteers recruited through newspaper ads) to obtain assessments of both the levels of acute and chronic stress that the subjects had been experiencing. Acute stress was defined as stress situations that had lasted less than a month. And, indeed, most of the incidents of acute stress that were reported lasted only a matter of minutes or hours. In contrast, situations involving chronic stress might have dragged on for months. The two major areas of stress they focused on were interpersonal stress and occupational stress.

Not long after the interviews were conducted, the subjects were quarantined in a hospital where they were given nasal drops containing a low infectious dose of a rhinovirus. While the subjects remained in the hospital, nasal secretion samples for virus culture were collected over a five-day time period. The major question posed was which subject would come down with an upper respiratory illness? What the researchers found was that while acute stress had little impact on the chances of developing an upper respiratory illness, the subjects who reported that they were experiencing either chronic interpersonal or occupational stress were much more likely to come down with the illness than the subjects not reporting being under chronic stress. The researchers described their findings as follows: "Although acute (lasting less than one month) stressful events did not alter susceptibility to colds, enduring chronic stressors (lasting one month or longer) were associated with greater susceptibility to rhinovirus-induced colds. Moreover, there was some indication that the longer the duration of the stressor, the greater was the risk for colds.... Persons experiencing chronic stressors associated with marked or severe long-term threats were between two and three times more likely to develop colds than those without such an experience."[36]

For most people colds are unpleasant experiences — runny noses and scratchy throats that run their course in a week or two. However, stress can have more serious and lasting adverse impacts on the body. Two cases in point are the gastrointestinal and cardiovascular systems.

The gastrointestinal system is notorious for problems that are either caused or exacerbated by stress. This linkage has been recognized in the medical community for years. I looked through a *Merck Manual of General Medicine* dated 1989 which estimated that 30 percent to 50 percent of referrals to gastroenterologists were for uncomfortable symptoms for which there was no clear pathological condition to account. The *Merck Manual* recommended that physicians consider the possible role of psychological stress factors when careful examination ruled out organic factors.[37] This is still very good advice for physicians.

Irritable bowel syndrome is an example of a disorder that often has a stress component. This syndrome, which affects a great many people, is characterized by abdominal pain, constipation, or diarrhea. The physician searching for organic causes for the symptoms may find none. This doesn't mean that stress is necessarily the prime suspect. There may be other reasons for the discomfort. Still, research suggests that stress is a factor that is important to consider. In a recent study looking at the heightened visceral sensitivity of patients with irritable bowel syndrome, the researchers noted that the IBS patients reported higher levels of stress than control subjects even before the experiment exposing them to stressors began.[38]

The following case illustrates the role that stress can play in irritable bowel syndrome.[39] The case presented by Catherine Youell and James McCullough concerned a 22-year-old female college student given the identification of "C." Colitis attacks — abdominal muscle tightening followed by severe cramps and urgency for a bowel movement — began in her junior year of college. The first attack occurred after a traumatic experience and since then whenever she felt under pressure. In time, she entered psychotherapy at the university. As she talked about her life, it became apparent that her stressful interpersonal encounters focused on the theme of being personally rejected. These encounters made her feel hurt and damaged. Moreover, she believed that the incidents which had hurt her had not been unintentional, but deliberate. The therapist asked C to consider alternative ways of interpreting these encounters and to seek confirmation for these alternative scenarios. As therapy progressed, and the patient began to view these situations more benignly, the colitis attacks markedly decreased and eventually cleared up altogether.

There is now an extensive body of research linking psychological stress to cardiovascular disease. Stress contributes to the risk factors for cardiovascular disease such as high blood pressure and may play a role in the progression of the disease. Although the magnitude of the risk stress poses is not yet clear, there is little doubt that stress emanating from such sources as one's job and relationships can have an adverse impact on the health of one's cardiovascular system. The "Type A" personality, harried and driven and often hostile, seems to be a good candidate for risk factors such as elevated blood pressure.[40] Hostility, which goes beyond merely feeling angry but adds an attitudinal component of active dislike, may be a particularly potent psychological factor for coronary heart disease.[41]

If, as the research indicates, that psychosocial stresses can have an adverse effect on coronary heart disease, we might expect that stress management programs would be beneficial for patients with heart disease. There have been a number of stress management programs set up for patients with coronary heart disease and evaluated for their effectiveness. The results have shown some promise. In assessing these programs, Kenneth Walton and his colleagues noted that some programs have reported substantial reductions for current cardiac events, in some instances greater than 50 percent. However, the authors expressed a cautionary note that some of these positive effects did not hold up over time.[42]

Here is an example of a recent study carried out at Duke University Medical School and reported in the *Journal of the American Medical Association*.[43] One hundred thirty-four patients with stable ischemic heart disease were given either the usual medical care or such medical care along with aerobic exercise training, or with stress management training. The stress management training program lasted for 16 weeks. The patients were tested on measures of emotional distress and cardiovascular functioning. The investigators, James Blumenthal and his colleagues, reported that both the exercise program and stress management training reduced emotional distress and improved the markers for cardiovascular risk. The fact that stress management programs appear beneficial for patients with coronary heart disease is further confirmation that stress pays a role in cardiovascular disease.

We have noted that one of the indicators researchers use as a measure of stress is the number of life changes that the subject has experienced. The association between life changes and illness has been established in studies carried out over the years. The number of major life changes a person has experienced can be an objective, albeit gross indicator of stress levels.

## *Some Reflections on Stress*

Stress isn't all bad. It depends on the amount of stress you are experiencing and how you deal with it. Stress is a mobilizing experience. A soldier in a combat zone needs to be on high alert. An actor about to perform may give a better performance when she walks on stage with butterflies in her stomach. The athlete about to compete on a basketball court or soccer field wants to feel that adrenalin flowing. Some people work best when they have deadlines to meet.

A reasonable amount of stress increases alertness and readiness to act. The problem arises where there is just too much stress. While some stress can certainly be useful, for many people a whole lot of stress can be disabling. Think of the actor who is revved up to the point of stage fright. An article in *Parade* listed some very big names in show business — such as Barbra Streisand, Cher, Donny Osmond and Donald Sutherland — who experienced this reaction.[44] Remember the first speech you gave to a large audience? Did it really help you perform better when your throat was dry and your knees were knocking? Li Robbins wrote a charming book recounting the tensions engaged women experience as their wedding date approaches.[45] Does it really make the wedding experience a better one to pile up a series of stressors that have to be surmounted before the event? Perhaps the most dramatic example of living with just too much stress was what happened to many soldiers during World War I as they lived in rodent infested, mud filled trenches and were subjected to sometimes daily bombardments of artillery. The profoundly disturbed condition that resulted from this constant exposure to trauma was called shellshock.[46]

I would like to return again to the distinction between acute and chronic stress as it will be central to our discussion. Confronting a thug on a street corner is acute stress. You face an immediate threat of sustaining serious injuries. Living in a neighborhood that is replete with thugs, drug dealers and violent gangs is living with chronic stress. The threat isn't immediate but is always around and never goes away. Many urban dwellers live in such problem filled neighborhoods; hearing gunshots is not all that unusual and the stressful environment takes its toll on the residents.

The more common causes of chronic stress, of course, are difficult, hard-to-change situations in your daily life. Financial problems — how are you going to pay that big, unexpected bill — chronic diseases that cause pain and disability, and as we have discussed, stress relating to school, tensions at your job, or at home with your spouse or children. Unless the experience of acute stress reaches traumatic levels, the effects on the body and mind are likely to dissipate fairly quickly. In contrast, the effects of chronic stress on your thinking and outlook, your mood and your emotions, and even your body are likely to be more damaging. For many people, chronic stress can be debilitating.

This principal focus of this book will be on ways of coping with chronic stress. While we will discuss the experiences of acute anxiety — panic attacks, agoraphobia, acute and post-traumatic stress reactions — the focus of the book will be on people who are experiencing too much chronic stress, typically a plethora of problems that are nagging, irritating, at times depressing — problems that seemingly won't go away.

In my thinking, I assume that every individual probably has an optimal level of stress that he or she can deal with, the right amount of stress to get you going, but not so much as to interfere with your ability to act or perform. Certainly, this optimal level of stress differs from person to person. Some of us do better in a quiet life while others welcome challenging, stressful situations. I can't imagine myself skydiving or climbing mountain peaks, but others relish it. People simply differ in this regard. The trick is to recognize what level of stress you're comfortable with — what impels you to action but doesn't hinder you. If you find that you are constantly exceeding the level of stress that you can comfortably handle, and often feel worried and tense as a result, then you need to lower the amount of stress you are experiencing. The book will offer some suggestions on how to do this, to cope more effectively with stress. These suggestions are based on clinical experience, my own research and the research of many other psychologists and psychiatrists. It is my hope that utilizing these techniques will enable you to gain a better sense of control over these stressors when they occur.

Before we begin Chapter 2 and our discussion of ways of coping with stress, please take a look at the brief survey below. You will see a list of some common sources of stress. Go through the list, asking yourself in each case whether this is a source of stress in your own life. Noting these sources of stress should be helpful as you read through the book and we offer suggestions that you might find applicable to your own life.

## *Common Sources of Stress*

| | *True for Me* | *Not True for Me* |
|---|---|---|
| *Your Job* | | |
| Uninteresting, boring | ( ) | ( ) |
| Conflicts with bosses | ( ) | ( ) |
| Conflicts with co-workers | ( ) | ( ) |
| High pressure to produce | ( ) | ( ) |
| Don't know how to do the work as well as I need to | ( ) | ( ) |
| Hours are too long | ( ) | ( ) |
| Little job security | ( ) | ( ) |
| Difficult commute to job | ( ) | ( ) |
| *Your Family* | | |
| Conflicts with parents | ( ) | ( ) |
| Concerns about taking care of aging parents | ( ) | ( ) |
| Conflicts with brothers or sisters | ( ) | ( ) |
| Conflicts with children | ( ) | ( ) |
| Concern about health of family members | ( ) | ( ) |
| Recent loss of family member | ( ) | ( ) |
| *Your Romantic Partner* | | |
| Want one, but don't have any | ( ) | ( ) |
| Difficulties getting along with | ( ) | ( ) |
| Not supportive enough | ( ) | ( ) |
| We don't share enough | ( ) | ( ) |
| Unsatisfactory sexual relationship | ( ) | ( ) |
| *Your Friends* | | |
| Lack of | ( ) | ( ) |

| | | |
|---|---|---|
| Do not have a real confidante | ( ) | ( ) |
| Conflicts with | ( ) | ( ) |
| Recent loss of a friend | ( ) | ( ) |
| *Your Education* | | |
| Need more | ( ) | ( ) |
| Having difficulty with a course | ( ) | ( ) |
| Concern about grades | ( ) | ( ) |
| Unsettled when taking tests | ( ) | ( ) |
| *Your Health* | | |
| Bothered by specific medical problems | ( ) | ( ) |
| Concerned about dental problems | ( ) | ( ) |
| Feel anxious or depressed | ( ) | ( ) |
| Bothered by physical limitations caused by chronic medical problems | ( ) | ( ) |
| *Your Finances* | | |
| Are a constant problem | ( ) | ( ) |
| Future prospects are unpromising | ( ) | ( ) |
| Lack adequate health insurance | ( ) | ( ) |
| Unpaid debts | ( ) | ( ) |
| *Your Living Arrangements* | | |
| Crowded | ( ) | ( ) |
| Noisy | ( ) | ( ) |
| Unpleasant | ( ) | ( ) |
| *Your Personal Growth* | | |
| Feel stifled, stagnant | ( ) | ( ) |
| Should be developing my potential more than I am. | ( ) | ( ) |

There are no scores for this kind of quiz. The quiz was not intended as a measure of anything. As you read along in the book, simply keep a mental note of the areas that seem to be sources of stress in your life and this should help you see the relevance of the discussion to your own life. In the last chapter of the book we shall return to this checklist as we try to apply the strategies for coping with stress outlined in the book to the problems of everyday life.

# 2

# *A Psychological Analysis of Coping Behaviors: What Do We Mean by Coping and How Do We Measure and Study It?*

My interest in coping behaviors began many years ago when I was fresh out of graduate school and had taken a job at the United States Public Health Service. I joined a small group of behavioral scientists — psychologists, sociologists and anthropologists — who were trying to better understand why people chose to participate or not participate in screening programs for chronic diseases such as heart disease and cancer. The senior members of the group had developed a predictive model which was very straightforward and rational in nature.[1] They postulated that people would avail themselves of medical screening tests if (a) they believed that they were susceptible to the disease, (b) believed the disease was serious and (c) believed that going through the screening procedure would be beneficial. For example, if a woman believed that she had a significant chance of developing cancer, and (as most everyone acknowledges) cancer was a serious disease and that screening procedures such as mammograms and Pap smears would be useful steps to take in dealing with this possibility, then she would be a likely candidate to see her doctor for these screening tests. At first blush this model seems very reasonable. However, the model assumes that people act in ways that are fully rational. And from Freud's time on, if not before, the suspicion has grown by leaps and bounds that people often act in ways that are far from rational. How often do we see people do things that are not in their best interest and fail to do things that are in their interest? This is certainly true when it comes to health related behaviors. Just think of a chain smoker or a compulsive eater.

You may have encountered a scenario like this. A husband complains to his wife that he has been feeling unwell. He has a number of disquieting symptoms including headaches and dizzy spells. She can see that he is genuinely worried about the symptoms and suggests that he make an appointment to see the doctor. However, he shakes his head and makes a vague excuse and finally says maybe the problem will go away. However, the symptoms persist and his concern mounts, but still he is reluctant to see the doctor. Finally, after some prodding from his wife, he admits to her, "I'm afraid of what he'll find."

I was convinced that we needed to add something to the rational model of preventive health behavior. As a minimum, we needed to take into account the way people responded to stress. Did they try to deal with the problem or did they try to avoid it in one way or another? It would be very useful if we had a way of measuring a response tendency like this.

I turned my attention to the psychological literature—looking through the psychological journals that published research on personality and personality measurement in the hope of finding a ready made instrument. Not only were there no proven ways of assessing coping behavior available, few researchers had even turned their attention to describing and measuring ways of coping with stress. I checked the *Psychological Abstracts* which lists and describes current psychological research. In the index of the *Abstracts* the word *coping* did not appear. The field of psychology had yet to shine a spotlight on this important problem. As we shall see, the situation changed dramatically during the years that followed.

I decided to make some initial attempts myself to develop an instrument that would characterize the way people cope with stress. I began with the notion that one could measure people on a scale who on one extreme would do whatever they could to avoid stress and on the other would actively seek stress out. I envisioned stress-seekers as people who skydived or might volunteer for the Army Rangers or otherwise thrived on excitement. With this concept in mind I wrote a large number of items presenting forced-choice situations. While I no longer have copies of the actual items we used, they looked something like this:

(A) I would like to go rock climbing.
(B) I would like to read a book.
(A) I would choose the most difficult courses I could get at the school.
(B) I would choose courses I knew I could succeed in.
(A) At a dance I would seek out the most attractive person of the opposite sex I saw as a partner.
(B) I would pick out someone who looked OK.

We made up a questionnaire of such forced-choice items and gave it to several groups of college students and then analyzed the data statistically using a procedure which I will describe shortly called factor analysis. I hoped to find a general approach-avoidance factor running through the responses to these questions, something like the "G" factor in intelligence. What we got instead, was a hodge-podge. Students who sought out challenging courses did not necessarily want to go rock climbing and vice versa. I was forcibly struck with the conclusion that coping with stress was much more complex than I had initially envisioned and required a much more subtle analysis.

This initial unsuccessful attempt to measure coping in very broad terms did have heuristic value. It seemed clear that to make progress in developing a usable measure for assessing coping behavior, we needed a better understanding of what coping was. How would we define coping? What behaviors or psychological processes would be included in a definition of coping and what would not?

The twin questions that had presented themselves—how to conceptualize coping behavior and how to measure coping—have continued to challenge researchers over the years. In this chapter we shall try to present some of the thinking that has emerged from psychologists working on these problems. Because the two questions are closely linked, progress on one question has tended to inform the other. Despite a great deal of research, however, there is yet no clear consensus on either how to conceptualize coping behaviors or how to measure these behaviors.

My own interest in coping behaviors was sidetracked for a number of years when I was offered an opportunity to direct a large-scale research project in Berkeley, California, which was co-sponsored by the School of Public Health at the University of California and the California State Health Department. After the project was completed, I returned to the Washington, D.C. area to join the staff of the Department of Psychiatry of the George Washington University Medical School. When I picked up again on my interest in coping behaviors, I found that the situation was now changing. Psychologists were not only interested in coping behavior but were doing excellent work. The attempt to develop broad-sweeping categories of coping behavior such as approach-avoidance had given way to a multidimensional approach which used a variety of more narrowly drawn coping behavior such as using prayer, distraction, and problem solving. And a number of self report measures were being developed and applied in interesting studies.

Before describing some of these measures of coping behavior and the studies they have given rise to, I think it is important to discuss how these measures are constructed and how we can judge their quality. Because measures of coping have played a very important role in expanding our understanding of coping behaviors, we need to have some appreciation of what goes into them and what their limitations are.

A paper published in the *Psychological Bulletin* by Ellen Skinner and her colleagues reviewed the attempts to date to define and measure coping behaviors.[2] The authors point out that there are two major approaches which have been used to address the problem. The first approach is a rational approach, one that involves a good deal of armchair reasoning. The second approach is more empirical, utilizing a statistical technique called factor analysis. Let's begin with the rational approach. Based on their observations of other people, or their knowledge of research previously carried out about coping, or better yet, drawing on a theoretical formulation in psychology that seems relevant, the researchers come up with a notion or framework of what is involved in coping behavior. They develop a concept of coping, define it carefully, and list behaviors and psychological processes which might be included under the definition. Then, they make up questions sampling the items in the list. I began my initial attempt to develop a measure of approach versus avoidance coping in this manner.

Perhaps another illustration would be useful in presenting this rational approach in devising psychological measures. Suppose researchers wanted to measure extroversion-introversion — that very familiar, yet very important measure of personality initially elucidated by the brilliant Swiss psychiatrist Carl Jung which has now passed into everyday thinking and language. In developing a measure of extroversion-introversion they would carefully spell out their definition of the terms, then list situations which might differentiate the two types of people. Then, they would make up some questions (items) asking about these situations. Here are some examples of items that could be answered yes or no.

"Do you enjoy being around lots of people?"

"Do you like to take long, solitary walks?"

"Would you like a job in which people work closely as a team?"

"Are you comfortable meeting people?"

To obtain a score for extroversion, the researchers might give one point for every question answered *yes,* reversing the scoring for items such as the second question. When they have drawn up perhaps 20 or 30 items, they may have a scale measuring extroversion. However, there remains a lot of work to do before they could justify making this assertion. In any event this is the essence of the rational approach to conceptualizing psychological characteristics and developing measuring instruments to assess them.

Many researchers have tried to develop classifications for coping behaviors using a rational approach. In their review article, Skinner and her colleagues listed over 40 inventories whose origins lay in rational analysis. Some of these inventories are based on the thinking of Richard Lazarus, a psychologist whose interest in coping and stress spanned five decades.[3] In theorizing about coping, Lazarus made a distinction between two broad types of coping efforts: (a) coping which is directed at dealing with the perceived source of stress (problem-focused coping) and (b) coping which strives to regulate one's personal emotions in adjusting or adapting to a stressful situation (emotion-focused coping).

The distinction between problem-focused and emotion-focused coping has been useful in organizing our thinking about coping and not only has found its way into several coping inventories (for example, the *Ways of Coping Questionnaire*) but has generated interesting research. Researchers have wanted to know under what conditions problem-focused and emotion-focused coping are likely to occur. Working at the University of Connecticut Health Center, Howard Tennen and his colleagues followed patients with rheumatoid arthritis, asking questions, daily, about how they coped with pain.[4] The questions used tended to fall into two groups which appeared to be similar to the categories of problem-focused and emotion-focused coping. Using pain medication and relaxation, for example, were considered to be examples of problem-focused coping while seeking spiritual comfort was thought to be an example of emotion-focused coping. The analysis of the data revealed an important difference between the two forms of coping. Problem-focused coping was often used regularly without emotion-focused coping, whereas emotion-focused based coping usually occurred on the same days as problem-focused coping. One interpretation of these findings is that emotion-focused coping frequently has the status of a fallback position. When you can't do something to alter a situation, then you turn to Plan B. How can I live with the problem? In situations where options of taking action to deal with the source of stress are severely limited, reliance on emotionally based coping can become a necessity.

In discussing their research on coping strategies used by children battling leukemia, John Weisz and his colleagues echoed this view, observing "that with relatively low-controllability stressors (e.g., leukemia and its treatment), the most adaptive form of coping may be that which focuses not so much on altering objective events and conditions as adjusting oneself to them."[5]

Lazarus' formulations are not the only basis upon which rationally-based coping scales have been developed. Some researchers have turned to the now voluminous literature on coping behavior, borrowing and reshaping ideas to formulate their own conceptualizations of coping behaviors while others have gone directly to the source — people themselves — and have interviewed them about how they cope with stress. Whether based on theory, previous research, inspiration or a combination of the above, there has been no shortage of effort, resulting in a number of rationally derived inventories for assessing coping behaviors.

The advantage of rationally sorting items into categories of coping behavior is increased conceptual clarity. Items appear to fall into distinct categories that make logical sense. The problem that arises is when the researchers think the items should fit together and it turns out that their preconceptions are way off the mark. Recall my own efforts to classify two types of reactions to stress, approach and avoidance. People simply did not respond in the way I anticipated they would.

The alternative to rationally defining patterns of coping behavior and measuring them is to take an empirical approach; one finds out how people actually respond to a series of items and by statistical analysis finds out what responses tend to cluster together. In accomplishing this goal, the method of choice is factor analysis. Examining what researchers have found using factor analysis will take us on a journey from the armchair and thinking cap to the computer.

Factor analysis is a statistical procedure that starts with a large number of variables (in this case items) and reduces them to a relatively small number of general factors that underlie these items. The procedure begins by computing the intercorrelations between the responses to all of the items and then extracts factors which can account for a large portion of the observed variance. The procedure involves a very large number of computations and was not widely used until the development of computers.

In a very rough sort of way I like to think of factor analysis as a sorting process that follows certain predetermined rules. In the wonderful series of books by J. K. Rowling about Harry Potter and his friends, a magic sorting hat assigned new students to one of the four houses in the school of magic. If Rowling had used factor analysis instead of magic to do the sorting, it would take us a step further than the sorting hat. Factor analysis not only would tell you which children are associated with what houses, it would define the characteristic of the houses, themselves.

Imagine for a moment that you sat down and drew up a list of 50 items, each asking about some way of coping with stress. For example:

"I pray a lot."
"I try to get extra sleep."
"I watch television."
"I take a long walk."

In devising scores for your projected inventory of coping behaviors, you would find it awkward to deal with 50 separate items each with an individual score. You would prefer to work with only a few scores indicating general patterns. To achieve this efficiency, you would need to know whether people's responses to the items group themselves into a few patterns. Let's further imagine that you administered your questionnaire, to say, 200 people. Then, you ran a factor analysis program on your desktop computer. The program would resolve the responses to the fifty items into a small number of factors that account for much of the variance in the responses of your subjects. Now, you would look at the factors listed on the printout of the data and see which of the original 50 items had the highest numerical loading on each factor. High loadings for several items on a factor enable you to identify the factor and perhaps give it a name. Factor analysis cannot be used only in this exploratory way; it can also be used to confirm the scoring of an inventory that you developed rationally. Skinner and her colleagues consider the use of confirmatory factor analysis the third approach to identifying concepts and measuring them. Confirmatory factor analysis was what I employed in my fledgling attempt to develop an approach-avoidance measure of coping behaviors. In this instance, the factor analysis failed to confirm.

Let's now turn our attention to some of the patterns of coping behavior that have been identified using exploratory factor analysis, beginning with a study that Roland Tanck and I carried out at George Washington University.[6] The study carries the minor distinction of being one of the earliest studies using exploratory factor analysis to identify patterns of coping behavior listed by Skinner and her colleagues. Tanck and I began with the assumption that coping could be viewed as a variety of efforts (which included both external actions and internal processes) that might act to reduce or diminish stress. Based on this assumption, we administered a short questionnaire to 132 undergraduate students. After asking some preliminary questions about current feelings of tension and depression, we inquired, "When you do feel tense, what things do you do to try to diminish or relieve these feelings?" We presented a list of 22 items which included both overt actions (e.g., "seek professional help," "take a trip or vacation") and internal processes ("just bear with the discomfort until it goes away," "daydreaming or fantasize"). Four alternatives were presented for responding. These were "never," "once in a while," "often," and "almost always." Responses were scored zero, one, two, and three respectively.

To see what patterns might emerge from the students' responses to these items we ran an exploratory factor analysis. The factor analysis extracted seven factors which accounted for 63 percent of the observed variance. When we made up the questionnaire, we had no idea what the factors would look like, but we were presently surprised by the clarity of the factors that emerged.

We named the first factor *seeking social support.* Items loading high on the factor were "seek company," and "talk the problem over with friends or family." In retrospect we now know that seeking social support is a very important way of coping with stress. College students have told us that this is what they do most often. In our subsequent studies with college students, we found that seeking social support was what the students did most often when they felt under stress.[7] As I suspect is true for most of us, the students turned to informal sources of help rather than formal sources, in spite of the fact that a counseling center and members of the clergy were readily available. In one study, we found that 95 percent of the students reported that they had at least, once in a while, talked to a good friend to cope with tension. The comparable figures for family members were somewhat lower (70 percent) and very much lower for therapists (15 percent) and clergy (7 percent).

Not only was talking with a friend the most frequently used strategy among the coping strategies listed in our inventory, it was also most often rated as helpful. Sixty percent of the students who talked with a good friend as a way of coping with tension reported that the strategy was helpful. The comparable figure for family was 42 percent with lower figures for the therapists and clergy. These data are certainly consistent with the commonplace observation that adolescents rely heavily on their peers for social support.

When we talk about everyday life, seeking social support may bring a plethora of images to mind. A young child talking to his mother after a bad day at school. A young woman talking with her best friend after having an argument with her boyfriend. A man seeking the comfort of his wife when experiencing self doubts about his ability to get ahead on the job. And sometimes, we hear about social support when it is not there, when it is absent — such as the wife who complains about her husband with the words, "When I need him, he is never there for me."

The belief that social support can help a person weather a time of stress has become institutionalized in our society in the form of support groups that offer help and support to people who are experiencing difficulties with physical and emotional problems.

In large metropolitan communities, support groups may be found for a wide variety of medical and psychological problems. Glancing through a newspaper in the area I live in, I see support groups listed for such diverse problems as anxiety, breastfeeding, cancer, clergy abuse, defiant kids, organ transplants, and ostomy.

Evaluations of support groups by their members tend to be positive. Support groups help their members cope with difficulties. There is the feeling, for some, almost a relief that they have found people who really understand what they are going through. For example, a study of members of prostate cancer support groups in Australia found that peer support was rated positively by most members and high satisfaction with the group was related to a perceived better quality of life.[8]

Social support groups provide face-to-face interactions and a sharing of problems, anxieties and fears. All of these things can have a positive effect on reducing stress. What happens, however, if the community in which one lives is too small to allow the formation of such groups? Can Internet groups provide an alternative? A study of Internet support groups for parents of children with special health needs indicated that for many people, the answer was yes.[9] The parents who were surveyed reported that they got more out of the group than they had expected. Ninety percent of the sample surveyed suggested that parents should join these groups as soon as possible.

The second factor that emerged was a pattern of *dysfunctional behavior*. Some items that loaded high on the factor were "just become ineffective-stop functioning well," "eat constantly," "daydreaming or fantasize," "spend endless hours thinking about things," and "become irritable and easily angered." There is a pattern here of turning inwardly, of ruminating and even obsessing, and in one way or another avoiding the issues confronting the person. When the person interacts with others, it is less seeking social support than a response of snappishness. The attitude is one of "leave me alone." This pattern of dealing with stress is all too familiar to psychotherapists. It is often part of a psychological malaise, increasing vulnerability to a depressive reaction.

We called this factor dysfunctional behavior advisedly, because the behaviors involved certainly did not appear to be adaptive. The reactions to stress seemed to disengage the individual from the chance of effectively dealing with the sources of stress and at the same time provided little comfort. This drawing inwardly and the irritability that accompanies it would make it harder for one to seek the support of other people. One can be pretty much left with only one's own resources to deal with the situation and an emotional state that is at best uncomfortable that could in time become wretched.

In a subsequent study, Tanck and I found that whether people who reacted with this pattern to stress began to develop the symptoms of depression depended in part on the level of stress that they were experiencing. When the level of stress was low, people who reacted with a pattern of dysfunctional behavior were not likely to report depressive symptoms. They seem to muddle through their difficulties without really feeling down. But when stress levels mounted, the report of depressed symptoms increased markedly.

The third factor was labeled *narcotizing anxiety*, using the term originally coined by the distinguished psychoanalyst Karen Horney.[10] The items loading on this factor included "drink alcohol," "use marijuana," and "seek sexual comfort." You have probably heard such siren songs as "have another drink — it will take the edge off," or "you'll feel more relaxed after smoking a joint." There is little doubt that using chemicals to diminish tension can be effective, but it is also clear that such use can be a two-edged sword.

Factor four is *problem-solving*. Two items loading high on the factor are "try analyzing the problem" and "take direct action to deal with the source of the problem." This is a straightforward idea, but not quite as foolproof as it might sound at first blush. The distinction between analysis and rumination can be murky. The former is useful in clarifying issues; the second can be destructive, resulting in a pattern of endless internal turmoil.

Factor five is *reliance on the professional health care system*. Two items which loaded highly on the factor were "seek professional help" and "take tranquilizing medicines." For the college students who filled out our questionnaires, this might mean visiting the counseling center at the university. For other adults, it might be visiting the family physician or seeking help from a psychotherapist. The students in our sample of college students infrequently turned to professionals in coping with stress. They tended to turn to their friends or look within themselves. The students who did turn to professionals for help with stress tended to have relatively high levels of depression.

The sixth factor, *bearing with discomfort*, has the quality of acceptance. This factor does not have the suggestion of coming unglued like our second factor, but suggests a kind of inward acceptance and readiness to deal with the worst. Two items loading on this factor were "just bear with the discomfort until it goes away" and "pray." One might think of a person who is patiently, perhaps courageously, undergoing post-surgical radiation or chemotherapy treatment for cancer. Acceptance as a coping technique has some similarity to the ancient philosophy of stoicism which advocated suppressing emotion and displaying an indifference to pleasure and pain. However, the resemblance is, probably, only superficial, for coping by acceptance has a flavor of reluctance to it; it is not a philosophy of life like stoicism. The individual acknowledges the difficulties and the pain involved in the situation, but has concluded that there may be few if any options to do anything about it, and that all that seems to remain open is to bear with the difficulty as best as one can. One thinks of the British phrase "keep a stiff upper lip" or the comment of the person of faith facing severe difficulties, "I turned the problem over to God."

The seventh and final factor was *escape.* Two items with high factor loadings were "watch TV or go to a movie" and "take a trip or vacation." What we are talking about here is doing something actively to get away from the problem, not simply shoving the problem out of mind, perhaps telling yourself, "I'm not going to think about this anymore."

One interesting aside about escape, or as some have termed it, escape-avoidance as a coping technique is that avoidance, seems to be characteristic of people who have eating disorders such as bulimia.[11] At least three studies have reported this finding, including a study carried out on a large number of women in Sweden. It is not clear what the tie-in is between avoidance and eating disorders, but it might have something to do with the often secretive aspects of eating disorders such as the purging that takes place in bulimia. Or, it may be that people who become obese simply avoid other people.

For an initial, exploratory study, the results were quite satisfying. We identified a relatively small number of patterns of coping behavior that makes sense and seemed consistent with everyday experience. But, the study was clearly only a beginning. Other researchers working from different perspectives from ours (and usually from each other) developed scales measuring coping behaviors and produced their own lists of factors. In their review article Skinner and her colleagues listed 71 attempts to identify and measure patterns of coping using exploratory factor analysis over a 25 year time span. Some of the patterns of coping behavior identified by these researchers are quite similar to the ones we extracted in our analysis. "Problem-solving" shows up often, as does "seeking social support" and "escape." While we talked about "narcotizing anxiety," others talked about "alcohol-drug disengagement." So, there is a lot of commonality in what researchers have found, although new ideas have been advanced as well. Here are some examples of alternative patterns of coping that have been identified using factor analysis: "minimization of threat," "selective ignoring," "focus on the positive," "introspective self-blame," and "wishful thinking."

Probably the most widely used inventory of coping techniques is the *Ways of Coping Questionnaire* developed by Susan Folkman and Richard Lazarus.[12] As mentioned earlier, Lazarus, a longtime researcher in the area of coping and stress, elucidated a view of coping that distinguished between problem-focused coping on the one hand and emotional regulation of stress on the other. Folkman and Lazarus developed a coping inventory that asked subjects to consider a real live stress incident they had experienced and then inquired how they reacted to it. They presented a series of items to the subjects that included many items dealing with problem-focused and emotion-focused coping. The current version of the *Ways of Coping Questionnaire* provides scores for a variety of techniques of coping such as confrontation coping (standing up for oneself), distancing, self-controlling, seeking social support, accepting responsibility, escape-avoidance, planful problem solving, and positive reappraisal.

Several researchers have subjected the *Ways of Coping Questionnaire* to factor analysis with results that are somewhat inconsistent. Nonetheless, this measure of coping has been widely used by researchers.

Coping inventories have been used as research tools in a variety of studies. For example, a number of researchers have been interested in learning how people cope with the stress brought on by medical problems. The list of medical problems studied is lengthy and includes potentially fatal diseases such as cancer and coronary heart disease as well as chronic, sometimes disabling conditions such as rheumatoid arthritis and disorders which often afflict children such as asthma. Tracey Revenson and Barbara Felton, for example, studied the psychological adjustments of patients with rheumatoid arthritis.[13] They recruited their subjects from the outpatient rheumatology service of a large metropolitan hospital. In questioning the patients they found that the main stressors generated by the disease were a restrictive lifestyle, limited movement and pain.

The researchers administered a number of self-report psychological instruments to the patients including measures of positive and negative emotional states, (e.g., "feeling very happy"), self report of disability, and a modification of the Ways of Coping Scale developed by

Folkman and Lazarus. The authors reported that in dealing with stress caused by the disease the patients "tended to rely on emotion-focused coping strategies, involving efforts to direct attention from the illness and minimize its stressfulness."[14] However, the use of the strategies did not seem particularly effective. For example, the use of wish-fulfilling fantasies was associated with decreases in positive emotional states and increases in negative emotional states. The authors observed, "despite their apparent intentions, emotion-focused coping strategies may not be effective in this regard, but rather may increase distress."

The question of how people manage pain continues to attract researchers. Recently, researchers in a Norwegian university gave the Ways of Coping Scale to patients in a pain management program. The researchers found that the way the patients thought about — i.e., appraised — pain influenced their coping behaviors. If they perceived pain as a challenge, they tended to opt for problem-focused coping. On the other hand, if they saw pain as a threat, they tended to utilize emotion-focused coping.[15]

The study of how children, particularly very young children, cope with medically-related stressors creates special problems. While there are coping inventories especially designed for children and adolescents, researchers have tried a number of alternative procedures to assess children's coping responses.[16] One team of investigators, for example, gave children facing medical procedures the choice of two sets of toys, one of which was medically oriented, the other not. Choosing or not choosing the medically-oriented toys would be an indirect assessment of the child's coping tendencies. Other investigators have interviewed the children about their expectations and reactions to medical procedures. In one variant, the researcher asked how the child would coach a friend on how to cope. Some researchers have turned to the parents of the child for information, interviewing them about the way the child coped with stress. Finally it is possible to carry out observations of the child during hospitalization.

A very different kind of study using a coping inventory was carried out by a research team working at the Karolinska Institute in Stockholm, Sweden. The researchers Kenji Kato and Nancy Pederson were trying to parcel out the relative contributions of genetic and environmental factors to a person's coping style.[17] The idea that there is a significant genetic component in the way we usually cope with stress strikes me as very interesting. I would have imagined that our coping styles were largely something we learned as we grew up. However, the study by Kato and Pederson indicates that this view of coping is probably oversimplified and needs to be modified.

Briefly, the researchers used a coping inventory that was developed by American researchers William Billings and Rudolph Moos. The inventory, which had been rationally developed, was translated into Swedish. When the researchers factor analyzed the inventory, they uncovered three familiar factors, "problem solving," "turning to others," and "avoidance." The researchers utilized a register of twins kept in Sweden. Contacting a sample of the twins, they administered the inventory to a group of identical (monozygotic) twins and a group of twins that were fraternal (dizygotic). Some of each group of twins had been reared together and some of each group had been reared apart. With this kind of research design, the researchers were able to use sophisticated statistical analyses to separate out the influence of heredity and environment on the responses to the coping inventory. They concluded that there is a "moderate heritability" of coping style.[18] So, while it is still reasonable to believe that how we cope is largely learned in our experience growing up, there is a significant genetic influence as well. If coping style is, basically, part of our personality, then this finding makes sense because we know that our genes have a very large influence on the makeup of our personalities.

Questionnaire measures of coping behaviors have been criticized on a number of grounds. Perhaps, most fundamentally, the basic assumption that a person copes the same way in a variety of situations has been called into question. If coping is a fairly stable personality trait, then coping inventories make sense. If coping varies significantly from one situation to the next, then more tailored measures of coping might be needed. In my fledgling effort to develop a measure of approach versus avoidance reactions to stress, I did find evidence that different situations led to different reactions.

In an article discussing the way children cope with medical procedures, Lizette Peterson discussed this issue. "One of the important movements within the adult coping literature has been the recognition that coping is, to some extent, a temporally and situationally specific process.... Although an individual may characteristically respond to related situations in a similar fashion, consistency across many dissimilar situations is not to be expected, even within the same individual. For example, how one copes with the news that surgery is necessary may be very different from the method used to cope with actually entering the operating room.... Thus, the accurate prediction of coping demands attention not only to individual differences, but also to different stressors."[19] Given this problem, generalized coping inventories (including the measure I developed with Tanck) may have an inherent weakness. A second criticism of coping inventories is that we really don't know how valid the measures are. When people report that they seek social support when feeling under stress, is that what they really do? While there have been some validity studies carried out on coping scales, for the most part, when people say they seek social support or try problem-solving or seek some form of escape, we assume that is what they really do. It is a truism about self report measures that people don't always give accurate responses. Sometimes they check off what seems socially desirable, or what makes themselves look good, or even what they think the investigator would like to see.

One of the issues relating to the validity of coping inventories concerns the fact that the accounts obtained are typically retrospective. A researcher might ask, "Think back to a recent event that caused you a lot of stress," and follow this with a series of questions about how the person reacted. There is usually a time lag between the stressful event and the researcher's inquiry. The longer the lag, the more tricks memory may play on what will be reported. A group of researchers at the State University of New York at Stony Brook have questioned the accuracy of retrospective reports of coping. In one paper, Christine Marco and her colleagues noted, "We and other researchers ... have reported evidence that retrospective coping reports may not be accurate representation of the actual coping behaviors used at the time of an event. For example, Stone et al. (1998) found that cognitive coping efforts were more likely to be forgotten on a retrospective recall and that behavioral coping efforts were more likely to be 'generated' on a retrospective recall."[20] A reframing of reality takes place in somewhat the same manner that a good story gets better with retelling over time.

The most trenchant criticism of self report measures of coping is that research using these inventories has not been very productive. The yield of interesting, worthwhile, meaningful data has not been commensurate with the effort that has gone into obtaining these data. The results have not been that impressive. Even the developers of coping inventory such as Richard Lazarus have expressed some disappointment.[21] Critics of coping inventories such as James Coyne and Melissa

Racioppo have used blistering language in their evaluation of research using coping inventories. In a critique of such research, they wrote, "Warning! Hundreds of studies have established that use of this instrument is unlikely to yield findings of substantive importance and that the risk of confounded and otherwise spurious results is high."[22] I suspect that the statement was intended to shake up the field, to persuade researchers on coping to quit barking up the wrong tree (relying on coping inventories) and try a different approach.

Spurious results are indeed a danger with coping inventories as they are with many personality measures. I once reported a relation between our coping inventory's factor of dysfunctional behavior with a measure of depression; however I was quick to point out that this was almost a tautology.

I believe many studies using coping inventories such as the ones described in this chapter are indeed useful. In this, I disagree with Coyne and Racioppo. However, I do agree with these authors that current inventories are clearly limited in what they offer, and researchers should be striving to develop alternative and hopefully better data-gathering techniques to study coping.

What then are the alternatives to relying on coping inventories? One approach is to try to reduce the errors inherent in retrospective data by obtaining measures of coping behavior closer to the actual events. One could use psychological diaries similar to the ones Tanck and I used in our studies of interpersonal stress. Diaries filled out nightly would limit the subject to reporting about what happened during the day. I like the procedure because it diminishes the errors involved in recall yet allows a reasonable amount of reflection in the responses. The disadvantage of using written diaries is that daily diaries pile up and it becomes a laborious job to score and analyze them.

Arthur Stone and his colleagues at Stony Brook have used modern technology to reduce retrospective errors about coping behavior to a near minimum. They drew upon the very creative work of M. Csikszentmihalyi and R. Larson who studied the behavior of adolescents using an electronic device to page the subject and then obtain data on what they were doing and feeling.[23] Stone and Saul Shiffman developed a procedure that uses an electronic diary—a palm-top computer with a 20 character LCD screen and an audible alarm.[24] At certain times during the day, the electronic alarm sounds and the subjects (typically recruited through radio and newspaper ads) are asked whether they have experienced an "issue or conflict" since the last time they were buzzed, and if so, did they use any of several coping strategies such as distraction, social support, and relaxation. This johnny-on-the-spot method of assessing stress and coping behavior would tend to minimize errors of memory and would lessen the tendency that many people have of putting the best face on a situation, the ego protective tendency to make oneself look good, or at least not inept. However, there are problems with the method. The Heisenberg principle stemming from quantum mechanics that trying to measure a phenomenon can interfere with what you are measuring applies in spades to self-report data obtained from human subjects when the researcher uses the same question over and over. People get bored, irritated, or simply try to dismiss the question, giving a perfunctory answer with a minimum of thought. Tanck and I included an adjective checklist to measure daily moods in our psychological diaries. After a time, many of our student subjects responded to the list of adjectives with as much thought as they gave to brushing their teeth.

When measured by an inventory asking for the way one usually responds, coping behaviors approximate the status of a personality measure. When assessed on a periodic basis using an automated electronic diary, coping behaviors are much more situationally determined. The immediate context for the assessments can make a large difference in how the person queried may respond. With such different approaches to measuring coping, it is not surprising that the results using the two methods can be quite different. Indeed, some of the results reported with the electronic monitoring device are not only different from what one obtains with more conventional approaches, some findings seem counterintuitive. For example, coping as measured by electronic diaries has no perceptible relation to mood. We know from other types of research that certain patterns of coping behavior such as seeking social support often have an elevating effect on a person's mood, even positively influencing a person's mental health. The quick, on-the-spot measures of coping apparently do not catch this. It may be that these brief time samples may not register the full meaning and impact of coping behavior.

One alternative to relying on coping inventories is to use observation of actual behavior. Instead of relying on self-reports, why not see what people actually do? The idea sounds more appealing than it actually is. In the first place, much of coping with stress as we currently understand it does not involve behavior; coping often involves internal psychological processes, and internal psychological processes are not readily discernible by even the most acute observers. Secondly, observation is not really practical except under conditions where people are confined in a fairly restricted space such as a hospital ward, schoolroom or playground. It is usually children who are so restricted, not adults, so much of the work using observation has been done on children. There are studies on how children respond to conflicts and aggressive acts and these do provide some information about coping behaviors. The observer can note whether the child becomes aggressive, withdraws, seeks the company of other children, or seeks the comfort and security of an adult.

A second approach to studying coping is to design experiments. Rather than try to measure coping as it naturally occurs, one can induce stress in subjects by some of the means previously elucidated (e.g., placing the individual's hand in very cold water, exposing the person to loud noise, requiring the subject to make rapid calculations) and study the reactions. One of the best studied effects of stress using experiments has been a series of studies done with very young children. In a special room with one-way vision screens, the toddlers are separated from their mothers and left alone for a period of time, then reunited to them. During the separation, the children react with various degrees of discomfort. Although the focus of these studies is on the kind of attachment the infants have formed with their mothers, the experiments tell us a great deal about the response of infants to the stress of separation.

One of the more interesting types of experiments does not try to induce stress experimentally and study reactions. Rather, the investigators use subjects who are already experiencing stress and teach them coping skills to see whether the acquisition of the skills will have a positive impact on the individual's mental health. There are studies which look at the effect of teaching individuals specific coping skills such as relaxation or meditation and there are investigations which teach people a whole package of skills. As an example of such a study, researchers in the Netherlands wanted to know whether teaching a package of cognitive and behavioral coping skills would help patients suffering from chronic low back pain deal more effectively with their illness.[25] Training consisted of 12 group sessions in which the patients learned to modify their experience of pain by using imagery and at the same time learned to improve their relaxation skills. Using a variety of outcome measures (activity level, pain intensity, and report of emotional states), the researchers concluded that teaching patients the package of coping skills was indeed helpful to the patients.

In evaluating these various approaches to studying coping, I think it is fair to say that while we have developed some very useful schemes for defining and classifying coping behaviors, our methods of studying these behaviors are far from ideal. Self-report coping inventories are easy to use and score and have provided some interesting data. However, we do need to know more about the validity of these inventories and what they are actually measuring. Alternative assessments based on observations and experiments are cumbersome and are likely to have only limited use. While we have learned a good deal about coping with stress using our current methods, there is a clear need for continued research and the development of new procedures.

# 3

# *Things to Avoid*

Some ways of dealing with stress are better than others. But, it's not just what you do, it is also how much you do it. Take watching television. Diversion can be a reasonable way to tone down feelings of stress. And, watching television is certainly the most widely used form of diversion in our society today. Watching a television show can take one's mind off of a pressing problem, which is often useful, at times even necessary. But imagine a person who, night after night, sits in front of the tube for hours on end spending the entire evening watching and absorbing a succession of situation comedies and crime shows. Or, think of a homemaker who spends the entire afternoon watching a succession of soap operas. Such a large investment in passive viewing may come at the expense of pursuing interests and activities which are more potentially gratifying. Or take a person who likes to discuss his problems on the telephone with his friends. Talking things over with friends is usually a helpful way of coping with stress. It allows one not only to ventilate one's problems, but also to hear what others have to say about them, thus providing some objective feedback for one's own thoughts and conclusions. But imagine a person who night after night bends the ears of friends, one after the other with hours of self-focused conversation. It may soon come to pass that when the phone rings the person on the other end may quickly excuse herself saying that she has pressing matters to attend to. Dinner may be on the stove or it may be this, that or the other thing. Our caller has worn out his welcome. Excessive reassurance seeking may turn off people who might otherwise be helpful. This tactic can be a counterproductive coping strategy that attempts to assuage one's doubts about one's lovability.[1] While talking with friends can be an effective way to cope with stress, it is not a short course to build self esteem. Attempting to put a friend into the role of a therapist on a continuing basis may eventually lead to rejection and the loss of the friend.

The classic case of a little being effective and a large amount being destructive is the use of alcohol to reduce tensions. A drink can soothe, intoxication can lead to all sorts of problems.

As is true for many things, in choosing strategies to cope with stress, there is probably a virtue in diversity. Just as a stockbroker might advise you not to put all of your money in one or two stocks but rather to invest in a number of stocks or alternatively a mutual fund, it's probably a good idea to have a number of ways of combating stress in your arsenal. If one approach doesn't work, you have others to rely on.

I would like to begin by discussing ways of coping with stress that are likely to prove less effective. These are approaches to coping with stress that you might want to avoid altogether, or a least not overdo. When we have considered these more suspect approaches, we will turn to the strategies that are likely to prove more effective.

## *Rumination*

Many problems in life lend themselves to traditional problem solving techniques. These techniques include such steps as defining the problem, seeking information, analyzing the situation, and using this analysis to decide on steps to best deal with the problem. Such traditional problem solving techniques probably work best when there is not a large interpersonal content involved and when the individual is not emotionally involved in the problem. Some examples in which traditional problem solving techniques are likely to be effective include a mechanic who must diagnose and repair a car that has strange sounds emanating from the engine, an administrative assistant in a large medical practice who is given the task of reorganizing the files to make them more accessible and at the same time conserve space and a stockbroker who tries to most efficiently allocate his client's assets into stocks, bonds, mutual funds and real estate investments.

In all of these undertakings, careful analysis of the problem is important in making good decisions. However, when problems involve a large interpersonal content or when you are emotionally involved in the situation, analysis as a problem-solving tool may not work as well. You may be able to be objective about setting up a file system but it is a lot harder to be clear-headed about a problem which involves a family member or a girlfriend or boyfriend. When one's thoughts are about a love interest, objectivity often is a casualty. Many people have a tendency to idealize their romantic partners, not seeing them in realistic terms.[2] The saying "love is blind" has a lot of truth to it. When difficulties arise in romantic relationships or in another highly significant area of one's life, it is very difficult to be objective about one's own role in the situation. Some people, given to inflating their own virtues, tend to ignore or deny their own culpability in the problems that have arisen in their relationships. Other people, particularly those with low self-esteem, often see the fault in themselves and have a tendency toward self blame. In either event, trying to figure out what is going wrong and how to correct the situation can be a very difficult undertaking and analyzing the problem oneself can sometimes lead to misleading, erroneous conclusions.

While self analysis can be a tricky business, ruminating — constantly going over the problem in your mind — is very likely to be harmful rather than helpful. The research evidence is quite clear that for people who have a tendency toward depression, rumination tends to worsen depressed feelings. In discussing their own research on rumination as well as the research of other investigators, Sonya Lyubomirsky and her colleagues noted, "An increasing number of studies provide evidence that ruminative responses are associated with longer and more severe depressed moods than are distracting responses. In the laboratory, manipulations of rumination or self-focus maintain depressed mood, whereas distraction or externally focused manipulations lead to significant relief from depressed mood.... Longitudinal studies of naturally occurring depressed moods show that people who respond to those moods with rumination report more severe and longer periods of depressed mood than people who use pleasant activities to manage their moods, even after controlling for the initial severity of the mood."[3]

To endlessly think about a problem is obsessive. And when these repetitive thoughts turn negative, it can be a real downer. To obsess about why things are going wrong can become a perpetual sword in one's side. When rumination occurs at night, it can lead to a sleepless night and fatigue in the morning. Have you ever had the experience of going to bed with a very troubling problem on your mind and finding yourself unable to sleep? You may go over and over the problem, looking at it from this angle or that, trying to find some satisfactory way to deal with it. But the solution eludes you or just isn't quite right somehow. Eventually, you look at the clock. It is taking you forever to fall asleep. And in the morning you feel very tired. This very common experience points out how ruminating can be self-defeating.

I had a patient once who was constantly going over in her mind unresolved problems with her boyfriend. She knew that such ruminating was a bad idea, but she said, "I can't stop it. I try as hard as I can, but I just keep doing it. I try to get him out of my mind, but when I'm home alone, he keeps popping into my mind." I had to tell her that she was not alone. There is no easy cure for rumination. It is unlikely that you can simply tell yourself to stop thinking about the situation and expect that to work. If anything, an attempt to suppress the idea that is plaguing you may only bring it back again. A psychologist, Daniel Wegner, developed a simple, but ingenious procedure for studying the effectiveness of thought suppression.[4] In a laboratory demonstration suggesting the futility of thought suppression, Wegner and his colleagues at the University of Texas in San Antonio asked their students not to think of a white bear. Then, the students were asked to signal when the thought of a white bear entered their streams of consciousness. During a five-minute period of attempted thought suppression, thoughts of the forbidden subject occurred at a rate of more than one per minute.

Unwanted, intrusive thoughts are part of the clinical picture in the psychiatric conditions obsessive-compulsive disorder and post-traumatic stress disorder. Patients afflicted with these disorders may develop multiple strategies for dealing with their unwanted thoughts and one of them is thought suppression. Christine Purdon of the University of Waterloo in Ontario has reviewed research relating to these clinical populations and has concluded that thought suppression is likely to be futile and probably counterproductive, much as it was in the experiments carried out with college students.[5]

You might find it interesting to try the experiment of the white bear on yourself. See if you can avoid picturing a white bear in your mind's eye. Unless you are unusual in this respect, you will probably find that you can't keep the bear out of your mind. So, simply saying, "I'm not going to think about this anymore," probably won't work with intrusive thoughts. I told my patient to try diverting herself with some other activity to see if that would help, for that is what the research suggests.

For people who find themselves obsessed with an unresolved personal problem, going over and over the issues involved in their minds, moving back and forth in their thinking, but never coming to a really satisfactory conclusion, I would say that the odds are that this is not likely to be helpful. Rumination is more likely than not to be counterproductive. My suggestion would be the same as I gave to my patient. Try diverting herself. Pick up a good book, one that is a page-turner, which grabs and holds your interest. Or put a movie on your DVD player, one that is really absorbing. Most likely, your problems will keep until tomorrow when your head will be clearer and you may have the opportunity to talk about the problem with someone else.

## *Self Defeating Mind Games*

Excessive self focusing can be self destructive. The patterns of thought that occur during periods of rumination are often downers, ultimately undermining one's self esteem. There are a number of such destructive thought patterns — self defeating mind games that people engage in. One should be aware of them and avoid them when one is trying to cope with stress.[6]

## *Comparison Traps*

Brenda was experiencing serious financial problems. Unpaid gas, electric and telephone bills lay on the corner of her old desk. And in today's mail she had received a very large bill from the dentist. She had needed a crown, there had been no choice and now she had no idea where she would find the money to pay for it. Brenda worked as a waitress. She had two young children, Denise and Joshua, and a husband, George, who had recently been laid off from his job in the textile industry. As Brenda and George had only high-school educations, he was finding it difficult to land a new job. So, supporting the family temporarily fell on her shoulders and her wages were simply unequal to the task. She frequently worried about money. When she did, she often thought about her girlfriend, Andrea. They had been best friends in high school. Brenda became pregnant with Denise in the tenth grade. Denise's father had never taken responsibility for his child and now lived out of state. Brenda subsequently married George who was a loving husband and good father, but now he could not find work. In contrast Andrea had finished high school, gone on to college, and then received training in computer programming. She had an excellent, well-paying job, bought herself a house in the suburbs, and was filling it with expensive, beautiful furniture. Andrea thought of the cramped apartment in which she and her family lived and the old, worn furniture that they made do with. The comparison made her feel she was a failure. Thinking about her friend's situation made her feel depressed. What she failed to remember was that there were good things in her life; she had two nice children and a caring husband. Andrea was alone.

Comparisons with other people are a trap. In some ways you will always come out second best. There will always be someone, somewhere, who looks better, dresses better, makes more money, is more successful in his or her career, is a better athlete, or more socially skilled. Comparisons can make you feel depressed. But it's a fruitless exercise, if you think about it. What other people have done in their lives shouldn't really matter to you that much. You are a unique individual with your own needs, ideas, and values as to what is important. A maxim I like is to live your own life in your own terms and try to improve in those areas where you need to.

## *Perfectionist Thinking*

If you agree with me that what's important is to think about your own goals and lifestyle and not worry about what other people are achieving, then the focus should be on what will make you satisfied and comfortable. Consider goals that are satisfying yet achievable. One mental set which is almost guaranteed to never give you peace of mind is perfectionistic thinking. If something must be done exactly right every time, you are likely to be chronically frustrated. To set unreachable goals is something like hitting your head against the proverbial stone wall. You will never really be satisfied with what you do. In the process you may not only make yourself unhappy, but make everyone around you miserable.

The earliest example of a perfectionist that I had the misfortune of encountering was my violin teacher. I was about seven or eight years old when I fell into the clutches of this man who always reminded me of a Prussian drill master. Lessons consisted of repeating violin exercises over and over and over again. I remember that what I did was never quite right and I was forced to repeat the same meaningless activity ad infinitum. It was like a first grade teacher not being satisfied with teaching her pupils the basics of reading but expecting the students to read *War and Peace* before moving onto the second grade.

It's hard to imagine perfectionists being really happy with what they are trying to do. I suspect that many such individuals live in a perpetual state of discontent, if not agitation. If the mischief perfectionists accomplish would be confined to themselves, it would be forgivable. But the harm they cause others is less so. A friend of mine used to tell me about his perfectionist father who insisted on looking over every bit of homework my friend ever did and correcting it. His comments to his child were often demeaning. With an air of disgust on his face, he would say things like, "Is that the best you can do?" "Can't you do anything right?" "You'll never amount to anything." My friend had to survive this assault on his self esteem before turning his own life around and achieving a great deal. A perfectionist with his own children he is not.

Researchers have developed psychological measures of perfectionist tendencies and have used them in research. These studies suggest that people with perfectionist tendencies are more vulnerable to feeling depressed and when treated for depression they do not seem to progress as well. Here are two illustrative studies. A group of researchers at UCLA led by George Brown asked undergraduate students to complete some psychological inventories that included a measure of perfectionistic achievement (e.g., "my life is wasted unless I am a success") and a measure of depression.[7] The students then took an examination that for many of them was their first college level examination. Prior to the exam, the students were asked to write down the grade that they expected to achieve. The researchers found that the students with high perfectionist leanings showed more of a tendency to become depressed after not performing as well as they had expected on the exam.

As part of a series of studies on depression carried out under the auspices of the National Institute of Mental Health, people who were receiving outpatient therapy for depression were monitored for their progress. Those patients who had been characterized as having perfectionist tendencies did not progress in therapy as well as the other patients.[8]

Most of us, fortunately, are not perfectionists. If we were, the world we live in could be unbearable. No one would ever be satisfied with what they were doing and we would be constantly in each other's faces. If you live with a perfectionist, wouldn't it be nice if that person would turn down the screws a notch? You might have some room to breathe. And if you are the one who is the perfectionist, does it make you happy or does it just leave you feeling edgy, cranky and riled up? Ask yourself this question: "If I eased up on myself and was a little more tolerant of others, would my world really fall apart?" Perhaps you might just feel a little more relaxed.

## *Guilt Trips*

Have you ever know anyone who seldom or never admitted making mistakes? Someone who always cast blame for mistakes and failures onto other people? A person who never took responsibility for his own failings? I have occasionally come across people like that. At its extreme we sometimes think of such people as having personality disorders. When something goes wrong, it is always someone else who is at fault. At the other end of the spectrum are people who are prone to place the blame on themselves. If something goes wrong, they are likely to say, "It's my fault." They may take responsibility when clearly fault may lie in other corners or at least should be spread around. People who blame themselves for things that go wrong are likely to carry the burden of guilt. Not surprisingly, people who unduly blame themselves tend to feel depressed.

There are frequently extenuating circumstances for mistakes or failure. In a work situation, one often has to depend on the work of other people. Their work may not be done on time, it may be poorly done, or not done at all. And, somehow, you must pick up the pieces and this puts you at a disadvantage in doing your job. You may be sick or there may be illness in your family that requires your attention and these realities can distract you from your work. There may be insufficient funds and resources to effectively complete the project. Extenuating circumstances are often real but the guilt-prone person may dismiss them and still see himself or herself as the culprit. The ability to see extenuating circumstances is a self protective mechanism. To always feel one should have or could have done more — to frequently entertain such regrets — can be self defeating.

Psychologists like to use "sentence stems" (the beginning of sentences) in some of their personality tests. They ask the person being tested to complete the sentence. Imagine how a guilt-prone person would complete these sentences.

"I should have..."

"I regret..."

"I failed to..."

"When things go wrong..."

"I didn't..."

" My conscience bothers me when..."

" I wish I had..."

Guilt is part of the human experience. It has an important place in the process of socialization, in the formative years when we learn the basics of getting along with other people. We learn to feel guilty when we do bad things to other people. Some people experience very little guilt. They don't care if they harm others. Think of hardened criminals. We call such people who feel little remorse about inflicting hurt or injury psychopaths or sociopaths. But self blame is nothing to indulge in when you are under stress. It is only likely to drag you down.

## *Overgeneralization and Catastrophizing*

Unpleasant events happen to all of us. Perhaps on the job, perhaps in one's own family, or in a dating situation. Maybe there were harsh words spoken at the dinner table or maybe a report you wrote at the office was criticized. Such things happen to almost everyone. No one likes to experience disappointment or rejection, but such experiences are almost inevitable. The important thing is not that these experiences are going to happen — they are — but what you make of them.

In evaluating events, your perspective on life events is important. When something goes wrong, if you have a perspective — a philosophical outlook — that you "can't win them all," you accept the unpleasantness, don't overreact and move on. Tomorrow, you could have a better day and hopefully more success. But suppose, instead of looking at what happened as a transitory event, something restricted to a time and place, and not necessarily indicative of what may befall you in the future, you generalize from this unpleasant experience to the rest of what's happening in your life and conclude that your life is in shambles. Far-fetched? Not at all. A lot of people overgeneralize from unpleasant experiences.

A classic case happens when you realize that a person, perhaps a co-worker, doesn't like you. That's unpleasant. It may upset you more if you have a very strong need for everybody to like you, even love you. As was true for perfectionist thinking, the expectation that everybody will love you is just not going to be fulfilled. Not at least for most people. If you are extremely careful in what you do and what you say, smile at everyone, never utter a controversial remark, never put yourself into a leadership role, it is remotely possible that you may achieve this objective. At least no one may dislike you. But if you hope to do something serious in the world, this is nearly impossible. Think of some of the great people of history. Abraham Lincoln and Martin Luther King were despised by many people. Even George Washington had many detractors. Surely if you want to accomplish anything you must give up the fantasy that all people will adore you. They simply won't. The situation may not be as bad as legendary baseball manager Leo Durocher's famous comment would suggest that "nice guys finish last," but surely being loved by everyone is an unrealistic idea.

A young patient of mine was constantly harping on how unpopular he was. On one occasion, the basis for his conclusion was the open hostility of one person on his basketball team. When I inquired one by one about the remaining members of the team, it appeared that he got along fine with everyone else. It was something that I had to call to his attention in the manner of a quiet cross-examination before he was able to accept the fact that he was not unpopular simply because one person didn't like him.

The young heroine in the novel *Pollyanna* played the "glad game." As I remember the story, she began to list the good things in her life, the things she felt glad about. The idea strikes me as a pretty good antidote to a tendency to overgeneralize about negative events. Unless you are in the depths of a depression in which everything looks bleak to you, you can probably point to a number of things that are going well in your life. It may be something that happened at work, something your son or daughter did, perhaps a satisfying conversation with a friend, or maybe you helped an elderly neighbor and felt good about it. If, in an overgeneralizing mind-set, you have piled the recent events in your life on the negative side of the scale, step back for a moment and put the good things that happened to you on the other side of the scale. In taking stock of the good things, you may find that the scales are not as out of balance as you had imagined.

One of the most perverse forms of overgeneralizing is to imagine that in the future all events will turn out similar to the unpleasant event of today. Logically this makes no sense whatsoever. But as I have pointed out to patients in response to their observations that "nothing will ever change" or "things will always be this way" that if they really believe this, they may actually bring this result about as a self-fulfilling prophecy by doing the things to achieve this eventuality. The ultimate result, of course, will be a feeling of hopelessness, a pessimistic attitude toward life and probably depression.

My introduction to the idea of catastrophizing came as a small child when someone read to me the story of Henny Penny, Chicken Little and their friends. You remember the story of the fretful fowls who on the basis of very meager evidence proclaimed that the sky was falling down. Their alarmist cries were picked up by the other residents of the farmyard, and the terrifying prospect of the sky crashing down on their heads soon became an accepted reality.

Catastrophizing is making mountains out of molehills, with an element of panic thrown in. In fact the mental process of turning events into catastrophes has much in common with the terrifying experience of panic attacks. Typically, during panic attacks the heart races rapidly, there is shortness of breath and the person may initially interpret these symptoms as a heart attack. The thought that one is experiencing a heart attack, of course, is frightening, creating additional stress which only compounds the physiological reactions.

I am not sure how far the distance is between overgeneralizing and catastrophizing, but I think that overgeneralizing may be a step on the road. The mental progression may go something like this: "I had a bad experience," to "nothing is going right in my life," to "things are spiraling out of control." Concluding that you are on the edge of a disaster accompanied by feelings of mounting anxiety is the antithesis of reducing stress. Most typically, the sky is actually not falling; it's only a few acorns falling from a tree.

## *Narcotizing Anxiety*

When talking about using alcohol or drugs to lessen feelings of stress, I like to use the term narcotizing anxiety. The phrase conveys the idea of dampening down feelings of distress, of taking the edge off uncomfortable feelings. The term narcotizing anxiety is not one of my own. It was coined by the distinguished psychoanalyst Karen Horney many years ago.[9] Certainly, many people very deliberately use alcohol as a means of reducing stress. Think of the busy manager returning from a stress laden day at the office, driving through congested traffic, and then greeting his wife at the doorway, "Boy, do I need a drink!" We are not suggesting by this illustration that alcohol is only used for stress reduction. People use alcohol for a variety of reasons that have little to do with stress reduction. Alcohol has a long tradition of use with meals, in celebrations and at other social gatherings. Still, it seems clear enough from both everyday observation and psychological research that many people use alcohol to diminish stress.

A very interesting study was carried out by a group of researchers working out of the University of Connecticut Health Center.[10] One hundred men and women were recruited from newspaper ads for a study of daily life. The subjects were first given some self-report personality measures to complete including some questions asking whether they used alcohol to cope with stress. Then, the subjects were given an electronic reporting device, a hand-held computer with which they not only recorded episodes of drinking, but the context in which they were drinking — whether they were alone or with others, whether they were home or away. At night, the subjects completed a form asking about both positive and negative interpersonal exchanges that may have happened during the day.

The subjects, paid for their participation, followed this monitoring routine for 30 days. Over 10,000 positive interpersonal exchanges and over 4000 negative exchanges were recorded. Alcohol was consumed on about three-quarters of the days.

The subjects who said they used alcohol to cope with stress did indeed consume more drinks than the other subjects and this occurred irrespective of the context of drinking. This higher usage of alcohol raises the question as to whether routinely coping with stress by drinking creates a slippery slope toward alcohol dependency.

Looking at the entire sample, the researchers reported that on the days in which negative interpersonal encounters were reported, people tended to drink at home and alone. Such drinking usually took place in the evening following negative exchanges earlier in the day. Positive interpersonal exchanges were associated with drinking with others.

The possibility that stress-related drinking might be a precursor to excessive alcohol consumption needs further confirmation in research. However, I have seen examples of this in my clinical practice which makes me suspect that this is often the case. One of my patients, Lois Nettles, particularly comes to mind. I remember her very well because she was one of the first patients I saw in private practice. People have a tendency to remember things that happened at the beginning and end of a series of events. What happens in the middle often becomes blurred. Lois was referred to me by a colleague, a psychiatrist who was overbooked with appointments at the time and thought that I might be able to help her.

Lois had a drinking problem. While it is not clear that she was an alcoholic, it was clear that she was overusing alcohol as a means of dealing with the stresses that she was encountering in life. These stresses came primarily from her marriage, both in her relationships with her husband and her children. Lois had married a man, Richard, who was extremely bright, an intellectual in his pursuits. He was a very competent scientist, receiving his Ph.D. from an Ivy League school. While Lois was warm, engaging and pretty, she was no match for Richard in intellectual brilliance. Richard pursued his career, received recognition, and grew intellectually. Lois stayed home, busy raising three children. What happened is an all too common story. These role decisions exacerbated the differences between Richard and Lois. Richard became frustrated and discontented with his wife. Lois became intimidated by Richard. Their interactions deteriorated from being humdrum and unrewarding to uncomfortable to nasty. Richard became adept at making biting, sarcastic remarks, belittling his spouse. Their children soon picked up his disdain for his wife and began to lose respect for her. In time, they ignored her. Lois' self esteem collapsed under this pressure and she began to take refuge in drink. But drinking only exacerbated the problem, for what ability she had to cope with Richard decreased when she was drinking. The situation was unequal to begin with, but under the influence of alcohol, Lois' ability to counter Richard's criticisms and to fight back was severely impaired. She could not think straight or respond intelligently. For his part, Richard reacted to her drunken state with just more sarcasm.

Richard left Lois and sued for divorce. Desperately unhappy, Lois sought psychotherapy. Lois came to see me from a considerable distance. She lived in the northern suburbs, a good hour's drive away. Still, she never missed an appointment. Mostly what I did was to be a good listener and support her through this trying period of her life. I am happy to say that she got better, was able to give up drinking, and by the time therapy had concluded she had a new job and a more positive outlook on life. She told me that she was getting along much better with her children.

Many people with alcohol problems are not so fortunate. They may require years of working with groups like Alcoholics Anonymous to effectively deal with their problems. Lois was a highly motivated patient, and I was very happy to see her recover.

Alcohol and its effects on relationships can be an insidious problem, one that may not show itself right off the bat, but which becomes clearer and clearer over time. In talking about his wife's drinking which ultimately led to his divorce, a young lawyer told me, "I had no idea that she was drinking that much. In the beginning she was secretive about it. One day I noticed a half filled glass of orange juice on the kitchen table. I was about to empty it into the sink when I took a sip. It was almost pure vodka. I tried to confront her about her drinking but it didn't do any good. It's just made matters worse. She just got defensive and very angry."

The current view is that light drinking is probably good for one's health and longevity. Excessive drinking, however, creates medical problems and can wreak havoc with one's interpersonal relationships. Heavy drinking is a very poor way to cope with stress. It impairs one's ability to think straight and to converse intelligently. Speech becomes rambling and repetitive. Drinking decreases inhibitions and impairs the critical faculty that we rely on in screening what we say and do. Remarks made when one is drunk are often harmful to other people and can do serious damage to one's relationships. Excessive alcohol use is associated with both verbal and physical aggressiveness. A nasty remark or a violent blow once given cannot be taken back. Heavy drinking may dim the pain of stress temporarily, but actions taken under its influence can be destructive and cause far greater stress in the long run.

To drink or not to drink? For many people, that is the question. For one group of people — those who drink moderately — the answer is a no-brainer. They may enjoy a cocktail before dinner, a glass of wine during the meal, or an occasional beer during a hot summer afternoon. The drink was a pleasant, relaxing experience. There is little urge, much less a compulsion to keep on drinking. The bottle is put away for another day. For another group of people the answer to the question is also a no-brainer. They have learned through years of bitter experience that they cannot handle alcohol. The destructive consequences of drinking have been legion. Their marriages have suffered, perhaps collapsed, and they have had difficulties working effectively. Eventually, they received help from organizations such as Alcoholics Anonymous and concluded that they should never take another drink. For the many drinkers in between these two groups the question can be an important one. If they find they are drinking until they are drunk, and it's becoming a regular activity, it is probably time to start looking for alternative ways of reducing stress.

Many people smoke. Some, perhaps a great many of these people, will tell you that they smoke because it helps them to deal with stress. Because of the strong links between smoking and cancer, heart disease, and lung disease, smoking is clearly a potentially self-destructive way of easing stress. Therefore, it is important to examine the links between smoking and stress. We know what smoking does to people's health. It is very harmful. Does it do anything for people? Does it in fact reduce stress?

If you have seen movies made in the 1940s and 1950s about the Second World War, you may remember scenes in airplane hangars, where the pilots are nervously fingering half smoked cigarettes before setting out for that next mission in their Spitfire fighters or Flying Fortress bombers. The images on the screen are of men under great tension and the cigarettes they are holding are clearly there to calm their nerves.

Researchers who have studied the relation between stress and smoking have concluded that the relation is, in fact, quite complicated. As we have indicated, many smokers will certainly tell you that smoking relieves tension. But some critics would argue that much of the tension relief experienced is really quelling the pangs of nicotine dependence, or worse, addiction — calming withdrawal symptoms. Still, smokers will tell you that they smoke more when they feel anxious, sad, or under stress. And, they do so with the expectation that smoking will alleviate their distress. These smoker expectations and beliefs are well documented in the research literature.[11] However, it is still unclear whether smoking actually reduces tension. Although, smokers report that smoking reduces tension levels, physiologically, smoking elevates cortisol levels, rather than reducing them. This paradox was observed by Nesbitt in 1973 who noted, "The physiological and psychological effects of smoking a cigarette are seemingly in contradiction to each other.... When smokers smoke, their level of physiological arousal goes up, while they report themselves as calmer and more relaxed."[12]

In a review article on smoking and stress, John Kassel and his colleagues noted that experimenters have placed smokers into mildly stressful situations and studied the effects of smoking on both their self reports of stress and physiological reactions.[13] The results have been variable. Smoking may affect one type of measure, but not the other in the same way. So, it is not yet clear how smoking affects stress levels. We simply have the self reports of smokers that it does.

We do know some things about smoking and stress. We know that stress plays a role in the initial decision to smoke. While peer influences have a marked effect on the decision of children and adolescents to smoke, stress is also involved. Kassel and his colleagues noted that "numerous studies have found associations between various indices of psychological stress and smoking uptake."[14] These stressors included childhood abuse, dysfunctional households, adverse childhood experiences, parental divorce, and negative life events.

So, people begin to smoke, in part, because they feel stress; when stress increases, they smoke more; and when they quit, they may resume because of stress. They believe that smoking helps them reduce stress, but physiologically smoking has the opposite effect. This is, however, more than an academic puzzle, for in time smoking is likely to destroy one's health.

While alcohol and cigarettes are clearly used by many people as ways of reducing tension, illegal drugs may or may not be used for this purpose. People look at different drugs in different ways. They may see some drugs as tension reducing but not others. Clearly, it is unlikely that a person would use a potent hallucinogenic drug simply to reduce stress and achieve relaxation. The motivation for using hallucinogens such as LSD, peyote, or mescaline would more typically be to achieve a state of enhanced experience. The user may hope to see intense colors, unusual geometric forms, and even experience profound visions. Indeed, in using hallucinogens, one may experience panic reactions, rather than relaxation. The users of cocaine are not so much seeking a means of reducing tension as much as they are seeking a high. What they are hoping for is an intense rush, a feeling of euphoria, a sense of extreme happiness and well being. Using cocaine may not reduce anxiety so much as it makes people feel restless, irritable and edgy. The most frequently used illegal drug, marijuana, however, is used by many people to reduce stress. For many people the marijuana experience can be a relaxing one.

In my book, *Marijuana: A Short Course,* college students discussed their attitudes toward marijuana use and what they hoped to achieve from using it. A state of relaxation is a typical response.[15] Some students freely talked about their need for stress reduction. Here is an example

Question: How do you usually feel before smoking it? Did you tend to be in any particular mood — feel in any particular way before you begin to smoke?

"In need of release from anxiety."

Question: What do you usually hope to get out of smoking marijuana?

"Relaxation, release from stress — relaxation."

Question: Now, please tell us in your own words what it is like to smoke marijuana. How would you describe the feelings and sensations you experience?

"Release from anxiety and inhibition...."

If marijuana can be relaxing, what are the downsides? There are several. First, like most drugs, marijuana does not have a single effect such as relaxation; it has a variety of effects, some of which may not be welcome. For example, marijuana use sometimes causes anxious and depressed reactions. Using marijuana can also interfere with one's ability to drive a car. Second, as marijuana is an illegal substance, the quality and strength of what one buys is unknown. One might end up smoking a joint which is a lot more potent than one expects. Third, marijuana is a gateway drug. By that we mean using marijuana may open up an interest in and desire to experiment with more powerful and more dangerous drugs. While it is true that most users of marijuana do not move on to harder drugs, it is also true that users of harder drugs frequently began their drug use with marijuana. When I was a consultant with a drug and alcohol unit in a Veterans Administration hospital studying heroin addicted patients, I asked them about their perceptions of various drugs. One of the interesting findings of that research was the favorable view that these patients had of marijuana.[16]

Having seen their lives nearly destroyed by heroin addiction, they now looked back upon their earlier experimentation with marijuana through rose colored glasses. I suspect that most of them wished that they had stopped right there and had not proceeded down the path to heroin addiction. Fourth, marijuana is an illegal substance. Getting caught using marijuana can lead to a criminal record, which no one wants.

Here are a few thoughts about eating as a way of coping with stress. In my clinical work, I've heard more than a few patients tell me, "I'm gaining weight because of the stress I'm under." Indeed, many people binge on food, which leads to being overweight and in some cases binge eating may be caused by stress. But, to attribute most cases of overeating to stress seems a very large stretch.

As a way of putting the issue in perspective, a group of researchers working out of the University of Helsinki in Finland surveyed over 45,000 workers obtaining data about various aspects of job-related stress.[17] They related the level of stress reported to a measure of the respondents' weight — their body mass index. If workplace stress were a key factor in overeating, we would expect to find a substantial relation between the two measures. There was a relation, but it was pretty weak. Stress on the job appeared to be a factor — but only a small one — in overeating.

Now, a large-scale study like this is a rather blunt instrument for examining the relation between stress and overeating. However, when controlled laboratory studies were undertaken in which people were exposed to mild stressors (e.g., scary movies, failing at a task, making a speech) there was usually no overall tendency to overeat. In one study men watched videos.[18] For half of the men, the videos were unpleasant. While watching the videos, the men were presented with several types of food (sweet, salty, or bland). The men who watched the unpleasant video ate only about half the amount of food as the other men. Clearly, they didn't reach for food as a palliative for whatever negative emotions the video generated. Stress may have turned off their appetites rather than the reverse.

Do people sometimes binge on food when they are under stress? Sure. In our coping inventory which asked about responses to feeling tense, Roland Tanck and I included an item, "eat constantly." Five percent of the students responded that they "almost always" did this while another 12 percent said they "often" did this.[19] Clearly, there are a fairly large number of people who respond to stress by binging on food. The question becomes, who are these people?

One robust finding in the research literature on stress and eating is that women who are exerting considerable effort to control their weight — who try to exercise restraint in their eating — are people who seem to let go of themselves under stress.[20] They appear to be the ones most likely to binge. It's something like a binder snapping under heavy physical stress.

If the person is overweight, then binge eating is an unhealthy way of coping with stress. Being markedly overweight is a prime factor for developing serious medical problems. A readily available supply of non-fattening foods such as fruit and vegetables to snack on is one way to try to control a binging tendency. If you are not overweight and the stress you are experiencing is to be super thin like the reigning supermodel, you might ask yourself whether it is all worth it. To be very thin is a current cultural pressure which makes as much sense as a cultural pressure in earlier days (circa 1890) for women to be pleasingly plump. Some women at this time were trying very hard to put on weight to be physically attractive.[21] This is something to think about before becoming too focused on dieting. The stress caused by the pressure to be thin may cause you to binge.

There is a tendency for many people in our society, today, to be overweight, even obese. However, research suggests that for most people the culprit is probably not stress. I suspect that the problem is too much good tasting food loaded with too many calories, coupled with not enough exercise to burn off the calories.

## *Feeling Trapped*

Have you ever felt in a bind? Trapped in a situation? Perhaps it was a meeting at work in which you were feeling very uncomfortable. You wanted to leave but you just couldn't get up and walk out. Or perhaps you were stuck in bumper to bumper traffic. In both situations you had few good options. Fortunately, you knew the situation was only temporary. Eventually, you knew the meeting would break up and so would the traffic.

Imagine a situation where you felt in a bind that was not transitory. Imagine that every day you awoke with a feeling that you were trapped in a bad situation. You recognize your situation is lousy, but when you think about making changes, you do not like the alternatives. The devils known are bad. The devils unknown may be worse. Your current circumstances are stressful. The thought of making major changes is even more so.

Christina graduated high school, but decided not to go to college. She never did well in school and did not like it. When her parents suggested she should get additional education to enhance her job opportunities, she said she was tired of school and would find a job. After two or three short term jobs working as a waitress, she finally found a somewhat better job working in an office doing low level work processing insurance claims. The job required only very basic knowledge of using a computer. Christina has now been in this job for six years. The work is repetitive, boring, and does not pay particularly well. But Christina has few job skills and she is afraid to try to find a better job, because she thinks she might not be able to handle it. Her experiences at school had eroded her self esteem and she had little self-confidence. She believes that the job at the insurance company is secure. She feels she can stay there as long as she wants to. She really needs the salary. But she realizes that there is no future there and it is a dreary prospect to remain there indefinitely. Fear of not being able to handle more challenging work keeps her locked in her present job.

Theresa's parents were both in their thirties when they married. Theresa's mother was 41 when Theresa, her only child, was born. Theresa's mother thought a second pregnancy would be risky. As an only child Teresa received a great deal of attention from her parents. She was loved and well cared for. Her childhood and adolescence were both pleasant. After high school, Theresa went away to college and took a master's degree in history. She began a career teaching at a community college.

Theresa had an active life. She liked teaching and participating in the activities at the college. She had many friends, dated frequently, often went out to dinner and the movies. She had one serious love affair, but she never married. When Theresa was about 40, her father had a stroke. Unable to cope with the situation, Theresa's mother asked her to come home and help out. Theresa took a leave of absence for a semester from the college and returned to her childhood home. What she found was very disquieting. Not only was her father a helpless invalid, her mother was showing initial signs of dementia. Given this situation, she decided to quit her job at the college and stay home to take care of her parents. In time Teresa found that she was in charge of everything, looking after the finances, running the house, preparing meals, as well as providing some nursing care for her father. Helping out had become a full time job. All the things that Theresa had liked to do, her teaching, her social life — all fell by the wayside. As the years went by Theresa found that she was trapped in the role she had taken on. The loss of what had pleased her in her former life was depressing. To leave her parents, however, was unthinkable. She found herself in a dilemma that had no obvious answer. As her mother's dementia increased the situation in the house became increasingly stressful.

The picture of a man or woman trapped in a dreary, loveless marriage was truer of the past than it is the case today. Novelists used to write about a woman with children somehow enduring a tyrannical husband or a husband being nagged to death by a shrewish wife. It wasn't that far back in our history that divorce was much harder to obtain and was considered disgraceful.

The bind of a bad marriage is no longer the chilling prospect it once was, at least not in Western societies. Today, divorce is commonplace. But the prospect of leaving an unsatisfactory marriage and going forth on one's own can still be a very troubling idea for many people. Becoming a single mother is a major step with significant potential disadvantages. It will very likely mean a decline in one's living standards. There will simply be less money to do more. It may also put the woman into a multiple roles situation, where she may not only have to work on a job, but keep up the house, shop, cook, and be responsible for the care of the children. It is a very large responsibility. And, of course, there are the effects of divorce on the children. Divorce can have both short and long-term negative effects on the children. So, the question often becomes, for both men and women, is it better to stay with a bad marriage and try to improve things or venture out on one's own?

There are many reasons for a marriage to turn sour, leaving one or both spouses dissatisfied and unhappy. Marriage counselors can offer a long list of reasons. A few of the more frequent causes are arguments about money, dissatisfaction with sexual relations, a lack of communication, and alcohol abuse. While there may be any number of reasons for a spouse to contemplate divorce, a physically battered woman's motivation to end a marriage should be crystal clear. You have probably read stories in newspapers and magazines of wives who ended up in emergency rooms after beatings by their husbands. What often happens is that after the beating, the husband pleads with his wife to return home, promising her that it will never happen again. But in time, it does happen again. And after another beating, the battered woman returns home once more. This repetitive cycle may be mystifying to outside observers. Why does she do it? It seems to be a classic case of a person being stuck in a bad situation, one in which there is the ever present possibility of serious injury. Why is the battered wife unwilling to leave? There certainly is a well grounded fear of the known situation, a husband who can lose control and become violent. Is it fear of the unknown should she break the relationship and must be on her own that keeps her there? I think there is often a good deal more involved.

There is hope — often misplaced — that things will get better. Memories of better times often sustain this hope. And there still may be feelings of love, perhaps only embers of what were once more vibrant feelings. But still there is love and the hope of a return to what once was.

In understanding why people remain in unhappy situations, it may be helpful if we analyze the nature of conflict situations. Psychologists like to talk about three types of conflicts. The first is a situation in which a person is torn between two choices. For example, a young woman graduating high school has been accepted by two prestigious universities — Stanford and Columbia. Which does she choose? Since she would be very happy to attend either university, it's not a wrenching problem. Whatever she chooses, she can't really lose.

A second type of conflict is the one we have been discussing where either alternative looks unpromising, perhaps even bleak. Our young woman who works in a dead end job in an insurance company but is afraid to look for a better job elsewhere, the daughter caring for parents in declining health, and the many men and women seemingly trapped in unhappy marriages are all examples of this type of conflict. So too are many of the women who are battered wives.

Some of the battered wives however represent a third type of conflict. This occurs in people who have both positive and negative feelings toward the same person. A battered woman may still care about the person who has hurt her. We call positive and negative feelings toward the same individual ambivalence. A certain amount of ambivalence in human relationships is normal. If we are pushed, we can all think of negative qualities in almost anyone we think about. Your doctor, minister or even your romantic partner can irritate you at times. But, to be wracked by fundamental ambivalence toward another does not bode well for a relationship.

As is true for the second type of conflict, having strong ambivalent feelings can be a wrenching experience. I remember a young man head over heels in love, but who knew deep down that there was very little, if any, chance that things would work out well. Realizing this, he still could not let her go and seek someone else who was attainable.

In an essay on "The Psychology of Doing Nothing," Christopher Anderson reminds us that while the failure to take action can be the result of a severe conflict, it can also result from more mundane reasons as well.[22] The person might be lethargic, insufficiently motivated, or someone who prefers to leave things as they are. Anderson talks about a concept of *decision avoidance* which applies to responses to conditions which are not threatening. He defines decision avoidance as "a tendency to avoid making a choice by postponing it or by seeking an easy way out that involves no action or no change."[23] Decision avoidance is characterized by adherence to the status quo, inaction, inertia, and delay. When there is a threat involved, when the situation involves stress, Anderson uses the term defensive avoidance, which is similar to what we have been talking about as an immobilizing response to conflict. Anderson's description of defensive avoidance helps flesh out a portrait of this reaction. "Defensive avoidance occurs when there may be risks to maintaining the status quo but the prospects for discovering better alternatives appear grim. The defensive response takes several forms: evasive, in which reminders of the decision are ignored and distractions are sought; buck passing, in which responsibility for the decision is shifted to others; and bolstering, in which the decision maker seeks reasons, in a biased manner, to support an inferior course of action."[24] Bolstering sounds like another term for rationalization. In either case, where there is a threat or no threat involved, the failure to act can have consequences in the form of lost opportunities for making needed changes.

Being stuck, feeling trapped in a situation which arouses considerable stress, is a situation that happens all the time. But, remaining immobilized, frozen in a situation, is a poor way to deal with constant stress. If you are in a real bind, not knowing what to do, you have probably already received lots of advice. Perhaps some of your friends or family members are even growing impatient with you for not resolving this situation. They may not fully appreciate how difficult the situation is for you. Still, their growing irritation pales next to the pain you feel about being stuck. My suggestion to people frozen in bad situations is to take another look at possible options. This time, try to really free up your mind and look at possibilities you haven't yet considered. Give your creative muse a chance. Let your imagination roam over a much wider range of possibilities than you have previously considered, even far out possibilities. Then, get very practical. Do some serious research on any option that looks plausible. The devils unknown in making a change may not look so forbidding when you have taken a really close look at them.

# 4

# *Better Ways of Reducing Stress*

## *Exercise*

Of all the ways of reducing stress that have some proven value, for most people nothing is more easily available than exercise. Almost any kind of exercise is likely to be beneficial. There is a park near where we live and on a Sunday morning in the spring, there is a procession of bicyclists, joggers, young mothers pushing baby carriages, and elderly men just ambling along. Set back slightly into the park is a tennis court which is usually occupied and not too far away is a public golf course. Whatever kind of exercise you choose, it is likely to be good for both your body and your mental health. The caveat is that you should undertake only the exercise which is clearly within your capabilities and if you have any doubts about this whatsoever, you should check with your doctor.

The reasons exercise works in reducing stress are not altogether clear but there is a great deal of research evidence to show that it does. Many studies point to the mental health benefits of exercise. In one type of study, the researchers might begin by taking psychological measurements, then institute an exercise program, repeat the psychological measurements, then compare the results with those of a control group not given the exercise program. Or, the researchers might compare the benefits of different types of exercise or perhaps different lengths of time that the exercise is undertaken. An example of the latter type of study was one carried out at Kyushu University in Japan.[1] The researchers T.

Nabetani and M. Tokunaga recruited healthy male graduate students and asked them to run on a treadmill at a pace at which they felt good, on two different occasions, once for 10 minutes, once for 15. Before, during, and after the exercise, the researchers administered a mood checklist to assess three measures of mood, feelings of pleasantness, relaxation, and anxiety. The researchers reported that both levels of exercise (10 or 15 minutes) affected the subjects' mood in a positive way. The researchers concluded that such exercise — whether 10 or 15 minutes in duration — had positive psychological benefits for the participants. These results suggest that doing some exercise is probably more important than how much you do.

Using a different approach to assess the psychological effects of exercise, S. G. Aldana and his colleagues at Brigham Young University carried out a large-scale survey relating leisure time physical activity and self reported stress.[2] They surveyed over 30,000 working adults, asking questions to assess both their levels of physical activity and self reported levels of stress. The results were quite clear. The adults who participated in even moderate amounts of physical activities had about half the rate of perceived stress as nonparticipants.

In reviewing the research literature on the effects of exercise on anxiety, depression, and stress, P. Salmon noted that exercise can have adverse effects as well as positive ones.[3] I had a patient, once, who simply overdid it and caused himself harm. To obtain the benefits of exercise, you need not train like an Olympian. Salmon also noted that the antianxiety and antidepressive effects of exercise have been most clearly established in normal rather than in clinical populations. Salmon's interpretation of the research evidence is that exercise may well have a stress buffering effect.

Exercise is not just for the youngster or twenty-somethings or thirty-somethings. Appropriate, medically approved exercise can have significant mental health benefits for older people as well. An interesting study indicated exercise can enhance self-esteem in older people and self-esteem is one of our bulwarks against stressors. In the study carried out by Edward McAuley and his colleagues, 174 sedentary adults (average age 65 years) were recruited to participate in a six-month long exercise program.[4] The subjects were randomly split into two groups. The first group walked for exercise, while the second group met in a gymnasium where they did strengthening and flexibility exercises. Both groups exercised three times a week. Both types of exercise led to higher levels of self-esteem as measured by psychological tests. The participants felt better about their bodies and themselves.

Studies such as the one carried out by McAuley and his colleagues point to the psychological benefits of exercise for people in almost all age groups. One of my favorite examples of the use of exercise for reduction of stress is Anna, a 53-year-old elementary schoolteacher who does a great deal of work with special education students. Anna says, "After days of chasing after kids, I look forward to my class of water aerobics exercises. I meet a lot of people I like in the class which adds to the fun of it." In the pool she goes through a series of standing and running exercises using foam weights and "water noodles" and then swims across the pool. Anna says, "The exercise makes me feel good. I feel relaxed and energized."

I usually recommended exercise to my patients who were experiencing high levels of stress or suffering from depression. My general rule was to do what you like doing. If you would rather walk than run, then, by all means walk, and walk about as far as you're comfortable walking. If you are seeking relaxation, don't make it a competitive venture. If the point is to relax, relax! Competition is terrific for many people. They thrive on it. But like workplace competition, the sports field can be stressful. If your ego is on the line, where is the relaxation? A pickup game of basketball is one thing. To strive for victory at all times is something else. A walk along the park untarnished by competitive strivings is my ideal of exercise undertaken for the purpose of relaxation.

Once you have chosen a form of exercise that you feel comfortable about, pick a time of the day that is convenient for you and unlikely to be compromised by other activities, and see if you can get into the habit of exercising then. I think you will find you will soon feel better.

## *Talking to a Friend*

It is probably something basic in our human natures — perhaps part of our phylogenetic heritage — but it is clear that the company, the touch, even the voice of another person can sometimes assuage anxiety. The social scientist is likely to call the phenomenon social support. But we all know what the term means when we receive a squeeze on the shoulder or a ready ear and a sympathetic voice. After a sudden, painful fall, the young child recognizes the comfort of his mother's soothing voice and encircling arms. And adults may experience a similar comfort when feeling sick and worried and they reach the friendly confines of their doctors' offices.

The crying child and the sick adult are seeking help. The person feeling troubled who calls a friend may be doing much the same thing. The result of the conversation may be similar to the relief the frightened child and the sick adult experience. The caller feels better. The level of tension drops. The body quiets.

Part of the magic in talking to others lies in the feeling that someone cares. As a college student wrote explaining why he felt talking with a friend helped when he was feeling tense and anxious, "Talking to someone that you know loves you and cares about you offers a great sense of comfort."[5]

Sometimes in these conversations, a catharsis happens. The person unloads pent up concerns. There is an unburdening, and a strong sense of relief.

Not only can one's emotions be quieted by a supportive response from another person, there may be changes in the ways the stressed-out person perceives the problem. Once personal problems have been cast forth into the more objective arena of dialog, it is no longer a situation where the individual struggles alone with problems and possibilities. Rumination — wrestling with unsolved problems — has ceased at least temporarily. Now there is a fresh perspective — the views of someone else who may evaluate the situation differently. Perhaps in the eyes of the friend, the problem does not seem catastrophic, perhaps even fixable. That type of reassurance can be worth a lot to someone who may be analyzing the problems to death.

There are many studies one could cite that attest to the buffering effect of social support when a person is facing a stressful situation. Here is an illustration. Eighty-four patients facing surgery in a German hospital were asked to fill out a psychological scale which measured the level of social support they felt they had relating to the impending surgery.[6] The patients were also assessed for the level of anxiety they were experiencing, the amount of narcotics they required for anesthesia induction, and later for the length of time they stayed in the hospital following surgery. It is not surprising that the patients who felt they had more support for the upcoming surgery were less anxious before surgery. Social support is a good bet as a buffer for diminishing stress.

What may be surprising was the finding that patients with higher levels of social support needed less narcotics and stayed in the hospital a shorter time after surgery. The impact of social support appears wide ranging.

When a person is faced with a stressful situation, the presence of people who are supportive tends to dampen the body's reaction to the stressor. A number of laboratory studies have shown that social support reduces cardiovascular reactivity to stressors. In a thoughtful article, Shelley Taylor and her colleagues noted, "Contact with a friend or a supportive other person during stressful events down-regulates sympathetic and neuroendrocine responses to stress and facilitates recovery from the physiological effects of acute stress."[7]

Taylor and her colleagues observed that coping with stress by seeking the company of other people is more common among women than men. This, I think, is an everyday observation and reflects the different kinds of training and experiences boys and girls have as they grow up in our culture. Research very clearly supports this observation. Taylor and her colleagues observed, "Research on human males and females shows that, under conditions of stress, the desire to affiliate with others is substantially more marked among females than among males. In fact, it is one of the most robust gender differences in adult human behavior."[8] In referring to a review of gender differences in seeking social support, Taylor and her colleagues noted, "Of the 26 studies that tested for gender differences, one study showed no differences, and 25 favored women."[9] In commenting on this difference, Taylor and her colleagues noted,

> "Across the entire life cycle, females are more likely to mobilize social support, especially from other females, in times of stress. They seek it out more, they receive more support, and they are more satisfied with the support they receive. Adolescent girls report more informal sources of support than do boys, and they are more likely to turn to their same-sex peers for support them are boys.... Female college students report more available helpers and report receiving more support than do males.... Adult women maintain more same-sex close relationships than do men, they mobilize more social support in times of stress than do men, they rely less heavily than do men on their spouses for social support, they turn more to female friends more often, they report more benefits from contact with their female friends and relatives..."

In referring to a study on social networks, the authors observed that "women were 30 percent more likely than men to have provided some time of support in response to network stressors, including economic and work-related difficulties, interpersonal problems, death, and negative health events."[10]

Evidence abounds for the importance of emotional support in all age ranges. Such support can be particularly important for the elderly. Writing in the *Journal of Gerontology*, Neal Krause reported the findings of a national survey of elderly people which inquired about stress, emotional support, and perceived health.[11] As expected, negative life events were associated with perceptions of poor health. However, high levels of emotional support in the areas of life that were most important to the respondents had a buffering effect. People with such support felt better. Emotional support helped them deal with the deleterious effects of stress. Krause's data also suggested that part of the stress-buffering effect of emotional support in the elderly lies in the protection of a person's sense of meaning in life. A sense of self efficacy may be fading with declining physical capabilities, but older people need to know that they still matter. Talking with and being close to others helps maintain their sense of identity.

While social support has a great deal to recommend it as a way of coping with the everyday stresses of life — the arguments, the hassles, the inevitable disappointments — like all coping techniques, the use of social support has its limitations. When a person is faced with a stressor of traumatic proportions, support from others can be beneficial, but probably more will be required to adequately address the level of stress aroused. A case in point would be a study carried out on the survivors of a disastrous supper club fire. The fire occurred on a Saturday night of a Memorial Day weekend.[12] The supper club was quite spacious; a very large crowd, over 2500 people, patronized the club that evening. A fire broke out and spread. Despite warnings given to patrons to exit quickly and orderly, many people were unable to escape. One hundred sixty-five people died as a result of the fire.

A team of researchers led by Bonnie Green monitored what happened to a group of the survivors for a period of two years. The researchers were looking for long term psychological problems that might result from the disaster. The researchers found that the survivors who had more natural supports in their daily lives (family, friends, and co-workers) showed fewer indicators of psychiatric symptoms. While social support was helpful, it was unlikely, in itself, to undo the effects of the trauma. If someone had a terrifying experience during the fire and its aftermath (e.g., exposure to disfigured bodies), the concern and support of others might help, but clearly might not be enough.

Given this perspective, let's talk about choosing a confidante. This may be very easy for you or you may find it difficult. If you are a lonely, isolated person, there may be no one who comes readily to mind. In that event you might try searching the Internet for a like-minded soul, but hopefully there are some existing possibilities. If I were to describe my idea of an ideal confidante, it would sound something like this.

You have a high comfort level with a person. You feel simpatico. You trust the person.

The person is a good listener. The person does not quickly toss out reams of advice to you, but first tries to listen and understand.

The person is not judgmental, and is not a faultfinder, which is the last thing you need.

The person is not locked into a single point of view, but can see different sides of a situation. You need some other perspectives, not just your own.

The person is not a gossiper.

If human touch can relax stress, wouldn't sex be even better? Yes, in some circumstances. But, it may be misplaced as an antidote for every source of stress that comes along. Sex can be a wonderful expression of the love two people feel for one another and if the tensions that a person feels are pent up sexual desires, then clearly sexual relations are an obvious remedy. However, sex seems like an inefficient and potentially complicated way to deal with the myriad of routine stressors that one has to deal with in life. Sex can have unanticipated and sometimes profound emotional effects on both parties. It is generally not an inconsequential act. In my studies on coping behavior, I did find some people who routinely used sex as a way of reducing stress. However, most of the people I studied relied on other ways of lowering tension which were more directly targeted to the problem causing the stress. If a term paper is due in the morning, using sex to reduce the stress of the deadline may send you to sleep with a smile on your face but it will leave your term paper unfinished.

If human companionship is reassuring and comforting, how about the companionship of animals? One could imagine a cartoon, more or less along the lines of Charles Schulz's *Peanuts* comic strip, in which an erudite looking dog such as Snoopy is holding a note pad and looking at its master, Charlie Brown, who is expounding on his cares and troubles. I imagine there are plenty of people who use their pets as sounding boards (at least they won't find fault), but more likely it's just the quiet companionship and physical stroking that is soothing. I have more than one friend whose cat ends up in bed at night.

I spoke with a young woman who loves animals and knows a lot about dogs. She described the dogs she has had as "devoted"—"that they were there for you." She said that "every night when I come home from work, they were there waiting at the door to greet me." The greeting always gave her a lift.

The calming effects that petting animals has on people have long been recognized. There are petting farms for children and therapy dogs are used at nursing homes, hospices and hospitals. The young woman who was telling me about her dogs told me about a friend of hers, a dog groomer who had his poodle — a gentle animal with wonderfully silky hair — trained as a therapy dog. Once a week, the groomer takes his dog to visit nursing homes and hospices where the dog is happily petted by the residents.

Sandra Barker, who directs the Center for Human-Animal Interactions at Virginia Commonwealth University, has been much interested in the therapeutic use of animals, also known as animal assisted therapy. She notes that studies have demonstrated benefits for animal visits in a variety of populations including psychiatric patients and the elderly. Using a group of health-care professionals as subjects, Barker and her colleagues studied the effect of a therapeutic dog on the stress hormone cortisol. During the visits with the dog, which lasted either five or twenty minutes, the subjects were encouraged to interact with the dog. The researchers reported that after either the five minute or twenty minute visit with the dog, cortisol levels decreased.[13]

While there is still much to learn about the effects of pets on stress, there is evidence which supports the observation that pets can have stress-reducing effects on the people they are around. Researchers have found decreases in self reported anxiety, fear, loneliness, and depression.[14] Another line of research has compared the reaction to stress of people who are pet owners with those who are not. In a study carried out by Karen Allen and her colleagues at the University of Buffalo, pet owners showed smaller cardiovascular reactions (heart rate, blood pressure) during stress tests (doing mental arithmetic and the placing one's hand in very cold water test) than people who did not own pets. Interestingly, the smallest reactions to the stress tests for the pet owners occurred when their pets were present during testing.[15]

A study that I find particularly compelling was carried out on very young children, ages three to six. The children were given two physical examinations, which for young children can be bewildering and unsettling. On one occasion there was a dog present during the examination, on the other there was not. The researchers, S. L. Nagengast and her colleagues, reported that the children showed significantly less cardiovascular reactivity and less behavioral distress when the dog was present. The image of the doctor, the dog and the small child together certainly is a pleasant, reassuring one.[16]

When considering pets for possible help in stress reduction, the attitude of the people involved is very important. The presence of a dog for people who are uncomfortable with or afraid of dogs is likely to be counterproductive. Can other pets be therapeutic? Probably. One study, for example, has suggested that watching fish in an aquarium might be helpful in lowering anxiety. Another study looked at a bird as a companion and the possible effects of this on depression.[17]

If you are fond of animals, a pet can help. Try the animal rescue league or a similar organization in your community. You may find a very special friend.

## *Diversion*

To divert oneself, if only for a while, from troubles and cares has to be a good thing. Turning away from pressure-filled situations, to allow one's mind to engage in other thoughts, to participate in activities that are not a normal part of a stressful routine is something like turning down the flame on the stove under the pot that's about to boil over. Shift in scene, shift in activity, shift in focus can reduce pent up tensions and provide some space away from the problems that nag one — perhaps allowing one to look at the problems differently. Seeing things in a different light sometimes enables one to find better solutions for problems.

One of the virtues of a good novel is that it takes you out of yourself and permits you to enter the lives of other people. In a good novel, you are able to identify with the characters. Their problems and predicaments hold your interest, even absorb you. For a brief stretch of time, you have stopped worrying about that problem on the job or the argument you had with your boyfriend. In a word, you have escaped from your own realities, and put on the shoes of someone else. For a brief period of time you may find yourself transported to J.R.R. Tolkien's peril filled world of the *Lord of the Rings,* or to Harry Potter's delightful school of magic or to a romance in the regency period of English history or you may be trying to solve a murder mystery with any of a number of fascinating detectives. Whatever your taste, if the book gives you a respite from the pressing concerns of the day, it's a help.

Television soap operas may be the ultimate form for turning one's attention away from one's own problems and experiencing those of another. These programs have millions of faithful viewers who seldom miss an episode. Do they do much to improve one's intellect and knowledge? Probably not. Do they provide an hour or more of escape from one's problems? Yes indeed.

For many people music is a diversion. For others, it may be part of the background sounds of daily life, emanating from a stereo in the corner of the room or from the radio in the car that is on during a long trip or for the daily commute through rush hour traffic. The realization that listening to music could have a soothing effect goes back at least to biblical times and the story of the boy David soothing King Saul with the sounds of a lyre. In a review paper published in *Cardiology*, looking at the effects of music therapy, Suzanne Hanser and Susan Mandel of the Berklee College of Music noted that music therapists often participate in departments of integrative medicine where music is used to stimulate positive thoughts and memories, pleasant associations and images.[18] In this way, music could be used along with the muscle relaxation technique we will discuss shortly or as an adjunct or follow-up to meditation.

Research suggests that music used either alone or in conjunction with other relaxation techniques can be effective in lowering anxiety in cardiac patients. In one study, for example, patients who were recovering from acute myocardial infarction reported less anxiety after listening to 20 minutes of music than patients in a control group who did not listen to music. The researchers also reported reduced pulse and respiratory rates in the patients who listened to music.[19]

Such results seem sufficiently encouraging to recommend listening to music as one means of reducing stress. The caveat, of course, is that not all music is alike, and one has to find out what works for oneself. I would doubt that music which is depressing would be very helpful to most people, and probably not songs that are associated in one's memory with sad experiences. Listening to music has the virtue of being easy to do and you may find it helpful when you feel stressed out.

The potential benefits of music therapy are illustrated in a case reported in Hanser and Mandel's article.[20] The subject, a 72-year-old cardiac patient, who five months earlier had undergone triple coronary artery bypass surgery worked with a music therapist during her hospitalization. The therapists instructed her to listen to the music and as she did so to imagine beautiful places.[21] When the patient did this, she found that she slept restfully for 12 hours and experienced pleasant feelings for some time afterwards. When she left the hospital she continued these music therapy exercises on her own and she felt that they proved very beneficial. She reported that when she retired to bed, she switched on the music tape and listened, and as she did so, many memories would filter through her consciousness, and in time she would feel very comfortable and relaxed. Then, she would fall into a deep, restful sleep. She reports now that she has never had such low blood pressure readings.[22]

Do you have a hobby that you enjoy? Great! If not, think about getting one. Some kind of pursuit that takes you away from your daily routines. Something that will expand your knowledge and activities. Looking through my county recreation department's offerings, I find a list of pursuits, avocations, and activities that is as long as my arm. There are opportunities to sing, sculpt, learn a language, bird watch, cook exotic foods, learn to play a guitar, enjoy folk-dancing, improve your bridge game, take classes in yoga—you name it. If it sounds interesting and relaxing, try it. These activities can be both relaxing and productive.

Do you like to garden? My neighborhood is full of gardens. Mostly the gardeners are women dressed in shorts, with hats keeping the sun off their heads, their hands holding garden tools or immersed in the soil. The image of the back yard gardener is about as peaceful and healthy a one as I can imagine. And the flower beds that bloom in the spring and summer are beautiful.

## *Prayer*

When Micah was confronted with a difficult problem, his response was, "I'll pray about it." Prayer came easily to Micah. His father was a minister. He is devoutly religious and has always prayed. He asks for help and guidance for himself and for others. Micah finds prayer helpful in dealing with stress. It helps him compose his mind and gives him a feeling of peace.

For religious people, prayer can have many positive effects. A deacon at one of our local churches, for example, told me about how prayer helped her. "When I have a situation that is unclear and I don't know what to do, prayer helps clarify things for me. When I am in a difficult situation, it strengthens my resolve so I can do what I have to. And when I am in a situation that is not in my control, it is reassuring to know that God is above everything and will take care of things in the end." As was true for Micah, prayer left her with a feeling of peace.

Being religious has been statistically linked to longevity and less illness. The findings of a half dozen studies have indicated that church attendance is a predictor of lower risk of mortality. For example, a study carried out at Duke University Medical School followed nearly 4000 older adults for six years looking at the relation of church attendance and mortality. The researchers, Harold Koenig and his associates, found that the risk of dying for frequent church attendees (once a week or more) was 28 percent less than for less frequent church attendees, even when the effects of such factors as health status, health practices, and social connections were statistically controlled.[23]

With regard to mental health, the studies reported seemed less consistent. Where there are tendencies observed, religious faith seems to be associated with positive mental health. For example, Koenig and his colleagues found that frequency of church attendance was associated with less depression and a better overall quality of life.[24]

While religion generally has a positive relation to well being, it does not always work that way. Research suggests some religious beliefs may not only be unhelpful, but they may be counterproductive. Kenneth Pargament, who teaches psychology at Bowling Green University, differentiated two types of religious coping, which he calls positive and negative.[25] Positive religious coping consists of such behavior as seeking spiritual support, seeking a spiritual connection, collaboration with God in problem solving, religious forgiveness, and a benevolent religious appraisal of illness. Negative religious coping includes a view of God as punishing, feelings of being alienated or unloved by God, questioning God's powers and attributing illness to the actions of the Devil. Pargament and his colleagues first obtained measures of religious coping on over 500 hospitalized elderly medical patients. Then, the researchers followed the patients for about two years. The measure of negative religious coping was associated with a higher risk of mortality. Although the increased risk of dying was relatively small (6 percent to 10 percent), these findings suggest that there may be an inequality among religious beliefs in promoting well being. The belief that one's distress may be the result of an indifferent or punishing God or the handiwork of a malevolent force may have a negative impact on one's well-being. It may be that people with such tortured views of religion turn hatred and destructiveness against the self.

Faith can be a very powerful resource in life and many people place very high reliance on their faith in coping with the stresses of life. In times of personal and public upheavals religious people can draw on their faith to help them through. A study carried out by David McIntosh and his colleagues provides a very nice demonstration of how faith and the social support offered by the church members can become intertwined as boosting mechanisms during personal crises.[26] The researchers studied parents in Michigan and Illinois who had lost an infant child to SIDS (Sudden Infant Death Syndrome). The researchers found the parents who were more involved in religious participation received greater social support. Greater social support, in turn, led to less agony in the weeks following the child's death.

In an investigation of community crises, researchers studied the reactions of survivors to terrorist bombings in Nairobi, Kenya.[27] They found that religion was one of the principal resources people utilized in helping them cope with the attacks. Interestingly, religious coping among the Kenyans (attendance at church services) occurred at a higher rate than was true for the American survivors of the bombing of the Federal Building in Oklahoma City. As is true for a variety of ways of coping, culture plays an important role in determining how people respond.

## *Progressive Muscle Relaxation and Meditation*

There are a number of procedures which one can learn that can induce relaxation. Perhaps the best studied of these procedures are progressive muscle relaxation and meditation. Let's discuss these briefly.

Progressive muscle relaxation was the brainchild of physiologist

Edmund Jacobson who developed the procedure and then wrote a short book about it that was published in the 1930s.[28] I used Jacobson's procedure with patients fairly often in therapy and found it was easy for them to learn. Sometimes I used a tape recording of instruction for progressive muscle relaxation that had been passed around from psychologist to psychologist. The voice on the recording was quite soothing and undeniably contributed to the ease that patients had in picking up the procedure.

The objective of progressive muscle relaxation is to relax the muscles of the body. Relaxed muscles are usually followed by a lowered pulse and lowered tension. In this relaxed state it is often possible for a therapist to help the patient deal with situations that arouse severe anxiety such as phobias. The technique, called systematic desensitization, asks the patient to imagine scenes which evoke the phobic reaction. Because the patient is in a relaxed state, he or she is more able to tolerate this imagery, and often the phobia loses its intensity. Systematic desensitization requires the active participation of a trained therapist.

Progressive muscle relaxation is relatively easy to master. The body contains a number of muscles many of which are easily identified. If you have the time and curiosity, you might look at an atlas of the human body to see where the major muscles of the body are located. But the important thing for our purposes is to learn to recognize how the muscle feels when it is tense and how it feels when it is relaxed

How does a muscle feel when it is tense? Try this simple experiment. Sit down comfortably. Now, flex the bicep in your right arm, as if you were showing off your physique in a contest of musclemen at the beach. Continue to flex the muscle until you feel the tightness in it. Do you feel the tension in the muscle? Now, let the arm rest. Let it rest on the armrest of the chair. Notice how the tightness quickly diminishes. See if you can continue to do what you are doing, to let the diminishing tightness proceed just a little bit further. If you can do this, the muscle may feel more relaxed than when you started.

In learning how to use progressive muscle relaxation, you will have to take a trip around your body, working with one muscle at a time, first tensing the muscle, then relaxing it, and then simply continue the process of further relaxing the muscle. I am not sure that it matters very much what muscle you start with. Here is a routine you might try as a starter. It is very much like the routine I used with patients in therapy. It is not my own invention. What I did was to modify the instructions from the tape I mentioned that was then in circulation among psychologists. I wish I knew who the author of the tape was so I could give him or her proper credit.

You can follow this routine by yourself or better yet enlist the cooperation of a friend to assist you the first time around. Your friend can read aloud the instructions below, hopefully in a pleasant, soothing voice. Before you begin, choose one of the chairs in your home in which you feel most comfortable, preferably one with an armrest. Now settle back in the chair, rest your arms, and try to get really comfortable. Okay? Now close your eyes. Sit quietly for a moment or two. Now ask your friend to read the following:

"All right. Let's begin. Make a fist with your right hand. Really squeeze your hand so it becomes a tight fist. Make it really tight. Can you feel the tension in your right hand? Now open your hand and let it relax. Notice the difference. Now, just continue to do what you're doing — letting your hand relax."

"Let's try your left hand. Make a fist. Once again, really tighten your hand. Feel the tension? All right, now let go and relax the hand. Feel the difference? See if you can let your hand relax even more."

"Now, let's turn to your arms. Try bending your elbows. Move your hands up to your shoulders, and push your fingers against your shoulders. Hold them there until you feel the tension mount in your biceps. Now, slowly release your arms, straightening them until they come to rest on your chair. Feel your arms relaxing. Just continue to do what you are doing, letting your arms relax. Let the tension of the exercise diminish and disappear."

"All right, let's try another exercise with your arms. This time, stretch your arms forward, out in front of you, as far as you can reach. Notice the tension building in your arms and shoulders. Now, let go. Let your arms fall easily to the side, coming to rest on your chair. Feel your arms relax. As they relax you will feel them grow more and more limp."

"Now, let's move to your shoulders. Hunch up your shoulders. Hold them in this position until you really feel the tension in them. Now, let your shoulders relax. Just continue to let your shoulders relax. And relax even more."

"Let's turn to your legs. Try pressing downward with both feet against the floor. Really hard. Feel the tension in your legs increase. All right, stop pressing. Release your legs. Notice how the tightness recedes. Feel the sensation of increasing relaxation."

"Finally, tighten your stomach. Pull your stomach muscles in as much as you can. Do you feel the tension? All right, now release your stomach muscles. Let your stomach muscles relax and continue to relax.

"Now, you have relaxed some major muscles of your body. You have relaxed, in turn, your arms, your shoulders, your legs, and your stomach. Now see if you can let all of these muscles relax together even more. Do it all together. Just let go. As much as you can, let the muscles go limp. Now, as you feel the increasing relaxation of your body, breathe deeply for a moment and enjoy the feeling of being even more relaxed."

When you have relaxed your muscles, you might try imagining a very pleasant scene such as lying on the beach in the sun. This pleasant imagery should complement the muscle relaxation and add to your overall feeling of relaxation.

When you begin using the procedure, pay attention to the tightness in the muscle, and then to the decrease in tightness, and if you can, allow the muscle to relax a little bit further. Once you have mastered this procedure you will probably find that you won't need to tighten your muscles one at a time to achieve a relaxed state. You may not have to tighten the muscles at all. You will simply relax all of your major muscles simultaneously and in doing so the tension in your body should diminish.

While progressive muscle relaxation is a relatively recent invention, meditation has an ancient lineage. Its roots lie in the cultures of ancient China and India and particularly in the teachings of Buddha. Meditation as a practice was developed in the context of Eastern philosophies and religions and the vocabulary of writers who describe the technique may include such terms as transcendental and mystic realization. As is true for the practice of acupuncture where one need not accept the concepts and vocabulary of Chinese medicine to appreciate the usefulness of the technique, one may practice meditation with or without adherence to the philosophies in which it was developed. Meditation can be a useful technique in and of itself for quieting both the mind and body.

When Monica experienced one of her panic attacks, she could hardly function for a while. The attacks took a lot out of her, knocking her off her equilibrium. These panic attacks, which had been going on for many years, threatened her career working as a biologist in a research institute. The attacks were shattering her confidence and disrupting the orderly way she wanted to run her life. The stress of not knowing when the next attack would occur was at times overwhelming. Monica tried several antianxiety drugs, but did not want to stay on them for she knew that they might be habit forming. At a party, one of her friends at the institute introduced her to an émigré from India who was highly skilled at meditation. When he taught Monica how to meditate, she found that the technique helped her diminish the intensity of the panic attacks and in so doing restored her confidence that she could control the attacks if they occurred. With the recognition that meditation afforded her an effective means of coping with panic attacks, the stress that had been building in her life largely dissipated.

There are scores of books written on meditation and a multiplicity of ideas on how to do it. One of the essential elements in mediating is to turn away from the pattern of your everyday thoughts and concerns and focus your attention on something else. That something else could be your own breathing. You might begin by paying attention to the rising and falling of your chest. Alternatively, you could repeat over and over again in your thoughts a specific word, perhaps one with a rising and falling cadence that echoes the act of breathing. Repeating a word or even a sound over and over has been called mantra meditation with the word or sound itself being the mantra. How long should you do this? I have no ready answer for this. Some writers suggest 20 minutes, perhaps twice a day. Some people meditate frequently and at length.

How do you concentrate on a word or on your breathing for a long period without your mind wandering off to what's cooking on the stove or to that unfinished report due at the office? Not easily. I find meditating for more than a few minutes difficult. But, if you can master the skill — and there are tapes that can help you in this endeavor, and better yet, classes on meditation from well-trained instructors — it is likely to be helpful. People who are very experienced at meditation can lower their pulse and blood pressure.

Probably the type of meditation that is best known in the United States is transcendental meditation (TM) which is based on ancient Vedic traditions. The popularity of TM in this country is largely the result of the efforts of Maharishi Mahesh Yogi, a scholar and teacher in the Vedic tradition. TM is taught in a standardized fashion in a seven step program carried out in a four to seven day time period. There is a TM organization and an active research program centered in Maharishi University located in Fairfield, Iowa.

When TM took hold in this country it was hyped and I suspect oversold as a potential cure for almost anything that ails one. TM was tried as a treatment for psychiatric disorders, hypertension, insomnia, asthma, inflammation of the gums, alcohol abuse, drug abuse, and stuttering. Such unbridled enthusiasm led to a skeptical reaction among some traditional scientists who sharply criticized the research basis for TM as inadequate. In 1984, for example, a psychologist, David Holmes, wrote a devastating critique of the claims that meditation diminished somatic arousal to stressors.[29] Sure, he acknowledged, TM might relax people, but no more than simply resting. Holmes observed that "not one experiment provided consistent evidence that meditating subjects were less aroused than waking subject."[30] He followed this conclusion with the trenchant comment that "there does not even appear to be one bad experiment offering consistent evidence that meditating reduces arousal more than resting."[31]

Such critical reviews are really important if only to goad researchers into producing more convincing data to show that what they believe is really so. What is even more convincing is when people who are disinterested in the outcome design and carry out the research. This tends to eliminate the allegiance effect we sometimes find in research when the advocates of a procedure may find results which others do not. Eliminating the allegiance effect becomes really important in research on controversial topics such as ESP and repressed memories of sexual abuse.

Fortunately, there is now a growing body of research on the effects of meditation. Research has been carried out on such basic questions as how does meditation affect cardiovascular reactivity and how does meditation affect stress hormones. In a recent study carried out in Spain, for example, levels of epinephrine and norepinephrine were assessed in the morning and evening for a group of people who regularly practiced meditation and compared with samples from a control group of people who did not meditate.[32] The researchers reported that the morning levels of both hormones were lower in the group practicing meditation and this was also true for the evening measure of norepinephrine. The researchers concluded that TM had a significant effect on the sympathetic-adrenal-medulla (SAM) system, which is one of the two major systems in our bodies for responding to stressors.

Meditation in one form or another — whether TM, mindfulness based stress reduction (MBSR) or the program developed by meditation advocate and researcher Robert Benson — has been used as a treatment or adjunct treatment for various diseases. The research suggests that many of the people who learn to use these meditation-based therapies feel better and the effects can be long lasting if meditation is practiced regularly. For example, in a study of patients with irritable bowel syndrome, which is generally considered to be a stress-related disease, a group of patients were taught Benson's system of meditation and then monitored for several months. Following meditation training, the subjects showed fewer of the usual symptoms of the disease such as bloating, belching and diarrhea.[33]

While meditation is not the panacea for all of the world's ills that some of its enthusiasts seem to suggest, it can be a technique that many people will find useful in coping with the stress they are experiencing in their lives.

Are there potential downsides to progressive muscle relaxation and meditation? Can using these techniques cause harm? Almost anything you try to reduce stress could have unanticipated effects, some of which could be adverse. Even a relatively benign procedure such as progressive muscle relaxation could cause problems for some people. I have read reports of people being treated for anxiety with progressive muscle relaxation who have experienced increased levels of anxiety during the treatment.[34] Such paradoxical reactions do happen. Millions of people try to meditate; I suspect that many people have difficulty in doing it, and as is true for progressive muscle relaxation, some people probably experience adverse effects. Working with a very experienced teacher may be the best guarantee of success.

## *Take Direct Action*

If you are clear what the sources of the stress in your life are, then it may be possible to take some actions to change the situation. Certainly, doing things to alleviate problems is more difficult if the cooperation of others is needed or if you are experiencing serious conflicts about the situation. Still, there may be things you can do. A few small steps may begin paving the way for real change. Who was it that said a thousand mile journey begins with a single step?

Sometimes it's helpful to think in terms of programmatic action. By this I mean developing a plan that approaches the problem in several ways — more or less simultaneously. Perhaps, you might even develop a comprehensive plan to address the problem. It is also useful to think in terms of a sequence of actions. Try some things now which seem relatively easy to do, and if all goes well, add some more difficult things later.

While problem solving is a straightforward approach to coping with stress, many people find themselves unable to do it. Some people feel blocked even before they begin. Sometimes, it's a state of mind, saying "I can't do it." Perhaps, there have been too many failures in the past or it may be an overreaction, catastrophizing a previous failure. Two psychologists working in Montreal, Melissa Robichaud and Michel Dugas, have described a concept they call negative problem orientation and tried to develop a self report measure of it.[35] These researchers saw three components in a negative orientation to problem-solving: a belief that the problem represents a threat to one's well-being, doubt about one's problem-solving ability, and pessimism about the outcome of one's efforts. To paraphrase the researchers, people with this orientation feel, "It's a bad situation, I can't fix it, and if I try, I won't succeed."

The researchers fashioned items sampling these ideas and constructed a scale which they administered to university students. Not surprisingly, the self perception that one cannot effectively deal with problems was related to measures of psychological distress and pessimism.

It is not an easy thing to break a mind-set that "I can't do it." In my therapy practice I encouraged patients to start with small steps. Doing something is better than doing nothing. And, a little success can be encouraging to do more. Just getting off the dime to try something may reduce the pressure you are feeling — the sense of being caught in a bind. What you do does not have to be ground shaking. A few small steps to begin may be all you need to start feeling better.

In the preceding chapter, I mentioned Christina who was trapped in a dead end, low-level job working in an insurance company at a low level job doing repetitive work using basic computer skills. Her major problem was lack of self-confidence. The thought of looking for a better job was so threatening that she just went on from day to day living with a situation that offered no future. Clearly Christina wasn't ready to make a big move, but there are some beginning steps she could have taken which potentially could make the big step — getting a new job — possible. For example, she could try to upgrade her computer skills. There is a community college not far away from where she lives which offers beginning, intermediate, and more advanced training. She could enroll in the beginning class to see how it goes. This would be a safe yet significant step for her to take. Perhaps after a semester of training, she might feel confident enough to begin looking for a better job.

Some people are extraordinarily shy when it comes to meeting people of the opposite sex. Their behavior may be frozen between desire on the one hand and fear of rejection on the other. When I worked with patients who were extremely shy, one of the things I tried to do was to help them take the first steps that would put them in a position to meet the kind of person they wanted to meet. I would tell them that basically, it came down to three choices: (1) they could avail themselves of the modern methods and technologies of meeting people (using the Internet, computer dating services, responding to advertisements in the "in search of" columns in the newspapers), (2) putting themselves into a situation — a place where people are, or (3) waiting for lightning to strike. Who knows? A handsome man or woman might move in next door. While it makes a wonderful script for a light hearted romantic comedy, don't depend on it. You may develop gray hairs while waiting.

Using contemporary methods for meeting people such as responding to a newspaper advertisement is probably for the bolder of us, the man or woman who can shrug off rejection or the disappointments that are bound to come such as the hapless person who shows up for that first blind date. After all, you are not likely to find people advertising themselves in the newspaper column or dating services as "unattractive, boring, and a perennial loser." Quite the opposite. But lots of people strike it rich. I know a man who used the Internet to look for a woman and ended up with a foreign bride who was both stunning and charming. The second approach — to go where the people are — is less direct than using a dating service but has few risks. You are under no obligation to do anything. You can get by as a passive observer or you might smile a bit and try a few nods. If you are a churchgoer, join a church where there are many people in your age group. If you like to walk, join a hiking group. There are softball teams, cooking classes, classes in yoga, just about anything that might interest you. Ask yourself, what are the things you like to do? Then, join a group that does something you like to do and that attracts lots of people.

If the task of meeting new people seems overwhelming, try a low-risk strategy such as the above. Do some research, first. And then some scouting. Get your toes wet before you take the plunge.

## *Preparation for Upcoming Stressful Events*

I know a mathematics professor who teaches at a community college. Many of the students who come to the college have a history of not doing well in mathematics and have to work their way through remedial courses before taking traditional college mathematics courses. But along with these generally underprepared students there are some excellent students with strong aptitudes in mathematics. It has been the practice of the teacher for some years to recruit these promising students into an honors program in which they carry out original projects applying mathematics to the analysis of scientific and social issues (for example, the regulation of drug doses in medicine). To receive their honors recognition, the students have to present their projects to an audience of fellow students and faculty.

For most of the students this is the first time they have ever done anything like presenting an original project to an audience. Not really knowing what to do or what to expect are conditions which can arouse considerable stress. To give the students confidence, the teacher rehearses the students. They present their projects to an audience of their fellow honors students. The teacher and the students offer suggestions and criticisms. After modifying the speech to reflect these suggestions, the students may run through the presentation again. This preparation, which gives the students a real feel for what they are doing, increases the students' confidence and when they do present, they usually perform well. Careful preparation reduces uncertainties and increases confidence. When the time comes you're more likely to be ready.

Stress preparation has been used to reduce the fear patients feel about impending medical and dental procedures. Experiments have been carried out which demonstrate that patients who learned about an impending medical procedure (in one study, for example, the procedure used was an endoscopic examination of the upper gastrointestinal tract) are less fearful about the procedure.[36] Videotapes have been used to inform patients about how the procedure works. Seeing what goes on fills an informational void that could be replete with unpleasant fantasies about the procedure.

The idea of preparing people to face up to coming medical procedures seems particularly useful for children. A visit to the hospital to talk with the nurse or doctor could allay a child's fears which could be monumental. Watching an older sibling successfully undergo dental treatment can be useful in preparing young children for their first dental exam.

Preparation to more effectively deal with stressful situations when they arise is of course part and parcel of the training of future soldiers, police, and firefighters. They have to learn what to expect and how to deal with it. When life threatening crises actually arise, reactions of fear are likely to occur whether or not there has been training but knowing what to do and having practiced it repetitively are probably the best guarantees that the individual will perform well, notwithstanding the fear.

In preparing for the stress-arousing situations of ordinary life, some people find it useful to visualize in their mind's eye not only what they will be up against, but their own responses as well. Some athletes visualize competitive situations on the playing field and how they will react. For example, in his book *Play Better Golf,* Jack Nicklaus described how he visualized upcoming golf shots before actually taking them.[37] Nicklaus likened the visualization process to movies playing inside his head. In his imagination, he saw where he wanted the ball to end up, then he saw it flying through the air and then in his mind's eye, he visualized the swing that would accomplish this.

Do such visualizations actually help athletes perform better? It certainly didn't hurt Jack Nicklaus, whose exploits on the golf links are legendary. An examination of research on this question suggested that visualization can be helpful, although probably not as much as actual practice. Shelley Taylor and her colleagues at UCLA have carried out a series of very interesting studies about the effectiveness of visualizing upcoming tasks.[38] In one of the studies, students who were anticipating taking the midterm exam in introductory psychology in a few days were given instructions about visualizing their preparation for the exam. They were told to visualize themselves studying and to hold this image in their minds. To push this idea further, the researchers offered the students some ideas as to how they might do this. They told the students to visualize themselves "sitting at their desks, on their beds or at the library, and studying the chapters, going over the lecture notes, eliminating distractions such as turning off the television or stereo, and declining a friend's offer to go out."[39] It goes without saying that this is terrific advice for a student preparing for an exam — something any guidance counselor would vigorously applaud. But, visualizing these acts added a new and potentially potent dimension. The students were instructed to try this visualization routine for five minutes every day before the test. The results of the study were intriguing. Compared to a control group, the students who used the visualization procedure spent more hours studying and averaged about eight points higher on the exam. Students take note!

While Taylor's research team found visualizing the process of what lies ahead can have a salutary effect, they also reported that simply visualizing a happy ending — fantasizing about getting an "A" grade — isn't likely to accomplish very much. Their research suggests that if you visualize, visualize how you will get to where you are going, not just the happy ending.

Role playing can be another helpful technique in preparing for stressful situations. Role playing is play acting without a script. To take an example, let's say you're going to be involved in a difficult interpersonal situation at work, perhaps asking the boss to shift you to a different assignment because you feel you need a change in what you are doing. You could describe the situation to your spouse, who could play the part of your boss. Run through an imaginary conversation as if your spouse were the boss. If it doesn't go as well as you'd like, try it again, perhaps using a somewhat different approach. After this practice, you may have a better idea of what you ought to say and how to say it. Generally speaking, rehearsal can be good preparation enabling you to face an upcoming stressful situation better.

## *Positive Mind-Sets*

In the preceding chapter we discussed mind games people play which exert a negative impact on individuals experiencing stress — mind games such as overgeneralization, guilt trips, and perfectionistic thinking which can turn an uncomfortable, stressful situation into a bleak malaise. These mind-sets increase the chances of really feeling depressed.

There are other mind-sets which seem to protect against a depressive tailspin. These mind-sets, such as optimism and hope, act in some ways as polar opposites to the negative mind-sets we discussed earlier. Many years ago a clergyman, Norman Vincent Peale, wrote a best-selling book entitled *The Power of Positive Thinking.*[40] And believe me there is something to it. The lyricists for popular songs recognized this truth long before the scientific community understood it. Remember such standards as "Look for the Silver Lining" and the hit song from the musical *Annie*, "Tomorrow"? The ultimate proponent of this mind-set was Charles Dickens' memorable character in the novel *David Copperfield*, Mr. Micawber, who while chronically struggling with financial problems was fond of saying: "Something will turn up." The research evidence clearly points to the stress-buffering effects of optimism and its related state, hope. In one of our studies, Roland Tanck and I administered a version of our coping inventory to university students that included the items, "Try to keep a hopeful attitude — that things will get better," "Try not to get down on yourself," and "Realize that almost everyone feels this way at times." The students who reported that they tended to use these coping strategies had lower scores on a scale measuring depression.[41]

Subsequent research has demonstrated that optimism and hope have a positive effect on reactions to stress in a wide variety of contexts. People facing the severe stress of a coronary bypass operation who were optimistic were better able to generate active coping strategies to deal with this stress. Optimism has been linked to survival time in AIDS patients and to immune system functioning in students facing the daily grind of law school. Children dealing with the severe stress of having their mothers incarcerated for a crime were less likely to develop psychological problems and conduct disorders if they maintained high levels of hope.[42] These are straws in the wind which suggest that being happy, optimistic, hopeful — having a positive frame of mind — might be helpful in warding off both disease and emotional problems and may help one in dealing with diseases better when they come. There is also some intriguing evidence which suggests that a happy state of mind might be associated with a longer life.

The study carried out by Deborah Danner and her colleagues working out of the University of Kentucky suggests that positive emotions experienced in young adulthood are predictive of longer life spans.[43] The subjects in the study were a group of nuns, members of the School

Sisters of Notre Dame. Back in 1930, the mother superior of the North American sisters requested that each sister write a short single-page autobiography, not to exceed 200 to 300 words. The brief autobiography was to include biographical information, interesting and edifying events of childhood, the influences that led to the convent, religious life, and outstanding events. When the autobiographies were written, the average age of the nuns was 22.

Danner's research team retrieved these autobiographies and analyzed them. The team looked for evidence of positive statements (e.g." the past year which I have spent as a candidate studying at Notre Dame College has been a very happy one."),[44] negative statements, and neutral statements. Relatively few negative statements were uncovered.

Using statistical analysis, the researchers related the number of positive statements to the nuns' longevity. The results were striking. As the researchers themselves put it, "This study found a very strong association between positive emotional content in autobiographies written in early adulthood and longevity six decades later."[45] The message seems to be, be happy and live longer!

Christopher Petersen, who has carried out a number of studies linking optimism and health, commented, "One of the striking correlates of optimism is good health."[46] Shelley Taylor and her colleagues arrived at a similar conclusion stating, "Rigorous research investigations from a variety of laboratories have now provided evidence, however, that such resources as meaning, a belief in personal control, and optimism not only help people adapt to stressful events more successfully but actually protect health. Although as yet we do not fully understand the biopsychosocial pathways by which such protective effects occur, the evidence is strong enough to justify considering these resources important weapons in the arsenal of prevention."[47]

If you are one of the fortunate ones with an optimistic, hopeful attitude, then you can probably withstand a lot. You have a better chance of getting through whatever it is that is bothering you. I don't know of any magic formulae to turn a pessimist into an optimist. I wish there were. If you are an optimist, be glad of it.

Can you overdo these positive attitudes? Yes, if you reach the point of total denial of reality. A case in point is the battered wife syndrome. The failure of some battered wives and romantic partners to come to grips with reality has led them to endure both physical and psychological abuse and in some cases has put their very lives at risk. But for the most part, optimism and hope are wonderful commodities to have in abundance and fortunate are those who have them.

Let's close with a few words about a sense of humor. The idea that a good laugh can be stress-reducing is hardly new. What is new or at least relatively new is that there is research evidence to support the idea.[48] Researchers have shown that after being exposed to comic videotapes, subjects have higher pain thresholds. Their arms might be immersed in very cold water or squeezed by a blood pressure cuff or they may be subjected to electrical stimulation, but after their funny bones have been tickled by a comedy routine, it takes more of whatever unpleasantness the experiment is doling out to make them report that they are experiencing pain.

There is some data which suggest that exposure to humor may affect the stress hormones. Using a very small sample of subjects, Berk and his colleagues showed them humorous videotapes and then took blood samples assessing cortisol levels. The researchers found that there were decreased cortisol levels with laughter.[49]

Researchers have wondered whether exposing people to comedy with its attendant mood elevation of good humor and laughter might have an effect on the immune system. Subjects have been shown comic videos of Mel Brooks and Carl Reiner, Bill Cosby, W. C. Fields, and Billy Crystal and assessed for a component of the immune system (S-IgA) taken from saliva samples before and after the tapes were shown. These immune reactions were compared with the reactions to educational and documentary videos. The results have not been all that consistent, although some studies have found increased immune functioning following exposure to the comedy tapes.[50] The evidence for a positive effect of humor on one's psychological state and physical health, while still somewhat sparse, appears promising. In one study, for example, exposure to humor was followed by less tension and anxiety. In another study, people who reported that they used humor as a coping mechanism reported better physical health than the people who did not use humor as a coping mechanism. In a third study, people who were "funny people"— i.e., who often used humor in their interactions, reported that they coped better with the everyday stresses of their jobs than their counterparts who were not humorous.[51]

The use of humor in interactions with others can be a delicate, sometimes tricky, business. The line between being funny and being offensive can easily be breached. Nonetheless, people who are caregivers often find the use of humor helpful in dealing with those that they are caring for. Nurses, for example, report that humor has enabled them to cope with the often difficult and embarrassing situations that they experience on as daily basis and helps create a more positive work environment. Indeed, the use of humor in the nursing profession appears to be widespread. A survey of nurses indicated a very large percentage of the nurses who responded reported using humor to help them deal with the stress of their jobs.[52] Finally, an interesting note concerning physicians. In an article in the *Journal of the American Medical Association,* it was reported that physicians who used more humor and laughed more were less likely to experience malpractice claims.[53] Humor may not only protect against stress, but lawsuits as well.

# 5

# *Improving Your Relationship Skills*

A large proportion of the situations that cause stress in our lives arise in our relationships with other people. From time to time almost everyone experiences problems in getting along with other people. We do not live in a world composed of saints. While you will find very nice people almost everywhere you look, there are others who are difficult, insensitive, even hostile. Take a moment and think back about your own experiences. Think about some of the people you have known over the years that you found it difficult to get along with. It's hard to imagine that you haven't encountered someone who was a real problem.

Even when you are with people who are generally nice, it helps if you are skillful in getting along with people. Such skills will keep interpersonal stresses down to a minimum. And a life without frequent quarreling makes it easier to enjoy one another's company and increases the chances of sharing satisfying, enriching experiences. So, with both the people whom you find difficult and those who are generally easy to get along with, you should find it useful to hone your interpersonal skills.

I would like to focus on two issues: sensitivity to what others are thinking and feeling and conflict resolution skills.

How well do you read people? Reading other people accurately can be a tricky business. The other day a friend of mine was telling me about a new teacher they had hired in the college in which she was teaching. She recalled the job interview two years back where the applicant had been quiet and laid-back, giving the appearance of someone who would fit in nicely with the department. She certainly appeared to be a cooperative kind of person. Now, two years later, she is like a tigress, power oriented, hyperaggressive and supremely manipulative. What ever happened to the woman who applied for the job? Or was she always that way?

Sometimes, it's really hard to tell about people. And to compound the problem, many if not most of us make only a modest effort to really understand people when we meet them. We do not pay close attention — and we often make assumptions such as "that person is like me," rather than trying to find out what that person is really like. Research suggests that, too often, we are both unobservant and self-centered in forming impressions of others.

The study of how people perceive each other falls under the psychological rubric of research on social perception. Researchers have given a good deal of attention to two questions which particularly concern us here: how accurately do people perceive each other (how accurately can they describe each other) and how do people believe they are being perceived by others? This includes questions such as "do they like me?" and "do they understand me?" You can readily imagine how serious inaccuracies in perception in either case could lead to misunderstandings between people and result in interpersonal stress.

The accuracy of perceiving others is partly dependent on an individual's motivation and mind-set. People who are in the role of jurors at a trial are likely to pay serious attention to witnesses. People at a party may see, hear and remember very little of what is going on around them. Researchers suggest that when people are explicitly put into the role of observers, they are able to rapidly form useful impressions of others. The observed individuals generate information in their body language, facial expressions, and in both what they say and how they say it. While what is said can sometimes be tightly controlled, it is harder to control one's nonverbal signals. A study found that judges who expected a defendant to be found guilty revealed their expectations in their nonverbal behavior rather than in what they said.[1] Impressions can form in a matter of moments from what psychologists have called "thin slices of expressive behavior" and sometimes these impressions can be surprisingly accurate.[2]

The catch in this process of rapid impression formation is that if the observer is to obtain maximum benefit from these impressions, he or she has to have a mind-set of paying attention to the other person. Hearing, sight and understanding have to be focused on the target. Thinking about oneself and one's own agenda reduces the chances of efficiently learning about another. Therapists and physicians are examples of people whose professional roles require a mind-set which focuses attention on the other person.

Although people emit a great deal of data about themselves in their interactions, much of it is lost on inattentive observers. Research dealing with the accuracy of our perceptions of others demonstrates that while there is indeed a statistical relation between the way we describe ourselves and the way other people describe us, there are often large discrepancies. We may see a person in a certain way, and the person may have quite a different self-perception. While it is not always clear who is right and who is wrong in these judgments, it is clear that a great deal is lost in transmission in social interactions and people may end up with skewed perceptions of the other person. The level of accuracy in assessing another person is likely to improve when the traits being considered tend to be stable over time rather than variable, clearly observable rather than based on inference and when the person doing the evaluating has a reasonable opportunity to get to know the other person.

One's beliefs about the way other people see one may be as important in the grand scheme of things as how accurately one perceives others. In writing a review of social perception studies, David Kenny and Bella DePaulo observed, "This concern about how others view them far exceeds any concern that they may have about how they view others."[3] Most people are concerned about making a favorable impression.

Researchers have found that the way you think others perceive you is strongly linked to the way you perceive yourself. If people see themselves as intelligent, they expect that others will see things the same way. This expectation is not confined to the judgments of a few intimates; rather it becomes a generalized belief. It often comes down to, "This is the way I am, and this is the way almost everyone sees me." As Kenny and DePaulo put it, "In reacting and reading others' reactions, people often see what they expect to see."[4]

In their examination of research, Kenny and DePaulo noted some interesting tendencies. The people who interact with a given individual are not nearly as uniform in the way they view that person as the person thinks they are. People's guesses about what other people think of them are generally right on the broad outlines, e.g., do people like me? However, when it comes down to the more subtle aspects of one's behavior and personality, everyone does not see you the same way and you may not be fully cognizant of the differences among people in the way they look at you.

While it is not surprising that people make errors in the way they assess new people who come into their lives, it may be surprising that people who have known each other a long time can be poor assessors of each other. This can be true even of longtime married couples. A large part of such misreadings comes from carelessness. Spouses often don't listen to each other. A study conducted by Neil Jacobson and D. Moore found that husbands and wives were poor observers of their spouses' behavior. Husbands and wives were given a checklist of fairly concrete behavior such as "we watched television together," and asked whether this happened during the past 24 hours. The couple agreed only about half of the time whether the event had happened.[5] For couples seeking marriage counseling the rate was only 39 percent.[6]

Once I treated a patient who was severely depressed. One of the things that bothered him the most was that he felt his wife did not really understand how bad he was feeling. He would try to tell her, but she just didn't get it. He asked me to telephone his wife and explain how depressed he was. I replied that I didn't think this was the right way to go about it; rather, he should bring her along to our next session and perhaps in our three way conversation the issue would surface naturally and could be aired. When she came, it was clear that she not only didn't comprehend the depths of his despair, but had brought her own agenda which she wanted me to push on her husband. Attempts to manipulate therapists are not all that uncommon, and I did take the opportunity to point out what I thought was happening and that they needed to really start listening to one another. The importance of good listening in a relationship cannot be overestimated. When married couples are asked by researchers to engage in problem-solving exercises, the results speak as much about the state of the marriage as it does about the couple's problem-solving skills. In a research review, Thomas Bradbury and Frank Fincham noted that "the problem-solving interactions of distressed spouses, compared with those of non-distressed spouses, are characterized by higher rates of negative behaviors, more reciprocity of negative behaviors, and a greater degree of predictability between spouses' behavior."[7] Negativity usually isn't confined to hostile behavior; it extends to perceptions, interpretations of events, and a historical record of memory in which grievances are deeply felt, often by both marital partners.

Not only are the spouses in a troubled marriage poor observers of each other's behavior, they often have a marked tendency to put a great deal of spin on their interpretations of events occurring in the marriage, tending to downplay the good things that the spouse has done and highlight the bad things. When the spouse does something positive, it may be viewed as unintentional, or motivated by selfish reasons or as aberrance from his or her general behavior. In contrast, a negative action of the spouse is likely to be viewed as an intentional act rather than as an inadvertence, the results of undesirable personality traits, deserving of condemnation, and a demonstration of lack of love for the complaining party.[8] With mind-sets ready to put the worst interpretation possible on a spouse's words and acts, it is not surprising that the interactions of distressed spouses so often end up in quarrels and recriminations.

Distressed couples tend to present a pretty bleak picture in the accuracy with which they perceive each other and in the way they communicate with each other. They often lack the interpersonal skills we have emphasized and sometimes present a worst-case scenario of what can happen when these skills are deficient. One might wonder whether anything can be done to alter the situation, to make things better? What about marriage counseling? Can that help? The answer is a qualified yes. I think it largely depends on (1) whether the couple has a strong motivation to stay together and (2) whether both parties are willing to entertain the possibility of doing things in new ways, to exchange what they are currently doing which is not working for behaviors which may work in the future. If both parties will take the opportunity offered by marriage counseling to consider and try different approaches in their interactions, then marriage counseling is certainly worth trying. However, if the counseling sessions become a mere extension of the home battlefield with the parties devoting their energies to convincing the neutral party, the counselor, that "I'm blameless" and "My spouse is the villain," counseling could turn out to be a useless exercise.

With the problems of faulty perception and communication so central to the development of tensions between spouses, it is not surprising that marital therapists often focus on these issues. The marital therapist may try to teach basic communication and problem solving skills to spouses, even giving them homework assignments to try to improve the quality of the couple's interactions at home. For example, the spouses might be asked to pinpoint the behaviors that promoted their partner's satisfaction and then to use this knowledge to foster the relationship.

Marital therapy is not a panacea. Writing in *The Journal of Consulting and Clinical Psychology*, Neil Jacobson and Michael Addis noted, "Most tested treatments report no better than 50 percent success ... all treatments are leaving substantial numbers of couples unchanged or still distressed by the end of therapy."[9]

Which couples are most likely to profit from marital therapy? Research suggests that it is younger couples and couples whose marital distress is not severe. Indeed, research suggests that teaching communication skills to engaged couples before serious difficulties begin can be helpful in preserving the forthcoming marriage.[10]

We have cited research reviews which suggest that our ability to accurately read other people is often far less than it could be and our perception of how other people view us can be seriously flawed. Because such misperceptions can create and exacerbate interpersonal stress, it seems appropriate to ask ourselves what can be done to mitigate these tendencies. There are some very basic, commonsense things one can try which could turn this potential weakness into a real strength. And the result might lead to more accurate perceptions of others, fewer misunderstandings and communication failures, and hopefully less interpersonal stress.

The secret is attentive listening! All of us can make an effort to listen better! Try removing yourself, your own needs and agenda as much as you can from the listening process and tune in to what the other person is thinking, and even better, feeling. The surest way not to pick up what a person is trying to communicate to you is to frequently interrupt. Interrupting not only conveys a message that it is only what you say is important enough to listen to, it may destroy the chances that you will understand what the person is trying to convey to you. Sure, there are times when you have to interrupt. When somebody is speaking without ending — or even pausing — to let someone else into the conversation you may have no choice. I once had a patient who talked in machine gun like fashion for the entire 50 minutes of the therapy session without caring to listen to a single word of mine. She would have done as well to save her money and talk into a tape recorder.

A simple rule that is too often disregarded is if we really want to understand someone, then we need to listen carefully to what the person has to say. If we have the impulse to contradict what the other person is saying, or add examples of our own, resist the impulse at least for the moment. Allow the other person to finish his or her sentence and better yet the thought. It is usually helpful to maintain periodic eye contact to show that you are interested. You may gain a better understanding of what the other person is thinking and feeling if you not only listen carefully but also study the speaker's facial expressions. You can usually tell when someone is pleased or happy. You can't mistake a smile. And you can often tell when someone is angry. An obvious case is a young child. Think of the facial expression of an angry young child. And sadness is often easy to discern. You may notice that the head is angled downward. And the mouth may be downturned. And, of course, there may be tears. Low to moderate levels of anxiety are not that easy to pick up through either facial expressions or body language. When you feel a bit on the panicky side, most people are unlikely to know it unless you tell them. A very high level of anxiety, however, may show itself in eyes that dart back and forth, nervous twitches, clammy hands, and an almost rigid posture. Some writers emphasize the importance of body language in communication, but don't ignore facial expressions as, sometimes, they can be very revealing.

If your companion is quiet and poker faced, what do you do then? If you want to know what's on his or her mind, you had better ask. A vaguely worded open ended question is as good an approach as any. Remember the old line from the movies — "A penny for your thoughts"? Something like that is a good opener. In conversation you don't want to give people the impression that you are prying — or worse, interrogating them. That may simply arouse defenses.

If what you are hearing is interesting and you want to hear more, it is usually easy to accomplish this objective. Nod your head, smile, look interested. Ask a gentle question that invites the speaker to continue, such as, "What happened then?"

In understanding other people, the content of their speech (what they say) tells you a great deal. The tone in which they say it adds to your understanding. Is the tone curt, friendly, angry, sad? Is it merry and gay? Is there laughter or tears? And ask yourself what is not being said. What is left out can give one pause to think.

The point of more attentive listening and drawing someone out when necessary is to better understand the individual—what he or she is thinking and feeling. As your listening skills become more acute, you may reach the point when you can begin to put yourself in the other person's shoes, to grasp what the situation looks like from his vantage point. We call the ability to grasp what another person is thinking or feeling *empathy*. It is something like what happens when we are watching a movie and for a brief period of time we become the hero or heroine and experience the emotions we see portrayed on the screen. Psychologists call this process identification, but it is a lot like empathic listening. Only with your friend, spouse, or child there is no script or contrived story line—what takes place in the scene before you, in this small world, is very much for real. By being empathic you may find yourself in a better position to help bring about a happy ending. And you can communicate that you know where the other person is coming from with words that are simple, yet almost magical, "I understand." It is a gesture of emotional support.

Not everyone is capable of empathy. Some people are too self-centered to even conceive of the value of understanding others and wouldn't begin to know how to make the effort. Some people that psychiatrists call narcissists are unable to escape from the binds of self interest to step into the shoes of another even for a while. But empathy is a wonderful skill, much appreciated by others who love to have a sympathetic ear. Try listening attentively and try to comprehend what the other person is thinking and feeling. I think that you will find it valuable as will the person with whom you are interacting.

We have talked about conflicts that occur within the individual and how these can arouse stress and even become immobilizing. It is often a struggle for severely conflicted people such as battered wives to resolve these conflicts one way or the other.

The roots of conflicts are often interpersonal relationships. Two people may want the same thing. For example, teenage children might quarrel about who gets to use the family car. Conflicts may arise about issues of control and decision making. The child may want to do something; the parents may not permit it. The child wants to go out and play; the parents say, "No. Do your homework first." Couples may argue about spending money. Spouses may feel differently about sex;

men often complain that their wives are uninterested in sex. For their part, wives are often aggrieved that their husbands don't pay enough attention to them, that they don't share enough. The list can go on and on.

Sometimes, conflicts between people are more apparent than real. Consider this commonplace illustration. A husband and wife plan to go out for the evening and are trying to decide which of several possible movies to see. The husband has a preference for a thriller but feels his wife has a different idea. He thinks they may end up having an argument and this possibility concerns him. What he is not aware of is that her primary goal is simply to go out for the evening and it really is not that important for her what movie they choose. The possible conflict the husband perceived was minimal, perhaps nonexistent.

Take a look at your own situation and think of some of the conflicts you have had with other people over the last few years. Ask yourself, were there times (A) when someone didn't do what you had hoped they would do? (B) Did something that displeased you, even made you feel angry? (C) Took advantage of you? (D) Said or did things which seemed unreasonable to you? When you had such conflicts with other people, how did you deal with them? Take a moment. Think back and reflect.

Conflicts can be resolved in many ways. Perhaps the most destructive resolution is a scenario in which conflict leads to anger, anger to harsh words, and harsh words to violence. Sometimes conflicts are resolved by the breaking of a relationship. A father may become estranged from his children. A conflicted marriage may end in divorce. A person may leave a job where relationships and the work environment have become hostile and tension-filled. And then, alternatively, instead of trying to resolve the conflict, a person may utilize a host of coping strategies and defense mechanisms to make the strained situation more bearable. The person may simply choose to live with the problem.

In a series of studies carried out with Yale undergraduates, Robert Sternberg and his colleagues found that conflict resolution could be described by crossing two axes which were labeled active-passive and intensifying-mitigating.[11] Examples of active-intensifying styles of conflict resolution would be participating in an argument, directing harsh, angry words at the other person, or being physically abusive. An example of an active-mitigating style of conflict resolution would be to seek the help of a third party to mediate the dispute. A passive-intensifying style might be actions taken behind the scenes to undermine the other person's reputation or withholding oneself in a sexual relationship. A passive-mitigating style would be giving in or waiting and seeing.

The styles of conflict resolution that characterize most adults are patterns that gradually evolved out of childhood and adolescence. You have only to watch some children at play to see how striking the changes can be in our approach to conflict resolution as we grow up. With children it is often a matter of might makes right. This is particularly true for boys where physical strength and athletic ability are highly prized. The ultimate example of this conflict resolution style is the playground bully who intimidates his way into getting what he wants.

A study by Mara Reese-Weber provides a nice demonstration of how conflict resolution styles tend to change with age.[12] The researcher gave out questionnaires assessing conflict resolution styles to samples of adolescents (average age of 16) and young adults (average age of 22). The measures of conflict resolution styles derived from the questionnaire were an attacking style (getting mad and yelling, saying something to hurt the other person's feelings) and a compromising style (listening, trying to understand, working out a compromise). The teenagers studied reported that their relationships with both parents and siblings were much more punctuated with attacking behaviors than was the case with young adults. Young adults were more likely to use a compromising style of conflict resolution. There are gender differences in both the level of conflict that occurs during adolescence and in the way the conflicts are resolved. As a rule, more conflict occurs between boys than between girls. Boys are more likely to use threats or physical force to resolve disputes while girls are more likely to use a mitigating strategy such as changing the topic, offering a compromise or simply leaving the scene. Girls are more likely to want to talk about the situation, boys to be coercive. In an experiment in which best friends were asked to discuss problems that have arisen between them, communication skills were judged by outside observers to be higher among girls than boys.[13]

By young adulthood, conflict resolution styles are well formed. Sternberg and his colleagues found that their students at Yale showed a great deal of consistency in the way they resolved conflicts. The college students' approaches were pretty much the same whether the conflict was with a same-sex peer, an opposite sex peer or a parent. The students expressed a clear preference for conflict-mitigating strategies over conflict-intensifying strategies, although some students got down on themselves when their responses were too weak or passive to protect their own interests. For example, one student reported a conflict with her roommate. "I have strong religious values that place great emphasis on the sanctity and seriousness of marriage, and thus I feel that premarital sex is very wrong, so that when two of my suitemates last year, one of whom had a boyfriend who came to visit many weekends, showed that they participated in and/or approved of premarital sex I was made very uncomfortable, especially the first few times the boyfriend came over."[14]

This student did not respond overtly, feeling reluctant to complain about the boyfriend's visits. She didn't want to start any fights. Still, she often wished that she had had more courage in expressing her convictions.

You will find couples where one party is so dominant and the other so compliant that one rules and the others submits. If both parties are happy in this arrangement, then so be it. More often than not, however, the partners are not that unequal and conflict resolution requires discussion and give and take. In some form or other, negotiation really is the adult way of resolving conflicts.

The compromising style of conflict resolution Reese-Weber assessed in her research has at its core a process we usually call negotiation. Negotiation, if carried out with sensitivity, can be a very useful way of diminishing interpersonal conflicts and thereby reducing the stress these conflicts engender. As such, negotiation is a very useful skill to master. In the framework suggested by Sternberg and his colleagues, negotiation would be considered as an active strategy with the possibilities open that it could lead to either mitigation or intensification of the conflict. This depends on the way the process is carried out and on the equity of the agreement. The advantage of negotiation in disputes between nations is that it is unlikely to leave bodies piled up in the streets, and in everyday life negotiation can help prevent shattered relationships. It is a rational, relatively simple way to resolve conflicts. While negotiation doesn't always work, as Winston Churchill once said, "It's better to jaw, jaw than war, war."

While our interest will be on the use of negotiation in a very informal way, let's begin by looking a little more closely at what is involved in negotiation. In its formal definition, negotiation can be described as a process in which two or more people try to settle what each will give or receive or alternatively perform and receive in an undertaking. What results from negotiations is an agreement in which expectations, benefits, and responsibilities are spelled out and made explicit. Because negotiations in the world of business often result in monetary agreements, the process has greatly interested economists who have developed elegant models which specified optimum outcomes from the process. An optimal outcome is considered one in which no alternative solution would improve the position of one of the parties without being detrimental to the other party. Translating this idea into the real world of everyday living, this means achieving the things that you desire without causing harm to the interests or frustrating the needs of the other person.

The word negotiation may bring to mind images of two groups of people sitting across a table doing some hard bargaining. For example, a group of union leaders facing a group of corporate executives bargaining about changes in wages and health benefits in the union contract. Or, it may bring to mind a one-on-one situation where a customer is bargaining with the salesman in an automobile dealership about the price of a new car. In both situations, the bargaining can be hard. In both situations, there may be winners and losers. The customer may leave the showroom, driving away in a new car feeling he had negotiated a good deal, or he may have left empty handed, feeling the car salesman and his associates were little more than pirates.

The model of winners and losers is not the best model for settling everyday human relations problems. In fact, it may not be the best model for any type of negotiation. Thinking one has gotten a bad deal leaves rankled feelings and lingering resentments that may smolder and resurge with a vengeance, poisoning later interactions. Far better to end up with a situation where all parties emerge with a sense that they have gotten something. The so-called win-win outcome.

It is difficult to achieve a win-win outcome in resolving a conflict if there is a very small pie to be divided. If two teenagers are vying for the use of the family car and there is only one night of the week on which the car is available, there is going to be a winner and a loser. If the pie could be expanded, say there were two nights in which the car could be available, then negotiations with an equitable outcome would not be difficult.

In seeking equity in negotiation, it can be very helpful to make a careful examination of what is in dispute and to enlarge this domain to increase the possibilities that something can be offered to both parties.

Scott and Meredith had been dating for almost five months. They had been physically attracted to each other from the start and as they got to know one another, they found that they were very comfortable with each other. They could talk for hours together without getting bored and always found the other supportive when problems were encountered. Adding to the positive glow in their relationship was the fact that they liked doing many of the same things. For example, they both enjoyed hiking, camping and sports. When Scott told Meredith that he loved her, she responded that she loved him, too.

In so many ways they were well suited for each other. When they talked about marriage, however, there was a problem. They came from very different religious backgrounds. Moreover, their parents were strongly committed to their respective faiths and expected their children to marry someone within their faiths. Both sets of parents were vocal about their objections and this was causing the children considerable distress.

One day Scott and Meredith sat down and decided to try to work out a solution to the problem. They decided first and foremost that the decisions as to where they would marry and what they would do afterwards would be theirs alone and no one else's. After all, they reasoned, it was their lives to live and not their parents'. Having made this basic decision allowed them to talk about many possibilities. Rather than beginning with a fixed position of "my religion or yours" they decided to expand their horizons for both themselves and their children. They talked about the possibility of celebrating holidays from both faiths. They talked about the possibility of exploring alternatives to the religions of their parents, perhaps finding something that they both might feel comfortable with. They talked about the possibility of exposing their children to a variety of religious ideas. In this back-and-forth discussion they came to some agreements as to what they would do, leaving some issues to be resolved in further discussions. In no case did either Scott or Meredith push the other into accepting positions which would be fundamentally unacceptable. While they knew that only time would tell whether their plans would work, their discussion left them with the feeling that they were on the road to a workable solution to the problem, a solution that would allow them to do what they wanted to do above all else, marry and spend their lives together.

As you can see from this example, negotiation can be a very informal process. There is no need for the two parties to face each other on opposite sides of a table. No need for a gavel, an agenda, or the other trappings the procedure might bring to mind. Negotiation can be as simple as two people discussing possibilities and coming to some agreement as to what they will do, and in some instances who will do what. Needless to say it is important to stick to the agreements made, whenever possible, if the process is to have any meaning.

The anecdote about Scott and Meredith also illustrates that the negotiators need not be adversarial. They can be partners, looking for mutually beneficial courses of action. Interestingly, women are more likely than men to enter negotiations with this perspective. The experiences of a boy growing into manhood in our society — largely because of the emphasis on sports — tends to be more competitive than that of girls, and this sometimes carries over into negotiations. There is considerable evidence pointing to gender differences in negotiations, particularly when the situation is seen as competitive.[15] Women tend to approach negotiations in a less confrontational manner than men, looking at the person across the table as someone similar to themselves. Men are more likely to see the person as very different from themselves. Men tend to see themselves as more powerful negotiators than women and during negotiations women are more likely to make self-derogatory remarks. These gender-linked differences reflect the different styles men and women often display in life, men being more competitive, women being more cooperative, and this sometimes carries over into negotiations.

Chances are that if a person is aggressive and argumentative during negotiations, he may get more from the negotiations — a larger slice of the pie. That may be all right in some kind of negotiations, but if it's a dispute between friends, lovers, or family members, the increased gain is not likely to be worth the cost. The poison left over from the exchange may be lethal. Perceptions of equity and fairness are crucial in maintaining harmony in close relationships. Striving for a win-win outcome is very important.

There is no inherent reason why couples or families cannot look at a negotiation to resolve conflicts as a cooperative process rather than as a contest of wills. The requirements are simple: a willingness to give up something — you can't have everything your way — and a sincere desire to search for common ground.

Attempts to institute negotiations, even informal negotiations in your close relationships, may run into some resistance, particularly if the other party is accustomed to deciding things unilaterally or is hard headed and difficult to get along with. A simple "let's talk about it" might be the way to begin.

To expand the pie, to increase the range of possibilities, you might find it useful to draw on some of the ideas involved in the technique called brainstorming. This is a procedure in which all parties are encouraged to throw ideas out on the table for discussion and there is very little criticism of the ideas when they are first offered. Being liberal about the possibilities initially advanced puts a wider assortment of ideas on the table. If an idea is subsequently viewed as impractical, it can be eliminated at a later time in the discussion. To make the negotiation process work, it is important to encourage openness and flexibility.

# 6

# *Defenses, Deliberate and Unconscious*

Sometimes we protect ourselves against stress without fully being aware of what we are doing. These psychological mechanisms are in a very rough way analogous to the way the immune system protects the body against invading microbes. You don't see what is going on internally when your infection-fighting cells are mobilized, but there are outward manifestations such as a runny nose and a congested head. And in a somewhat similar way the individual often engages in defensive maneuvers to keep levels of anxiety from becoming overwhelming. One can think of psychological defense mechanisms as something like an iceberg: a little showing, a lot more submerged. The individual may have some awareness, a little awareness, or no awareness at all of the defense mechanisms operating in his psyche. Some of the classic defense mechanisms are thought to operate on a purely unconscious basis.

One way of thinking about defense mechanisms is to look at them from a developmental perspective. As we grow up, it is possible to observe changes in the kind of defense mechanisms we use. A young preschool child may use simple, transparent defense mechanisms such as denial. Flying in the face of reality, the child might protest, "I didn't do it. I didn't hit him!" A few years later the child may have given up denial in favor of projection. In response to her own feelings of anger, a teenager might say, "She hates me. She's got it in for me." Phoebe Cramer and Francis Kelly, who have been studying defense mechanisms in children, noted that the average child will shift from using denial as the primary defense mechanism between the ages of six and eight.[1] If children continue to rely on such mechanisms as denial as they mature, we might interpret this as a sign of developmental lag.

Since the times of Sigmund Freud, who first elucidated the idea of defense mechanisms, and his daughter Anna, who wrote what is perhaps the seminal book on the subject, psychoanalysts and psychologists have proposed a fairly large number of psychological processes and behaviors as possible defense mechanisms.[2] We are going to discuss a few of the more widely known of these, beginning with defensive maneuvers and defense mechanisms that are more accessible to consciousness, and moving on to those which are not. However, before we do so, it is essential to consider the ways in which researchers have tried to study defense mechanisms because this has proved historically to be a perplexing problem, severely limiting what we can be confident about. Put simply, the question is how do we study a phenomenon that may be largely or even totally out of our awareness?

One would have to answer, "Certainly not easily. Perhaps, not at all." A psychotherapist who has worked with a patient a long time may pick up on some of the defenses the patient is exhibiting — but it's strictly the psychotherapist's observations of the patient and the inferences made on the basis of the observations. This, certainly, is not the kind of objective procedure that would make a research person comfortable. Researchers need tools that can be applied objectively and lend themselves to replicable studies.

As we have indicated, the study of defense mechanisms has proved to be a formidable challenge for research psychologists. Still, researchers tend to be inventive and not easily discouraged. They continue to try.

The psychologist's first line of attack is likely to be a self report scale. Self report instruments work fine for many aspects of personality, for example, measuring extroversion, anxiety, or depression. People who report on self report scales that they are severely depressed usually are. Psychologists have tried to extend the use of self-report measurement to defense mechanisms. However, for the reasons I have given, one has to be skeptical of what such instruments really measure. Years back, a psychologist developed a scale to which he affixed the magic name of Repression-Sensitization.[3] As repression cuts to the heart of Freud's theory, the scale aroused widespread interest. Along with a host of other hopefuls, I tried using the Repression-Sensitization scale in research, relating scores of the scale to measures of dream recall, dream content, and dream associations. I found that the Repression-Sensitization scale predicted very little about dreams, reinforcing my skepticism that self report scales could measure repression.[4]

One of the more recent and widely used attempts to measure defense mechanisms using self-report inventories is the Defense Style Questionnaire developed by Michael Bond and his colleagues.[5] The scale tries to measure a range of defenses that are ranked in an adaptive hierarchy. In reviewing research with the inventory, Bond noted that people who use what are considered more adaptive defenses tended to have better mental health. This seems reasonable and suggests that the inventory is tapping into some aspects of emotional health. Still, for the reasons I have given, I remain unconvinced that any self report scale would be able to adequately measure the traditional defense mechanisms that are believed to be largely unconscious in nature.

If we accept the thesis that trying to measure unconscious mechanisms through self report is illogical, what are the alternatives? One obvious approach is to take a leaf out of Freud's work. He discovered the existence of defense mechanisms through careful listening to patients. Perhaps modern day clinicians can start the quest for the assessment of defense mechanisms by doing the same thing, and then trying to shape what they are doing into a research tool. There are some practical problems to resolve in doing this. For one thing, Freud was a rare genius. Most of the rest of us who practice psychotherapy are not. Also, contemporary training in psychotherapy emphasizes cognitive and behavioral techniques, not the psychoanalytic methods of Freud. This is quite reasonable because cognitive and behavioral techniques are effective and efficient treatments for many types of psychological problems, while psychoanalysis can be a long, drawn out process. However training in cognitive and behavioral techniques does not sharpen the skills needed to identify defense mechanisms.

Anytime a researcher wants to adopt a procedure developed by Freud (which tends to be open-ended with few boundaries) as a research tool, it means having to rein in some of Freud's brilliance and setting up some rules of order so that the procedure can be made objective. This task was accomplished in an interesting way by J. Perry.[6] Perry developed rules and instructions which allow clinicians to make judgments from the content of patient-therapist interviews as to whether certain defense mechanisms appear to be in use. The clinician who makes these judgments, of course, has to be specially trained to use the procedure — to be able to spot the kinds of verbalizations and behaviors in the interviews that Perry and his colleagues want them to report.

Can clinicians' ratings about these indicators of defense mechanisms be objective? Studies have shown that they can to a reasonable extent, although the agreement between an independent rater reviewing a videotaped interview and the therapist who actually conducted the interview is far from perfect.

There has been some interesting research relating clinician-rated defense mechanisms to symptoms of depression. Researchers have reported that people who tend to be depressed are more likely to use defenses such as acting out, passive aggression, and apathetic withdrawal.[7] It looks as if such defenses are not effective ways of coping with stressors and are unlikely to fend off the onset of depression.

A third approach to measuring psychological defense mechanisms involves the use of a projective technique called the Thematic Apperception Test (TAT). The TAT consists of a series of pictures such as a boy looking at a violin. The subjects are asked to make up a story for each picture, relating what is going on in the scene, what led up to the current situation and how it will all come out. As only the bare bones of the story are suggested by the picture, the rest of the story has to come from the subject's imagination and experience. The results can be interesting and revealing, although one cannot usually determine what the significance of the story is for the person without really knowing a lot about the person.

Phoebe Cramer has developed a manual for scoring TAT-evoked stories to establish the presence or absence of certain defense mechanisms such as denial, projection, and identification.[8] For each of these defenses she lists a number of markers or categories. For example, for the defense of projection, one of the categories is the attribution of hostile feelings or intentions to a character in the story. Each time the researcher sees evidence of one of these categories in the story, it is noted. These notations are summed over four of the TAT stories yielding scores for denial, projection, and identification. Cramer reports that analysts show substantial agreement in making these judgments.

The use of Cramer's technique in research is illustrated by a study in which children with conduct disorders (children who persistently violate accepted age-appropriate social norms and the rights of others by such behaviors as lying, cheating, and stealing) were compared with children with adjustment reactions (children experiencing difficulties brought on by stressors). The researchers hypothesized that children with conduct disorders would show more evidence of denial and less evidence of identification in their TAT stories than children with adjustment problems and this was indeed the case.[9]

Although these studies are interesting, my view of the state of the art of studying defense mechanisms is that researchers are still groping at the margins, trying to get a handle on a very difficult problem.

Now, let's consider some of the defensive maneuvers and mechanisms that we suspect are at work trying to protect us against anxiety and stress.

For some of these defensive maneuvers, we are pretty much aware of what we are doing. For others, we may have no awareness at all and it would take a psychoanalyst to point them out. Thought suppression is an example of a defensive maneuver which we are usually very conscious of. A troubling problem has been filtering through your consciousness to the point it is plaguing you, and you resolve, "I'm not going to think about this anymore. I'll put it out of mind." As we pointed out, this resolution, no matter how determined it is, is likely to fail. The more determined you are not to think about an unresolved problem, the more likely it is going to pop up anyway, like one of those annoying pop ups that clutter your computer screen when you search the Internet.

Another defensive maneuver that we may have some recognition of is a tendency to anticipate the worst outcome. Imagine for a moment that you are a recent college graduate who has sent out applications for admission to a number of law schools. Included in your list are Harvard and Yale. During the weeks you wait for an answer, you keep telling yourself over and over that there is no way you are going to get into either of these prestigious law schools, and so you have prepared yourself for the worst — that you will be rejected. When it happens, you simply shrug it off. Your maneuver of expecting the worst has protected you against feeling too badly.[10]

Is having low expectations a good idea? While there will be times when low expectations are useful — particularly when they are realistic — keeping expectations low is not in general a good rule in life. Low expectations may lead to low effort and you could end up with a self-fulfilling prophecy for mediocrity. Trying doesn't necessarily mean you will succeed but not trying almost guarantees that you won't.

Putting a positive spin on events often has the flavor of a defensive maneuver, and it is something most of us do routinely. An exception, of course, would be people who tend to become depressed relatively easily. They usually put a negative spin on events, which if not contradicted can help bring on depression. But, for most of us, we tend to characterize the positive things that happen to us as things we can take credit for—at least in part—that are likely to last, and have some impact in our lives. On the other hand, if something negative happens to us, we are likely to attribute the event to someone else's doing, view it as a temporary thing, and minimize its consequences. This self serving view of events is a widespread, robust phenomenon. In fact, it is so robust one might think it is hard wired into our biology. However, as Amy Mezulis and her colleagues noted in a review article on this tendency, Asians tend to show this self-serving bias in a less pronounced way than people in western countries, which suggests that cultural experience plays a role in the way this bias develops. Unless carried to an extreme, this self-serving bias often serves a useful purpose, protecting our self-esteem. In a real sense, it is anti-depressive.[11]

We often see this positive spin—the self-serving view—exaggerated in children. Children frequently engage in wishful thinking which carries with it reassurance and comfort. However, this usually diminishes as the years pass and reality begins to force the child to view events with a less rosy perspective.

It is hard to say how much awareness we have of this tendency to put a positive spin on events. It is such a routine, widespread thing that I suspect that we give it little thought. When the self-serving process involves minimizing the consequences of negative events, it has much in common with the classic psychological defense of rationalization. What rationalization does is go a step further, introducing reasons to explain and justify our positive spin on events.

Rationalization is a way of explaining away unhappy events such as failures in a way that makes them more palatable. Rationalization is another protective maneuver that we might have some hazy awareness of when we are doing it. Rationalizing is a game we play with ourselves, on ourselves. Finding acceptable reasons for our lack of success in an endeavor is a fairly benign process. It often helps protect our self-esteem, can be face-saving with others, and usually does little harm. When you tell yourself that the girl who rejected you when you asked her out wasn't really your type anyway, it keeps you from feeling deflated. With your self confidence remaining at a high level, you may feel comfortable about going right ahead and asking another girl out. Or, if you were not chosen for that part in the school play, and you told yourself that rehearsals would have really taken too much of your time—fine. All you have to do is half believe it and you may feel better.

In terms of where rationalization stands in a hierarchy of defense mechanisms, I see it as relatively mature and often adaptive. Can fooling yourself chronically be a problem? Sure.

Many years ago a psychologist offered a distinction between two types of rationalizations which has remained useful to this day. The distinction is between rationalizations which are sour grapes and sweet lemons.[12] Sour grapes rationalizations are excuses offered that the goal that was desired but not attained was not worthwhile in the first place. Following failure to attain a goal, one changes one's perception of the goal, devaluing it in one way or another. Following a failure to get the job she was interested in, a woman rationalized, "The more I thought about working there, the more problems I saw." This conclusion, which was followed by a list of "for instances" did wonders to protect her ego in this failed initiative. The other category, sweet lemons, is making a virtue out of a necessity. After an automobile accident which left his car with some unseemly dents, the driver rationalized, "My car will be in the shop for a week. Still, it will do me a lot of good to walk for a while. I need the exercise."

One of the nice things about rationalization is its plausibility. The excuse used for yourself may sound quite reasonable. Saying, "I didn't get the job because I was older and I'm sure they wanted someone younger" is not only plausible, it may be true. Of course, there are times when rationalizations are so far-fetched that they can be laughable. In a study of mothers who smoke, one of the reasons advanced for smoking was, "I did it for the sake of my children."[13]

Sometimes the experience of interpersonal stress includes a strong dose of anger. An encounter with a friend, co-worker or family member can leave you tense, upset, and fit to be tied. The difficulty that arises with being angry is that there are few useful ways to deal with these feelings. While expressing anger at the offending person may offer some immediate relief, this has the considerable drawback of potentially damaging your relationship with the person. Fights can do that. Not all of the time, of course. Some couples have blow-ups, then kiss and make up and everything is all right. But don't count on it. Bruised feelings can be a big problem. Holding anger in isn't that good an alternative, either. My colleague Arnold Myersburg used to talk about swallowing angry feelings. If this tendency reaches the point where the anger is directed inwardly and you get angry at yourself for what happened, that can be a real downer and make you feel depressed. So, there are really not any great options for dealing with angry feelings. The advice I usually offered to my patients was to first cool off and then look for solutions to the problems causing the anger. This can take time and be a difficult undertaking. I admit that my prescription for dealing with angry feelings offers no immediate satisfaction. If you try what I suggest, you may not feel a bit better. But compared to the alternatives, there will be times when you will find it is the best thing to do.

One thing that does happen — all too often — is that angry feelings arising from a stressful interpersonal encounter get displaced. There is a kind of transfer from the source that elicited the anger onto another target — a target of convenience that is usually more defenseless than the offending party. The angry husband returning from the office, all worked-up and stressed out from an exchange with his boss, blasts the horn in traffic, swears at the failings of other drivers, and when he returns home chews out his wife and children, and proverbially kicks the dog. Such displacement of anger is a defensive maneuver which may act as a safety valve temporarily reducing the individual's tension level, but is hardly fair to those who are the recipients of the outburst and may generate a lot more ill will than the momentary reduction of stress is worth. Have you ever had the experience of someone getting angry at you for no apparent reason? You wonder what brought on the storm. Was it something you did? But nothing comes to mind. And then it turns out later that he or she had been upset by someone or something else. I am not sure how much insight people who do this routinely have about their actions. Some people may have little or no insight.

While defensive maneuvers such as rationalization can be useful at times, the defense mechanism of denial strikes me as being really dysfunctional. I think of denial as a situation which is clearly obvious to almost everyone but to the individual in question who denies that things are the way they are. An all too common example is a woman having an affair with a married man who believes that the man will divorce his wife and marry her. The affair may go on for years. The woman's friends point out that despite his promises, he will never leave his wife. Nonetheless, she persists until the bitter end, having lived in a state of denial.

My favorite example of denial comes from the classic movie *Never on Sunday.* The heroine, an endearing lady in a shady profession, was fond of retelling the stories of the ancient Greek playwrights. Only, in her retelling of these grim, bloody tragedies, with the body count rising higher and higher, she concluded with the characters all going away happily to the beach. Denial of the realities may keep tension down for a while but is often a recipe for disaster. The battered wife who keeps thinking her husband will reform may end up in the hospital. The constantly drunk man who says, "I can handle liquor" may never get the help he needs. The couple who routinely overspend, run up huge credit card debts, and think there is no problem may be heading for bankruptcy. As a psychological defense, denial has little to recommend it.

Projection is one of the classic psychological defenses. Projection is attributing to other people thoughts and feelings that you have yourself. We do this routinely in social perception when we assume that the person we meet is similar to ourselves. It may take some time and perhaps some disillusionment to find that in important ways, this is simply not true. Where projection assumes the character of defense mechanisms is when we are uncomfortable with having certain thoughts or feelings and by not acknowledging them and attributing them to another, we can escape the responsibility for having such feelings. I would imagine that projection could involve any number of unacceptable feelings, but probably the prototype feelings are those of hostility. "He hates me" may be another way of saying deep down, "I hate him." Interpersonal stress often includes a component of anger. In relationships, it is difficult not to feel angry with someone, even for a brief time, who you perceive as having wronged you. Feeling disrespected by another person, believing you are being treated unfairly often arouses angry feelings. When these feelings arouse cross currents such as the stricture, "I'm not supposed to feel angry," or the idea, "I can't afford to be angry with this person," the end product of this conflict may be an unconscious resolution — projecting the anger onto the other person. Complicated? You bet. Provable? Not easily. But, the same could be said about most aspects of Freudian-based psychology.

Perhaps the ultimate defense against uncomfortable feelings is repression. The concept of repression was the brainchild of Sigmund Freud and has been controversial ever since he annunciated it. Repression is something like thought suppression although we usually think of repression as a more automatic process. Ideas which are potentially disturbing get banished to a zone of the mind — a place Freud called the unconscious. The unconscious has some superficial similarities to the recycle bin in a computer. When you want to delete a file, click the mouse on the appropriate spot and the file is gone. As Freud described the unconscious, it was much more of a dynamic system than the recycle bin. Ideas could creep out of the unconscious, filtering back into consciousness, albeit usually in a disguised form. Freud pointed to dreams as an example of such disguised forms.

Does the unconscious exist and does it work the way Freud believed it did? Some things do take place in thought processes without our awareness, but it is a large leap to accepting Freud's concept in its entirety. And if something like the unconscious is working within our brains, does it act as a safety valve for us or just add to our troubles? I can pose these questions but I don't think anyone can really answer them with certainty.

Defensive maneuvers such as expecting the worst and defense mechanisms such as repression very likely have an impact on the amount of stress we experience. How much, it is hard to say. But in any event, these are processes over which we have very little control. To deal with stress effectively in an assertive manner, we need means which give us a real sense of control over stress — means which make the stress we experience more manageable. We have discussed some of these ways in the preceding chapter and we will consider additional ways in the chapters that follow.

# 7

# *When Should You Consider Professional Help?*

There are certain circumstances in which a person should really seek professional help to deal with stress-related problems. There are other circumstances where seeking professional help is something one may want to consider — an option to put on the table and give serious thought to. One would ask such questions as how much would this help me? Would this make my life better? And there are circumstances in which professional help is clearly not needed.

I am going to discuss some of the stress-related conditions that I believe require professional help. These conditions are as follows: acute stress disorder, post-traumatic stress disorder, panic attacks, a limiting or disabling phobia, and when stress is accompanied by or followed by bouts of depression.

Acute stress disorder is a relatively recent concept in psychiatric thinking.[1] Acute stress disorder happens to some people who have experienced a traumatic event. Think of such horrific experiences as war, a serious automobile accident, being raped or mugged, or being exposed to a natural disaster such as a flood, tornado, or earthquake. We are talking about an event that threatens death or serious injury to you or those around you.

People respond differently to such threats. Some people shake them off. Others do not. An acute stress reaction to these threatening situations is a reaction of intense fear, helplessness, or horror.

The person experiencing an acute stress reaction following a traumatic experience may feel in a daze, unreal, experience emotional numbness, and perhaps what is the most clear cut benchmark of acute stress disorder—symptoms of dissociation such as amnesia. The person cannot recall important aspects of the experience. Memory for what happened seems partially or totally blotted out.

During the days and weeks following the event, the person with acute stress disorder may re-experience the traumatic event. Images relating to the event may intrude into the person's thinking. The person may experience nightmares and flashbacks. Heightened levels of anxiety, bouts of insomnia, and subjective feelings of numbness are other symptoms of the disorder. And, finally, there is a marked tendency for the person to avoid anything that may evoke memories of the event.

After a massive earthquake in the San Francisco Bay area—it measured 7.1 on the Richter scale—psychologists asked university students in the San Francisco Bay area to report any nightmares that they experienced. The frequency of their nightmares was twice as high as reported by a comparable group of students in Tucson, Arizona, and what was particularly revealing, many of the nightmares were about earthquakes.[2]

The symptoms of post-traumatic stress disorder are much like those of acute stress disorder. Nightmares, flashbacks, intrusive thoughts relating to the traumatic experience, exaggerated startle reactions and insomnia are typical symptoms. So too are a numbing of emotions and a tendency to avoid reminders of the traumatic event. The distinction between the two conditions has mainly to do with the time of onset of symptoms and how long the disorder persists. Acute stress tends to occur fairly soon after the event—certainly not more than a few weeks after, and tends to resolve itself within a month. Post-traumatic stress syndrome may occur years after the event and tends to be a chronic long-term problem. Episodes of acute stress disorder are often followed by post-traumatic stress disorder.[3]

My introduction to the problem of post-traumatic stress disorder was with veterans who had served in the jungles of Vietnam. One of my patients who served a tour of duty there could not tolerate loud noises. Such noises would really upset him, bringing back vivid memories of explosions. He needed quiet both at home and in his work situation to begin the process of recovery. My patient had served his country well, but ended up having to cope with nightmares, flashbacks and periods of disability.

Surveys suggest that perhaps 50 percent to 60 percent of the American population at one time or another has been exposed to a traumatic event.[4] Natural disasters, automobile accidents, sexual assault, severe burns, domestic assault, being mugged or robbed — so many things can happen, and for many of us, they do, at least once. Yet as Emily Ozer and her colleagues point out in a review article on post-traumatic stress disorder, only about one-tenth of the population has been diagnosed with the disorder.[5] Why is it that most people who have experienced trauma get over it while some do not?

Ozer and her colleagues explored this question by examining the findings from over 60 studies dealing with post-traumatic stress disorder and subjecting them to a meta-analysis. The researchers identified half a dozen factors that appeared to make a difference in whether exposure to trauma eventually led to post-traumatic stress disorder. Here are some of their findings. Having experienced an earlier trauma helped set up the individual for the disorder. It is something like the old proverb about too many straws breaking the camel's back. The experience of repeated traumas may have a cumulative effect leading to an emotional breakdown.

Having prior psychological problems such as depression increases a person's vulnerability to reacting to a trauma with subsequent post-traumatic stress disorder. No great surprise here. When a person already feels distressed, the last thing needed is a major traumatic event. If the traumatic event involved a perceived threat to the person's life, the chances of later developing post-traumatic stress disorder are increased.

Those who reacted to the trauma with intense emotion such as helplessness, fear, and shame had increased risk of developing post-traumatic stress disorder. If the experience was extremely disturbing, the chances increase for a subsequent reaction.

If the individual reported dissociative experiences, such as loss of memory during or immediately following the event, the chances of later developing post-traumatic stress disorder are increased.

Social and emotional support following the traumatic incident decreases the chances of a subsequent case of post-traumatic stress disorder.

Summarizing the results of the meta-analysis, if a person is vulnerable to begin with and the experience of the traumatic event is profoundly disturbing, the odds increase that there will be a subsequent reaction of post-traumatic stress disorder. Interestingly, the researchers observed that if these traumatic events occurred in civilian life, the chances were higher that post-traumatic stress disorder would ensue than if the events happened during combat. I have no ready explanation for this.

Panic attacks can be very frightening experiences. These attacks have been described as an experience of overwhelming fear. The cognitive or intellectual component of this fear is in part a reaction to the internal sensations of one's body mobilizing to deal with an emergency situation. In a panic attack, your body reacts as if you are being threatened with imminent danger. It's really not the case, but try telling yourself that when your heart races, breathing becomes difficult, you begin gasping for air, you are gripped by chest pains and you begin trembling and shaking. Small wonder you think you may be having a heart attack. You wonder if you are about to die.

One of the things about panic attacks which make them so troubling is that they can come out of nowhere — out of the blue. You might be sitting in a classroom, you might be working at an office, or even walking in the park. One minute you feel okay, and the next minute you are falling apart. You feel out of control. A case reported in one of the clinical journals in psychology described a young woman with several young children who suffered from panic attacks.[6] Often, these attacks occurred during stressful situations. However, sometimes the attacks occurred when she was feeling all right. Before a recent attack, she had experienced a stressful morning, dressing her children and getting them ready for a trip to a restaurant. It was a hassle getting them organized and to the restaurant on time. But she managed it. After settling down and ordering the meal, she felt everything would be all right. She began to relax, enjoy her meal, and then, suddenly, the attack hit her.

At such heightened states of alarm, panic attacks usually don't last long. Your body isn't programmed to stay at such a mobilized level indefinitely, so in a short while panic attacks usually subside. But while they last, the attacks can be extremely unnerving.

What happens to many people who experience panic attacks is that they begin to entertain the thought — and in some people the thought may rise to the level of an obsession — when and where will I have another attack? You have the sense you are carrying around a ticking time bomb. Recurrent panic attacks can have a demoralizing and debilitating impact on one's life.

In our description of panic attacks, we highlighted the role of thought processes (cognitions) in increasing the intensity of panic attacks. Current thinking about panic attacks holds that the patients' cognitions play a central role in deepening the attacks. David Clark and his colleagues describe the process in psychological terms. "Cognitive accounts of panic disorder ... have proposed that individuals who experience recurrent panic attacks do so because they have a relatively enduring tendency to misinterpret benign bodily sensations as indications of an immediately impending physical or mental catastrophe. This cognitive abnormality is said to lead to a positive feedback loop in which misinterpretations of bodily sensations increase anxiety, which in turn, strengthens the sensations, producing a vicious circle that culminates in a panic attack."[7]

The important role that cognitions play in panic attacks has been supported by research. Researchers have asked patients suffering from panic disorders to record their thoughts at the time of the attacks — if they are able to — or recall them soon afterwards. The researchers have found that the thoughts expressed during panic attacks are about anticipated catastrophes — e.g., heart attacks, seizures, death, losing one's mind.[8] Other studies have found that the presence of such catastrophic thoughts differentiates panic disorder patients from patients with other types of anxiety disorders.[9] Research, then, clearly supports the view that people who suffer from panic disorders misinterpret the signals coming from their body. The implication from such studies is that if people can learn during therapy to reinterpret their body signals in a non-catastrophic way, the severity of the panic attacks should decrease. As we shall see in the chapter dealing with psychotherapy, psychologists have taken this idea and run with it, developing very effective treatments for panic attacks.

There is a long list of phobias — situations that can arouse intense fear. You could start with acrophobia (fear of heights) and continue to xenophobia (fear, hatred of strangers). Fear of animals, for example, is a fairly common phobia. It is the kind of phobia one might pick up in childhood from hearing threatening stories about animals or having a bad experience with an animal. Some people have intense reactions to the sight of blood. And of course there is claustrophobia, that feeling of dread while being in a small elevator or in a closed space such as the tunnel often used in MRI exams. While many people have phobias, most are an inconvenience at worst and are hardly disabling. Many phobias, such as intense fear of snakes or spiders, usually have little impact on one's daily life. It is very easy to avoid snakes and a thorough vacuum cleaning should dispense with any spiders. There are treatments that can help you get over these fears, but, why bother? Avoidance of the situations that arouse anxiety is easy. On the other hand, if you have a phobia about heights, flying in airplanes, attending school, or dating, that could be a much larger problem. Avoidance carries a much higher price tag. And finally, if you have agoraphobia—literally fear of the marketplace, but in practical terms fear of being away from your home—that can be a huge problem. I have worked with patients who experienced intense anxiety when they were only a block or two away from their homes. Agoraphobia can turn one's life into that of a housebound recluse.

Chronic feelings of anxiety are often associated with depression. Imagine for a moment that you are a researcher and you have administered two psychological tests, one measuring anxiety and the other depression, to a very large group of people. Imagine a group of people about the size of the audience that watches a college football game. When you analyze the results you will probably find that most of the people you tested will score rather low on both anxiety and depression. Most people are not all that anxious and people who are not experiencing high anxiety levels in life are not likely to be depressed. You will find a relatively small group of people who report that they are feeling anxious, but not depressed, and another group, also relatively small, who will report feeling depressed but not anxious. And, you will find a fairly large number of people who will report feeling both anxious and depressed.

While anxiety and depression are related emotional states, we all know intuitively that they are not the same things. Psychologists have done extensive studies trying to pinpoint the differences, but I think what it comes down to is that anxiety is more of a physical experience than depression. When you are acutely anxious you may feel your heart pound, your hand tremble, experience difficulties in breathing and you may sweat profusely. You usually do not feel such physical reactions when you are depressed. When you are depressed, you may only feel worn out and fatigued. Depression is more of a state of mind than an acute physical reaction. When depressed, you may feel like a failure, even suicidal, but your body is relatively quiescent. You may even find it difficult to get out of bed in the morning.

Why are anxiety and depression related? There are different reasons one could imagine involving both physiological and psychological explanations. One of the possible scenarios that I have observed in some of my patients is that when they experience chronic stress, it can become a very uncomfortable existence. They can reach the point where they just can't deal with it anymore. Collapsing into a depression takes you out of the daily struggle. The fight is over. They have lapsed into a protective shell in which nothing seems to matter. They have lost interest in everything. In this shell they can't be hurt any longer. Of course, it doesn't work out that way. Depression can be a miserably bleak experience. In this scenario, they have only exchanged one set of horrors for another.

If you are experiencing any of these conditions, acute stress disorder, post-traumatic stress disorder, panic reactions, disabling phobias, or depression, I would certainly recommend that you have at least a consultation with a person trained and licensed in a mental health profession. If you are free of such difficulties, but are living with more stress than you can easily handle, then seeking professional help is an option you might want to consider. Your decision might depend on such factors as how uncomfortable you are feeling, whether the level of stress you are experiencing is affecting your ability to do what you want in life, and how it is impacting the people who are near and dear to you. If the level of stress you're experiencing is making a shambles out of your life, then by all means go and see somebody. In the next chapter we will explore the kind of help that may be available.

# 8

## *Using Prescription Drugs to Cope with Stress*

Popping a pill to deal with a problem is as American as apple pie, or at least that is what the pharmaceutical corporations would have you believe. There has been no shortage of advertisements suggesting how unhappy looking people may feel much better after using the corporation's antidepressant medicine. In the fine print are listed some of the unpleasant side effects the drug may cause. But if fine print conveys any message, is it not to be too concerned about these facts? If these disclosures were really important, surely they would make more out of them. Right?

Not that there is anything wrong about using medications to deal with emotional problems. The drugs can be very useful. But the advertising blitz would have you believe that drugs are the best way to deal with emotional problems, and perhaps the only way. The advertisements don't even suggest there are alternatives. For millions of people who are experiencing psychological problems, there are very good alternatives.

Drugs do have several distinct advantages. First, drugs are convenient. Taking a pill with a glass of water is a lot easier than driving to a psychotherapist's office and spending an hour in sensitive, sometimes difficult dialogue. Second, antianxiety and antidepressant drugs can often be obtained from your family physician. If you tell your doctor about the stress you are experiencing, the doctor may give you a prescription for an antianxiety drug or an antidepressant if that's what is indicated. Alternatively your doctor might refer you to a specialist to make the diagnosis and decision. For some conditions such as acute stress or a severe depression, the use of drugs may be an essential part of treatment.

The negative side of drugs is that reliance on drugs does not provide you with the insight you may need about what is bothering you. Moreover, drugs tell you nothing about better ways to cope with stress. Many people experience unpleasant and sometimes intolerable side effects from drugs. And in the case of drugs used to diminish anxiety, there is a potential for drug dependence.

In the modern era, the first major class of drugs that was widely used to relax people who were experiencing high levels of stress was the barbiturates. It wasn't that long ago that phenobarbital was the drug physicians would most likely prescribe when one of their patients was very upset or distraught. The drug was inexpensive, effective and had a sedative effect. I can almost hear the lines from one of those memorable black and white movies, circa 1940, in which the kindly, gray-haired doctor says reassuringly to the worried husband, "I'll give her something to calm her down. It will help her sleep." That something would have been phenobarbital.

One of the problems with barbiturates was that they became one of the drugs easily abused by drug abusers. When I was a consultant in the drug and alcohol unit of a Veterans Administration hospital, I asked heroin addicted patients which drugs they had used along the way to becoming addicted to heroin. Many of these patients reported that they had tried barbiturates.

As a prescription drug, phenobarbital can be taken in tablet, capsule, or liquid form.[1] The drug is usually taken one to three times a day, and if taken in a single dose, usually at bedtime. Phenobarbital has been used in the control of anxiety, of seizures, and in the short term treatment of insomnia. Because phenobarbital can be habit forming, it would not be the treatment of choice for reducing stress on a long term basis. Tolerance for the drug can develop after extended use and the drug may lose its effectiveness at the dose taken. After extended use of the drug, it is prudent not to discontinue use of the drug abruptly. Because of the possibility of withdrawal symptoms such as anxiety and insomnia, it would be wise to discontinue use under the supervision of a physician who may recommend reducing the dosage of the drug gradually before ceasing use. The side effects listed for phenobarbital include drowsiness, headache, dizziness, depression, excitement, upset stomach, and vomiting. Phenobarbital can reduce the effectiveness of oral contraceptives. If a woman is using phenobarbital and becomes pregnant, she should contact her doctor immediately.

The continued search for antianxiety drugs with fewer problems than phenobarbital produced a new drug, meprobamate (e.g., trade name Equinal) which came into wide use in the 1950s.[2] The drug, which appears to be effective in lowering anxiety levels, is considered relatively safe when used at normal doses. When discontinuing the drug after prolonged use, the prescribing physician may want the patient to gradually reduce the use of the drug before stopping it entirely. The most frequent side effect of the medicine is drowsiness.

The most frequently prescribed tranquilizing medications today are a class of drugs called benzodiazepines (BZDs). These drugs are believed to enhance the action of the major inhibitory neurotransmitter in the central nervous system. This enhanced action induces sedation in the user, muscle relaxation, and lowered anxiety. Benzodiazepines have proven useful not only in the control of anxiety, but also in alcohol withdrawal, in the control of seizures and as a muscle relaxant.

Two of the better known drugs within the family of benzodiazepines are diazepam (e.g., brand name Valium) and alprazolam (e.g., brand name Xanax). Both diazepam and alprazolam are effective drugs in controlling anxiety. Both should be used with caution.

Diazepam was discovered by Leo Sternbach, a chemist who was born in an obscure province of the onetime Austro-Hungarian Empire that was dismembered at the end of the First World War.[3] He received a doctorate at the University of Krakow and worked for a Swiss drug company until the outbreak of World War II when he fled to the United States. He began working on the development of a drug to rival meprobamate as an anxiety reducing agent. Eventually, he discovered diazepam and the drug was marketed in the 1960s under the name of Valium. Heavily marketed, the drug proved to be a huge success. Valium became the most frequently prescribed drug in America. In an obituary article about Sternberg in *The Washington Post*, Patricia Sullivan noted that the drug was at the top of the list of most common pharmaceuticals from the late 1960s to the early 1980s.

Well known celebrities including Hollywood actresses said they used the drug and some said they had become addicted to it. With rising concern about problems from overuse of the drug, sales began to decline. But, during its heyday the widespread use of Valium was a cultural phenomenon.

Diazapam may be taken as a tablet, as an extended-release capsule, or as a liquid.[4]

Here are some red flags for diazepam.

Women who are pregnant should not use the drug.

With elderly people, it may be advisable to use lower doses of the medicine.

People whose activities require high alertness should use the drug with caution because of the sedative effects. This caution extends to driving and the use of machinery.

Among the possible adverse affects listed for diazepam are drowsiness, tiredness, lightheadedness, and indigestion.

Diazepam can be habit forming. Tolerance for the drug may occur with long-term use, decreasing the effectiveness of the drug. After prolonged use of the drug, abrupt discontinuation of use may cause withdrawal symptoms such as anxiety and insomnia. Alprazolam, another widely used benzodiazepine, has been used successfully in the short term treatment of anxiety and panic disorder. In one study 82 percent of panic disorder patients had a favorable response to the drug. Interestingly, 43 percent of the patients who received a placebo also responded favorably which points to the power of belief that one has a way of coping with stress in controlling stress reactions.[5]

The key word here is short term because the possibility of dependence on the drug rises with the passage of time as well as with the dose. If the user develops tolerance to the drug, he or she may eventually require larger doses of the drug for it to be effective.

Alprazolam may be taken in tablet or liquid form. As is true for most antianxiety drugs, drowsiness is a common side effect. The user may also experience other possible side effects such as light-headedness, tiredness and changes in sex drive. The drug should not be used during pregnancy. Because abrupt cessation of the drug after extended use can cause withdrawal symptoms, such as anxiety and sleeplessness, the drug should be discontinued under the supervision of a physician.

Overdoses from using benzodiazepines are not infrequent. In a recent year there were about 40,000 incidents of overdose reported by poison centers in the United States.[6] Using these drugs in combination with alcohol or other sedative drugs can be hazardous and should be avoided.

It is important to remember that most antianxiety drugs have the potential for drug dependency. When used prudently, antianxiety drugs can be helpful in dealing with problems of acute stress, but they have potential drawbacks as a long term treatment for stress related disorders.

Given these cautionary notes, it makes good sense that antianxiety drugs should be used under medical supervision. The physician prescribing these drugs for you should not only know what other drugs you are taking, but also be fully aware of your medical history. When you begin the process of discontinuing the drug, you should go over the withdrawal procedure carefully with your doctor.

# 9

# *Psychotherapy*

When you are considering professional help to cope with chronic stress, the principal alternative to asking your doctor for medications is to consult a psychotherapist. Sometimes the term talking therapy is used as a way of distinguishing psychotherapy from reliance on drugs, but I have never liked the term for the talk that takes place in therapy is pretty far removed from what one is used to in everyday conversation. The talk in therapy is all about you, your life, your relationships, your dreams, your frustrations, your conflicts, and your fears — what makes you the unique individual you are. Sound interesting? Then, read on!

As we start out, it is important to note that psychotherapy is not a one-size-fits-all profession. Going to a psychotherapist is not like going to the dentist to have your teeth cleaned or to an optometrist to have your vision checked — situations where the procedures are generally well defined and standardized. Because there are widely different approaches to doing therapy, it is important to know something about the range of possibilities before choosing a therapist so one can select the kind of therapist who best fits one's needs.

This profusion of approaches to doing therapy is a relatively recent development, having mostly taken place during the last few decades. If you were seeking a therapist in the 1940s or 1950s, chances are that most of the therapists you would have encountered would have been psychoanalysts. In those days psychotherapy was almost thought of as psychoanalysis.

From time to time you may have seen cartoon caricatures of psychoanalysts — you remember the bearded analyst sitting on a chair and the patient reclining upon a couch. Psychoanalysis really fired up the public's imagination in the early and middle years of the 20th century. Alfred Hitchcock made a nail-biting movie, *Spellbound*, which was all about recovering lost memories of a murder with the aid of psychoanalysis. The patient was a young, very handsome Gregory Peck, the psychoanalyst the beautiful Ingrid Bergman.

Psychoanalysis was and remains a long, drawn out process, designed by its creator, Sigmund Freud, to probe into one's inner self, one's depths. The procedure can be unsettling and may require the patient to come to grips with some very uncomfortable ideas. Not only was psychoanalysis lengthy (it could take years to complete) and sometimes torturous, it was also expensive. It became a fashionable activity for the wealthy and the elite.

While psychoanalysis is still widely practiced today (and the people who do it may swear by it with an almost religious fervor), there are now shorter, less probing, and for many people equally if not more effective alternatives. These alternatives include behavioral, cognitive, and interpersonal therapy. Even the adherents of Freud's theory have recognized the need to develop more focused, more time limited forms of therapy which they call brief dynamic therapy.

One of the principal objectives of traditional psychoanalysis is to dredge up material from the unconscious and make it accessible to the patient, thereby reducing the pressures that these unconscious thoughts, are exerting on the individual's behavior. According to Freud's theory, these unconscious thoughts, which are often ideas the person would not normally want to admit to, are the driving force behind the person's symptoms. It is the pressure that these thoughts exert for release and the counter pressures the mind exerts to keep them buried in the unconscious which is tying the individual up in knots. If the analyst is able to help the patient bring these thoughts to the surface through such techniques as free association to dreams or just the patient's free flow of ideas and the patient is able to confront these ideas and accept them for what they are, then he or she should feel better. While this is not a very elegant statement of Freud's thinking, I believe this is the gist of what he was saying. The big questions that arise are (1) Does the mind really work the way Freud envisioned it did? (2) Is the bringing forth of unconscious ideas a necessary condition for making a person feel better? The answer to the first question is still somewhat murky. One major problem is that psychoanalysts have been historically reluctant to test their ideas in an objective and transparent way. A second problem is, as we mentioned in the chapter on defense mechanisms, it is extremely difficult to design useful psychological measuring instruments or sound experiments to study phenomena that are out of our conscious awareness. So, it has always been difficult to evaluate the extent to which the theory is valid. The answer to the second question is clearly *no*. The evidence is overwhelming that therapies which do not probe for unconscious material can be very effective in helping people. In any event, traditional psychoanalysis as psychotherapy is certainly costly and inefficient. To those who assert that it is, nonetheless, more effective than competing therapies, I would ask, "Where is the research evidence?" I have yet to see any.

Let's talk about behavior therapy. The behavior therapist who is a purist would not be very concerned about looking for the causes of the patient's problems. If the patient had a symptom such as a phobia, the therapist would focus on the symptom and try to get rid of it. For example, if a person were suffering from agoraphobia and reported that it was terrifying to venture a block from home, the behavior therapist would go right after the phobia and try to diminish it — and if possible get rid of it. Even the most vocal critics of behavior therapy would have to admit that this would be enormously beneficial to the patient.

The proponents of deeper therapy, however, would argue that the underlying problems causing the phobia have been untouched by the behavior therapy procedure and that these unresolved problems may give rise to other symptoms. Maybe. But, maybe not. The argument that other symptoms would arise is more theory than fact. The person who has gotten rid of the phobia could not care less about this academic dispute. After shaking off agoraphobia, he may be as happy as if he won a prize in the lottery.

The techniques of behavior therapy seem particularly effective when one is experiencing anxiety that is elicited by a specific situation, such as is the case in phobias. When anxiety is more general, when one feels under chronic stress, the usefulness of behavior therapy seems less clear. If you are experiencing chronic stress, the behavior therapist might want to teach you progressive muscle relaxation or perhaps refer you to someone who can teach you meditation, or possibly to someone who can give you biofeedback training where you can learn to recognize the internal signals of your body — how to sense when it is relaxed — and how to bring this state about. For the behavior therapist, the idea is that you can help people who feel under chronic stress most easily by doing the obvious — teaching them how to relax.

The techniques the behavior therapist uses to diminish anxiety reactions to specific situations are interesting. In therapy I have used one of these techniques, systematic desensitization, to help people better cope with phobias and found it very useful. Remember, systematic desensitization involves first teaching the patient the technique of progressive muscle relaxation, and then asking the patient to imagine a series of scenes that relate to the phobia. This procedure usually begins with a scene that arouses very little anxiety. For an agoraphobic that might mean imagining opening the front door a crack and looking outside. If the patient feels very anxious, the therapist might stop right there. But in a state of deep muscle relaxation, that is not too likely to happen. So the therapist would proceed to step two — perhaps walking outside a few steps and turning around. What I have found is that if patients can tolerate the scene in their imagination, they can often do this in reality. When it comes to serious activities, such as that first drive to the mall, the patient might want to have a friend along to provide that extra sense of security and comfort.

I liked using systematic desensitization because it is a conservative procedure. Another behavior therapy technique that has been called implosion therapy can also be very effective, but for the patient it has more of a sink-or-swim flavor. Implosion therapy is based on the theory that what you have learned to fear is perpetuated by your avoidance of the feared situation. If you are somehow imbedded with the feared object and cannot avoid it, and you find that, in time, nothing bad really happens to you, then your fear of the object will diminish and perhaps vanish altogether. For example, if you have a fear of snakes and are placed in a room with fearsome looking but harmless snakes, the theory would hold that you would, in time, feel less afraid of snakes. Well, implosion therapy doesn't usually ask you to sit in that snake infested room, it just asks you to imagine that you're there. In your imagination, you try to make the feared object as vivid as possible. The therapist will attempt to describe scenes which recreate the sights, the sounds, and even the smells of the experience that has frightened you. Your task is to make it real in your imagination and then wait it out until your fear subsides. Unlike systematic desensitization, the implosion procedure doesn't first relax you. You are simply thrust into the melee.

The clinical journals in psychology contain case reports of implosion therapy. Here are two examples. In the first example a young boy had an inordinate fear of bodily harm. In particular, the sight of his own blood terrified him.[1] He thought that if he started bleeding, he would bleed to death. The problem had its origin with his younger sister, who had a bleeding disorder that prevented her blood from clotting. His fears manifested themselves in crying at the slightest sight of his being cut or bruised. To prevent injury, he began to avoid all situations in which he might hurt himself. That meant shying away from the rough and tumble games and sports that many boys his age relish. In what appeared to be related problems, the boy developed both asthma and insomnia.

The boy improved greatly after only two sessions of implosion therapy. During each session he was asked to imagine as vividly as he could a series of scenes that was portrayed to him by the therapist. Examples of scenes that he was asked to imagine included slipping and hitting his head on a rock, then seeing blood trickling down on his nose, eyes and mouth. During the treatment sessions he became extremely anxious. He wept and trembled. The sessions exhausted him. But the treatment helped. His insomnia began to dissipate within a week. His asthma vanished as well. He began to play with more abandonment and had more fun in school. While the treatment was clearly effective, it was no doubt a very rough experience.

The second case involved a young adolescent boy who developed a severe case of school phobia.[2] The symptoms set in after he had been away from school for some time because of a prolonged illness. On the day he returned to school, he became extremely anxious and developed chest pains which were so severe that he had to be taken to the doctor. The doctor gave him tranquilizers which temporarily calmed him down. However, on the next morning, he resolutely refused to return to school. His fear of returning to school was so intense, nothing could make him go back

The therapist decided to try implosion therapy. The therapist asked the boy to imagine a series of scenes relating to school — all of which elicited considerable fear. For example, he was asked to imagine being dragged by his mother to the school against his will, confronting the principal — who was described as hostile, even sadistic — being forced to answer questions thrown at him by teachers, questions that he didn't know the answers to, and interacting with students who jeered at him and taunted him.

The first session of implosion therapy aroused a great deal of anxiety. As was true in the first case, the boy wept and trembled. He also complained of chest pains. At the end of the session, he, too, was physically exhausted. Surprisingly, the next morning he felt much better, went to school and attended his second implosion therapy session without protest. By the sixth and final treatment, all of his anxiety about school had disappeared. Thirteen weeks after the last session, researchers inquired about the boy's health and state of mind and found that he was doing well and had no anxiety about going to school.

In both examples the treatment worked very well. The turnaround in the second case was dramatic. The first day of treatment, however, was extremely stressful, almost traumatic. It was as if the patient had to go through hell to get rid of the problem. I prefer systematic desensitization for obvious reasons. It is a much gentler procedure. But I can certainly see the potential of implosion therapy for helping those suffering from prolonged post-traumatic stress disorder resulting from combat. This technique could be an effective way to deal with a seemingly intractable, agonizing problem.

You may have wondered whether behavior therapists have taken the next step, not settling for the patient's experiencing the feared situation in imagination, but instead directly confronting the situation as it exists in reality. The answer is yes. This kind of direct exposure therapy has been tried successfully where the feared situation can be reproduced. For example, people with fears of spiders were urged to remain close to harmless spiders and in time their fears dissipated. The acid test came when a spider was placed on the subject's arm. If the subject could tolerate the creepy, crawling insect strolling on his or her arm, it was a pretty good sign that the phobia had been cured.

Modern technologies are providing a new tool for the treatment of phobias — simulation of the situations that produce the phobic reactions in the treatment center. Computer generated virtual reality techniques can make you feel that you are on a high cliff or enclosed in a small elevator without your really being there. You can experience the fear but know at the same time that you are really safe.

The use of virtual reality techniques as a treatment for phobias is relatively new.[3] In the mid–1990s, a psychologist, Barbara Rothbaum, teamed up with a computer scientist, Larry Hodges, to develop the procedure and published a paper that studied the effectiveness of the new treatment for acrophobia, the fear of heights.

The use of virtual reality devices for treating phobia is still limited because of the expenses involved in buying and using the equipment but it is now expanding and in time may become widespread. The cover of the July-August 2005 issue of the *Monitor on Psychology* features a picture of the device in use. The patient wears oversized headgear which blocks out sights in the room and responds to an artificial world controlled by the therapist.

Imagine for a moment that you are the patient and you are being treated for that very inconvenient phobia, fear of flying. Inside the headgear covering your face, a small screen flips down and displays computer generated images that give you the sensation of being inside a commercial airliner. Then, you hear the noise of engines and there you go, up, up, and away. Or imagine you are being treated for fear of spiders and the image on the small screen is of a tarantula climbing on the kitchen counter. What you have here is exposure therapy without exposure. The best of all possible worlds. Meanwhile, outside the artificial world enclosed in the helmet, the therapist keeps a tight lid on things, controlling the length of exposure of each scene and the sequence of what comes next. Does virtual reality work for everyone? Probably not. And the availability of the technique at the present time is still limited. However, it's the most interesting and intriguing treatment for phobias that has yet come along.

Social phobias — which can make a shambles of one's chances of establishing meaningful relationships which are so important in life — are difficult to treat. Shyness is something that most of us experience during childhood or adolescence, but most of us get over it at least to the point of being able to talk to people and feel a degree of ease in meeting people of the opposite sex. But, imagine someone who remains super shy and feels panicky at the prospect of asking someone out for a date. There are many such people. Writing in the *Monitor on Psychology*, Melissa Dittmann noted that a very large number of people suffer from this destructive phobia. Citing data provided by the National Institute of Mental Health, she put the figure at 5.3 million adults.[4]

My own approach to treatment of social phobia was to first do some probing to look for the causes of the problem in childhood and then when I had some insight into what had transpired, to use the behavioral technique of systematic desensitization to lessen anxiety levels for situations which were arousing acute anxiety. I would follow this with role playing exercises which involve meeting people of the opposite sex and conversing with them. Too often, however, I found a disconnect between what seemed to go well in therapy and what took place subsequently in real life. Some patients' social interactions remained frozen.

Richard Heimberg, a psychologist at Temple University, has been working on this problem a long time. He suggests the use of cognitive-behavioral therapy to help people change their thought processes which seem to buttress the phobia, such as the idea that other people are evaluating them negatively. The therapist can readily point out that other people probably have something entirely different on their minds than thinking about you — that like you, they have their own concerns. Heimberg also uses anti-depressant medications and role-playing social interactions. When his patients are deemed ready, he gives them assignments to venture forth into interactions with people in the real world. The hope is that these coping skills learned in therapy will help the patient experience successes rather than another demoralizing failure.[5]

Cognitive therapy, which we have just alluded to, comes from the word cognition, which means thoughts or ideas. The basic idea underlying cognitive therapy is that a person feels bad — perhaps tense, perhaps depressed — because the patient operates on the basis of belief systems which bring on difficulties. A typical trouble-producing belief system is perfectionistic thinking. It is pretty difficult to feel good about yourself if you are convinced that everything you do doesn't measure up. The cognitive therapist would try to change such belief systems — to push aside this dysfunctional belief — in favor of ideas which allow the individual a greater possibility of the pursuit of happiness.

Or take another example. Imagine you are a college student about to enter a classroom to take a mathematics exam. As you enter the room your mind is full of self-defeating thoughts. "I'm no good at math," "When I see the questions, I know I won't be able to answer them," "If I fail the test, it will show how stupid I am," "People will look down on me if I fail," "My whole world will fall apart after I take this test." With this kind of mind-set, when you encounter a really difficult question on the exam, you are likely to come unglued. A cognitive therapist will try to show you that these kinds of attitudes are exaggerated, unwarranted, and are likely to interfere with rather than facilitate your performance on the test. The therapist would try to assist you to develop a less threatening mindset about taking examinations.

Cognitive therapy seems like a sensible approach for helping people who are experiencing stress. If the therapist in his diagnostic inquiries can identify patterns of thought which promote stress, he can point the way to alternative beliefs which do not engender such stress. Cognitive therapy techniques have proven effective in treating depression. Cognitive therapy also appears to be an effective treatment for panic attacks. Because the patients' thought patterns — misinterpreting benign signals from the body as heralding an impending catastrophe — are an important part of the process that occurs in panic attacks, cognitive therapy seems tailor-made as an approach to treating this disorder. Psychologists who are expanding the applications of cognitive therapy have developed treatment procedures for panic attacks. One of the better studied programs runs about 12 weeks. A shortened adaptation of that treatment program for panic disorder was developed by David Clark and his colleagues at Oxford University.[6] In addition to face-to face interactions between patient and therapist, this treatment program utilizes homework assignments and relies heavily on self-study modules. The patients read the modules and complete the written homework assignments before going over them with the therapist. The researchers' description of the modules conveys a sense of how the therapy attempts to modify thought patterns.

> Module 1 gave case illustrations of the panic attack vicious circle and used a series of questions about thoughts and feelings to help patients identify the vicious circle in one of their own recent panic attacks. Thought challenging was introduced, and ways in which attention to body cues, avoidance, and images might maintain negative interpretations of body sensations were explained. Module 2 focused on patients' worst fears about the sensations they experienced in attacks and helped them to generate alternative, noncatastrophic explanations for the sensations. Module 3 introduced safety behaviors, explained how they prevent cognitive change, and helped patients identify their own safety behaviors. Module 4 reviewed the outcome of experiments in which patients were encouraged to drop safety behaviors during their attacks and in feared situations, helped patients identify triggers for the attacks, consolidated the alternative explanation that had already been developed, and outlined a relapse-prevention program.[7]

Clark and his colleagues evaluated their abbreviated program, comparing it with the 12 week program that Clark had also been involved in developing. The researchers found that the two forms of the program were equally effective. In a follow-up evaluation, conducted one year after the patients had completed the treatment programs, it was found that over 70 percent of the patients previously suffering from panic attacks were now free of them. Cognitive therapy appeared to be very effective in dealing with panic attacks.

At first blush, behavior and cognitive therapy appear to be very different approaches to conducting therapy. Behavior therapy tackles symptoms directly, while cognitive therapy examines the thoughts and beliefs that may underlie the symptoms. While the two therapies obviously have a different focus, it wasn't too long before psychologists began to realize that there was no inherent conflict between these two approaches. They began to wonder whether using both techniques with a patient might produce better results than relying on either alone. Thus it was that clinicians began to experiment by combining both approaches with patients. The therapist might examine the thoughts underlying stress reactions and at the same time try one of the techniques designed to induce relaxation. And so it was that a hybrid therapy developed which is now called cognitive-behavior therapy. There is now a large body of research demonstrating the effectiveness of cognitive-behavior therapy in treating emotional difficulties.

Interpersonal therapy, which focuses on the patient's relationships, has always made sense to me as a treatment for people suffering from chronic stress. Clearly, not all of the stress people experience is engendered by difficult relationships. Financial worries, health problems, and job situations are obvious alternative sources of stress, but there is no doubt that for many people difficult relationships are a big contributor to stress. Even before interpersonal therapy came into formal existence, I am sure that most therapists found themselves inexorably drawn into dealing with such issues.

The therapist trained in the technique of interpersonal therapy will tend to focus on certain problems. The therapist will look for disputes that the patient may be having with people that are significant in the patient's life, recent or ongoing transitions (such as changing jobs, divorce, birth of a child), the experience of loneliness, and evidence of abnormal grieving after experiencing loss. The therapist will explore how the patient has been coping with these problems and will work with the patient to develop more effective ways to deal with these situations.

With these snapshots of different approaches to psychotherapy in mind, let us turn to the question of how to pick a therapist. Here are some basic things to consider.

1. Therapists come from several professional disciplines, most frequently psychiatry, psychology, and social work. There are good and not so good therapists coming from each discipline. You can't really tell how good a therapist is by the discipline label. You have to work with the individual therapist to find out.

   Having a medical degree, psychiatrists are able to prescribe medications. That can be an advantage if you are looking for medication. That could be a disadvantage if your interest is in learning how to cope more effectively with your problems, because some psychiatrists may rely primarily on medicine to help you rather than psychotherapy.

   You are very likely to find that there are licensing requirements in your state for members of all three disciplines. This means that the person practicing therapy has not only obtained the needed degrees in an appropriate graduate or professional school but has passed written exams to demonstrate satisfactory knowledge of the field. Licensing indicates that the practitioner has basic competence and has been following ethical standards.
2. How do you go about locating a therapist? In small towns and rural communities, there may not be much of a choice. There may only be one or two practitioners within driving range. In metropolitan areas, there are likely to be many choices. Most states and some cities and counties have professional organizations in medicine, psychology and social work and these organizations usually maintain referral lists. If you are looking for a psychologist in my state, Maryland, you can dial the number for the Maryland Psychological Association and the receptionist will give you the names of several people practicing in your area. You might well ask further whether there are people who offer specialties in the area you are looking for. For example, do they offer stress management?

   Of course, ask about fees. You may find wide differences in fees and the amount you pay may be no indication of how good the therapist is. Some therapists may give you a reduced rate if you have financial need. You might also try university counseling centers and community mental health clinics.
3. If you are able to, try to talk with the therapist on the telephone briefly before you make your appointment to get a sense of what the therapist is like. At the least, you want to find out if the therapist has had experience working with cases that are similar to your

own. For example, it you are suffering from panic attacks, find out if the therapist has worked with such problems. Ask how the therapist treats such problems.

4. In regard to the therapist's orientation think about the things we have discussed in this chapter. Ask yourself what kind of approach you feel would be most valuable for you. For example, if you feel that it is important to explore in detail your early childhood experiences — that this is the key to your problems — you may want to consider a therapist who is psychodynamically (psychoanalytically) oriented. If, on the other hand you want to focus immediately on your current pressing problems, you may want to consider someone who uses cognitive-behavioral or interpersonal approaches. If you feel you need a person who can help you with a wide range of possibilities, then look for someone who describes his approach as eclectic. So, by all means, ask about the therapist's orientation.
5. The personal qualities of the therapists are very important. You need to work with someone whom you like and trust. If you don't have such feelings, you're not likely to make much progress. If you cannot relate well to the first therapist you choose, find another one.

# 10

## *Some Alternative Approaches to Controlling Stress*

Just about everything that we have discussed so far fits into a mainstream approach for dealing with stress. We have outlined some common sense strategies that one can consider trying oneself—strategies that require little or no outside assistance. And we have talked about seeking professional help from physicians and psychotherapists, also very mainstream ideas. Now, I would like to discuss briefly some alternative approaches to dealing with stress that you might want to give some thought to: hypnosis, therapeutic massage and herbals.

My first exposure to hypnosis was watching Grade B films that were shown as part of a double feature at a local movie theater when I was a child. The prototype film featured an insane doctor played by someone like Bela Lugosi of *Dracula* fame who would hypnotize his victims into doing something terrible, something they would not normally do. The method of hypnosis used by the villain might be gazing into the victim's eyes with a stupendous stare or perhaps swinging a locket back and forth to induce a trance. While these cinematic portrayals had next to nothing to do with the reality of hypnosis, they must have left a bad taste in me because I never considered learning how to use hypnosis in my therapy practice. I had been totally turned off.

The use of hypnosis dates back to the late 18th Century, to the time of Franz Mesmer, who was apparently such a master of the technique that his name remains almost synonymous with hypnosis. We still use the term mesmerize. Over the years, hypnosis was used for parlor games, theatrical performances, by police detectives trying to enhance the memory of witnesses about the details of a crime scene, with occasional spectacular successes, and by psychotherapists. With such a mixed bag of applications, hypnosis has always enjoyed an uneven reputation.

Putting aside the hocus pocus about hypnosis, the basics of the procedure involve suggestions offered by the person in the role of the hypnotist to the subject awaiting to be hypnotized. The hypnotist might begin with an explanation of what hypnosis is all about and then offer a series of suggestions to the subject. The suggestions might begin with the idea that the subject is feeling relaxed, and then proceed to feeling drowsy, even sleepy. The hypnotist then may then add suggestions that the subject's hand is feeling warm and later that his right arm will rise in the air. Many people will react to this series of carefully worded suggestions by becoming drowsy, feeling warmth in their hands and raising their arms. Their actions appear to them to be involuntary. When people are in a hypnotic state, they became very responsive to the hypnotist's suggestions. If the hypnotist tells the subject to immerse his hand in very cold water and that he will feel no pain, chances are he will not feel the pain he would normally experience. In one experiment, highly hypnotizable subjects were given the suggestion that they were of the other gender (female subjects were told that they were male, and male subjects that they were female). The subjects became so convinced of this that when they were asked to state their names, they invented names of the other gender. The experimenters concluded that the highly hypnotizable subjects "experienced a transient delusion about their sex that was compelling and resistant to challenge."[1] If the hypnotist tells the subject that he or she will not remember what transpired during hypnosis, it is unlikely that there will be any recall.

What actually happens in hypnosis is not entirely clear. One of the theories advanced is that during hypnosis the mind experiences a kind of temporary disassociation, with part of the mind becoming amnesiac to the other part. It is as if there was some kind of barrier between streams of consciousness. While something like this may be happening, despite considerable research on hypnosis, we are still not really sure.

Hypnosis can be very useful in the control of pain. Major surgeries including appendectomies and hysterectomies have been successfully performed without anesthesia while patients were under hypnosis. Hypnosis has been used to quiet the pain of people suffering from burn injuries. Hypnosis has also been used in the control of more commonplace pain, such as headaches.[2]

There is, as yet, less evidence to show that hypnosis is as effective in the control of stress as it is in the control of pain. Hypnosis has been successfully used in treating disorders which may be stress related such as asthma. And there have been studies showing that the technique can reduce anxiety in people who are easily hypnotized. The technique also has been used successfully in the treatment of phobias.[3]

There is some research evidence indicating that hypnosis can be useful in helping people cope with some forms of acute stress. A study carried out on patients undergoing elective plastic surgery under local anesthesia and intravenous sedation found that patients given hypnosis reported less pain and anxiety than patients given other stress reducing techniques. Not only were the self-reports of anxiety and pain lower among the hypnotized patients, their vital signs were more stable during the surgery.[4] Another study found that adding hypnotic induction to techniques of cognitive-behavioral therapy lowered the risk for patients diagnosed with acute stress disorder from developing subsequent post-traumatic stress disorder.[5] While these studies do not directly address the question of the usefulness of hypnosis in the control of chronic stress, they do suggest the potential usefulness of hypnosis in coping with some types of acute stress.

Although the research evidence that hypnosis is effective in the control of chronic stress is not nearly as overwhelming as it is for the control of pain, the presumption is that it may be useful if, and this is a big if, you are easily hypnotizable. Some people are readily hypnotized, others are not. If you are, and a hypnotist can put you through a few simple exercises that can tell this quickly, then it may be worth trying. If I were considering hypnosis for help with any kind of psychological problem, I would look for a hypnotist who was also a licensed psychotherapist. Hypnosis carried out by a trained therapist would be more likely to be integrated into the overall therapeutic approach.

In Sam's life it is difficult to find time for him to relax. Sam is a successful businessman who owns and operates a consulting company that deals with computer networking. Because it is a small company, Sam finds himself heavily involved in fulfilling every contract the company has obtained. He puts in lots of hours, travels far and wide and is frequently under the pressure of meeting deadlines. One of the ways Sam has discovered to cope with the stress that is engendered by his heavy schedule is to periodically visit the office of a licensed professional who performs therapeutic massage. Partially covered by a sheet, Sam stretches out on the table, and for the next half an hour or so feels the skilled fingers of the therapist work their way into his soft tissue, his back, shoulders, neck and fingers. For a while he chats amiably with the therapist, then lapses into state of deep comfort. When the therapist is finished, he feels a great deal better.

While hypnosis has a history of 200 years or so, therapeutic massage goes back over 2000 years. Scholars have unearthed the use of massage therapy in such ancient cultures as Egypt, Greece, Rome, and China. The father of medicine, Hippocrates, indicated that massage was useful in dealing with stiffness. While massage was apparently in wide use in the Greek and Roman worlds of two millennia ago, it largely disappeared from medical practice until a century ago. This is a shame, because massage therapy can actually help people while a lot of other things doctors did in the dark ages of medicine probably were ineffective, if not harmful.

As is true for psychotherapy, there is no single form of massage therapy universally practiced. If you look in the yellow pages of a telephone directory in a large metropolitan area you are likely to see different types of massage therapy advertised. You may see Swedish massage, deep tissue massage, and Shiatsu, among others. Although all therapeutic massage involves rubbing the soft tissues of the body, the length of time of the massage and the technique used may vary.

Therapeutic massage is a helpful treatment for many physical problems. And it is clearly beneficial in the reduction of both transitory and chronic feelings of anxiety.[6] Therapeutic massage can reduce heart rate and blood pressure. In a recent review of studies examining the effects of a massage therapy on the stress hormone cortisol, Tiffany Field and her colleagues noted that significant decreases were observed in cortisol levels averaging about 30 percent. Continued treatments over time may be as helpful for many people as psychotherapy in reducing anxiety. Therapeutic message is certainly a plausible strategy to consider if you are troubled by chronic stress. With scientific data pointing to its effectiveness, it is not surprising that therapeutic massage is rapidly growing in popularity. If you decide to try massage, don't confuse therapeutic massage with what is offered in massage parlors. The difference is huge.

I will close this chapter on alternative approaches to treating stress with a few brief comments on the use of herbals. My general feeling is that until a very authoritative source, preferably a government agency, gives the green light indicating that an herbal preparation is both safe and effective, one should exercise caution in using it. Useful information on many herbals can be obtained from the National Center for Alternative and Complimentary Medicines.

I would like to mention two herbs that appear to have some value in dealing with psychological distress, one in the control of depression, the other in the control of anxiety. St. John's Wort (Hypericum perforatum) has been shown to be effective in a number of studies for treating mild to moderate depression. The herbal Kava (Piper methysticum) has been studied for its effects on anxiety. This herb, used for many centuries among Pacific Islanders in ceremonial and social occasions seems to have relaxing effects. Most of the scientific research that I have seen on Kava was carried out in Europe. These studies point to the effectiveness of Kava in lowering anxiety. Kava does have side effects which have been described as transitory. The red flags for Kava are warnings from the Food and Drug Administration that it could have adverse effects on the liver.[7]

Any time one considers the use of an herbal preparation for the treatment of emotional distress, one should be very careful to make sure that the herb does not interact with medicines the individual may be currently taking. Informing your doctor that you are using herbals is very important.

Another important thing to remember if you use herbals of any kind is to be certain that the company that produces the herbal is reliable. Be sure that the company has high quality control standards and has a reputation for producing quality products. A story on the front page of the *Washington Post* is a reminder that there are companies in this industry which are anything but reliable. The *Post's* story tells of a man who was suffering from prostate cancer. The man purchased a product which he thought was an herbal treatment for prostate cancer. The man died. It turned out the substance had been mixed with pharmaceuticals which included an artificial estrogen and a blood thinner. The combination proved lethal. The company pleaded no contest to felony charges of selling contaminated goods.[8]

If you use herbals, use companies that have a solid track record.

# 11

# *The Goal: Improving Self-efficacy*

Think about the following words: *confidence, control, empowerment,* and *self-efficacy.* Now, think about these words: *self-esteem, hardiness, resiliency,* and a word from the lexicon of psychology that you may not be familiar with, *ego-strength.* One of the things that all of these words or phrases have in common is that they denote characteristics that can be buffers against stress; they can mitigate the impact of stressors so you don't feel as upset when the stressors act on you. Not only may you not feel as upset, your body may not show the intensity of reaction in the production of stress hormones. Your pulse and blood pressure may remain normal or at least not rise precipitously.

The first group of terms deals with perceptions and attitudes. These are more readily malleable, more subject to change than the characteristics in the second group, which are more akin to enduring personality traits. It is the explicit assumption underlying this book that acquiring the kinds of coping skills discussed in the preceding chapters can increase one's sense of control and raise one's confidence so that when stressors arise — as they inevitably will — you will be able to more effectively cope with them. That increased sense of control, in itself, can make an important difference in how you will react.

Psychologists use the term self-efficacy to describe the sense that one has a reasonable measure of control over events and this includes one's emotional and behavioral responses to stressful events. Indeed, research suggests that self-efficacy can be an important buffer against stressors. To cite two examples, in a study carried out on patients suffering from headaches, a relation was found between the frequency of stressful events reported by the patients and the frequency with which they experienced headaches. In view of what we know about the relation of stress and physical symptoms, this is not surprising. However, it was also found that this relation was moderated by the patient's perception of self-efficacy. The relation between stress and headaches was stronger for the patients who were evaluated as low on self-efficacy and weaker for the patients who were evaluated as high on self-efficacy. Self-efficacy appeared to buffer the effects of stress on headaches.[1]

In a similar vein, in a study of college students carried out at the University of Florida, researchers found that students' confidence levels in their ability to solve their problems and their perceptions of their control in solving problems related to both lower stress levels and report of physical symptoms.[2]

A very creative psychologist, Julian Rotter, carried out some important research on the concept of perceived control.[3] Rotter offered a distinction between people who saw the ability to obtain the things they wanted in life as falling largely within their own control and those who saw these things as being largely under external control. The former group, sometimes called internals, placed great store on their own efforts while the latter group, sometimes called externals, saw themselves as something akin to sitting on a raft being buffeted about by the waves. For the externals attaining success was pretty much a matter of chance.

In a study carried out at Emory University, people were exposed to a noise stressor and monitored for cortisol levels. In one experimental condition, the subjects were told that they would be able to control the noise level. While this option did not make a difference for many of the subjects in affecting cortisol levels, it did make a difference for the people classified in Rotter's scheme as internals. When internals believed that they could control the stressor, they showed a smaller cortisol response to the stressor. The belief within you that you are in control seems to make a difference.[4]

A sense of control over events can help a person weather a storm even when the situation is far from promising. A group of researchers at the University of San Francisco studied patients who had experienced heart failure. Using a variety of psychological instruments, they obtained measures of perceived control, anxiety, and depression. The researchers found that not only did the patients with higher levels of perceived control report less emotional distress, when they were asked to walk for six minutes, they walked longer distances than the other patients.[5] The suggestion here is that if you think you can, then you just may.

Personality characteristics such as self-esteem and hardiness can also have this moderating effect on stressors. Researchers, for example, studied children making the often rocky transition from elementary school to junior high school. Think back for a moment to the time when you left your small elementary school with few students and a single teacher to enter a much larger school full of unfamiliar faces, with students shuffling around the corridors from class to class. The change can be pretty unsettling to a child. The researchers reported that the children with high self esteem made this often difficult transition with much less distress.[6]

Self-esteem, hardiness, and resilience are very desirable qualities in coping with the stresses of everyday life and may be particularly valuable in coping with the extreme stressors that may come our way on occasion. While these characteristics are formed in childhood and are reasonably rooted by adulthood, they are not immutable. One's self-esteem can and does change as a function of experience. Parents, teachers, peers, therapists — all can affect self-esteem, sometimes raising it, sometimes diminishing it. But, it seems to me, raising self-esteem is a more fundamental and difficult task than the one we have set forth for ourselves in this book — of describing an array of techniques to increase our sense of control when we encounter stressors. If an increased sense of control, in turn, increases self-esteem or resiliency, so much the better.

# 12

## *Putting It All Together*

To increase our sense of control when we encounter difficulties, we may need to make some changes in the way we cope with problems. Before considering possible changes, it is usually a good idea to assess where we are. It is not always easy to make such appraisals, and for many important assessments about ourselves, objectivity can be the first casualty. However, there are some things about our patterns of behavior which are not only very clear, but usually each individual is the best judge of his own situation. Let's begin by once again posing the question we asked at the end of the first chapter: what are the major sources of stress in your life at the present time? In thinking about this question, it may be useful to glance again at the checklist provided at the end of the first chapter which lists common sources of stress — the kinds of stressful situations that can happen to almost everyone. Ask yourself again, what are the situations in your life that are causing you distress?

As you looked through this list, did you mentally check one or two of the situations listed as sources of stress or did you check more than that, perhaps many more? While even one very distressing situation, such as a turbulent romantic relationship, can be enough to make one's life miserable, having stress arousing problems coming at you from all directions can be overwhelming. In one of the studies I carried out with Roland Tanck, we found that the more problems people had to deal with, the more likely they would report feeling depressed.

A second area of assessment that is important to make concerns the use of ineffective coping techniques in dealing with stress. In Chapter Three, we discussed a variety of techniques that tend to be ineffective, such as ruminating about unresolved problems, perfectionistic thinking, overgeneralizing, and making catastrophes out of manageable issues. If you are habitually doing any of these things to cope with stress, this may be a good time to reconsider what you are doing and to look for alternatives.

A third area of assessment would be to consider the ways of coping listed in Chapter Four, for these coping techniques have a better chance of being effective. Are there any techniques described here that strike you as a potentially good fit for yourself? Either something that you may be doing now that you might want to step up, or something that would be new for you but which sounds interesting, and most importantly, comfortable to try.

A fourth area of assessment would be your appraisal of the desirability of seeking professional help. If professional help makes sense, then by all means explore its availability.

In the introduction to this book I suggested that one-size-fits-all strategies for dealing with stress are not likely to be satisfactory. The ways you would cope with a deadline for a job you have been assigned at work, respond to a rash of puzzling physical symptoms, or deal with a difficult child are likely to be as different as night and day. To cope with the deadline at work, you may have to look for a quiet place where you can concentrate and work on the project. The unusual physical symptoms might warrant a quick call to your doctor. To cope with a difficult child you may need all the listening skills you can muster.

Prayer, meditation, and muscle relaxation are useful techniques to quiet yourself when you are upset or you feel you are going over the edge. All of these are effective ways of quieting and calming yourself so you can plan intelligently and act in a rational and purposeful way. They all can help lower the level of tension that you are experiencing and perhaps forestall rash acts which are generated by anxiety or anger. So, too, can tranquilizing medicines or a telephone call to a good friend or taking a long walk help when you are experiencing acute stress. But none of these acts are likely to solve the problems of the deadline at work, the unusual physical symptoms, or the difficult child. These stress reducing activities may make it easier to concentrate and focus on the task at hand, but to deal with each particular source of stress calls for plans that are tailored to the individual circumstances.

As a way of reinforcing the ideas presented in this book, I would like to offer some thoughts about coping with a few of the stress situations that most of us will encounter. Obviously, the specific circumstances that anyone will experience will differ from person to person. They will be as varied as the life stories each of us has to tell. But, here are some general thoughts that may be helpful.

Let's talk first about troubled relationships — spouses having difficulties, lovers experiencing distress, troubles with a boyfriend or girlfriend — the kind of thing we read about in novels, watch on the afternoon soaps, or that brings some of us in acute distress to a therapist's office. It's hard to go through life without having moments, and sometimes months, of distress relating to a romantic partner. We love someone, we want to be loved in return, we want to experience joy in a relationship, but we are not dealing with saints, but only with fallible people who may come into the relationship with a good deal of baggage — previous unhappy relationships, their own needs and problems — who are not always sensitive to their partner, and who can make mistakes by the bucketful. It is a wonder that couples get along as well as they do. But they can and they do, and as a rule of thumb, a person is much better off in life with such a relationship. What a nice, comforting thought it is to have someone special to share things with and who is there to help when troubles arise.

Still, the ups and downs, the stresses of love are legendary. So, let's imagine for a moment that a troubled relationship is causing you distress. If you are not in such a situation, try putting yourself into the shoes of someone who is. Simply imagine for a moment that the major source of distress in your life is your relationship with a romantic partner. And then consider how could you (or if this is a reality) how can you go about lessening this distress? How can you make things better? The question is of paramount importance to millions of people and the answer is not likely to be a simple one. Sure, a person can opt out and break up the relationship. Get divorced, if married. Call the whole thing off. Just leave and look for someone else. And, sometimes there is an attractive person waiting in the wings which makes breaking up less of a risk. But, it's not usually so easy to sever a romantic relationship. You and your partner may still have strong feelings for each other, and if that is the case breaking up will very likely leave you feeling sad and lonely.

Then how can one repair a troubled relationship? How can one make it better? While there is no magic formula, there are things that can help. I would stress three things: attentive listening, informal negotiation, and not overgeneralizing when there are problems.

An important first step is to try to better understand your partner. What is your partner thinking and feeling? What is really important to your partner? What would get over the threshold of a ho hum response and really make a difference? Probably the best way to find out is to encourage communication by listening attentively, and if you can empathetically. When you discover what it is your partner needs and wants, you can make the effort to provide some of these things. What better way to show that you understand and care?

Conflicts in a relationship are almost inevitable. If you are like most people you probably have conflicts within yourself. How can you expect not to have conflicts with others? Interpersonal conflicts can be resolved by brute force and domination and some people who are overly passive and submissive seem to like it this way, although one wonders what resentments may be smoldering underneath their habitual acquiescence. But most of us are not happy being trampled on. And a romantic relationship without some mutuality in decision-making is unlikely to prosper. The key to resolving conflicts is some sort of negotiation. I prefer very informal negotiating. Perhaps quiet talk with some give and take on both sides. Whenever possible, think creatively. Try to enlarge the pie to enable win-win situations to emerge. This may be one of your best bets to promote domestic tranquility.

We have talked about overgeneralizing. In romantic relationships it is important to keep a sense of perspective. Sometimes people overgeneralize from the minor disappointments and irritations in the relationship and rush to judgment that the relationship is not worthwhile. Hurt feelings often lead to overreactions. When harsh words are spoken, regret may follow. When problems arise in the relationship, try to keep in mind the things you really like about your partner. Maybe it's the way your partner looks or smiles or greets you or feels in your arms or a hundred other things that mean a lot to you. Put it all together and you may conclude that there is a lot here that is important to you and worth trying to keep and nurture.

There are no simple rules to improving a romantic relationship, but as we have seen there are things one can do to make it better. And when things get better, stress levels should decrease. It is certainly worth making the effort. And if outside help is needed, marriage and couples counselors can often be helpful.

Let's turn to another area on the checklist that is a source of stress for many people — the millions of people who are attending school, whether it is high school, college, or receiving graduate or professional training. At times students at all levels experience some stress. Many students experience considerable stress. Early in the book I mentioned a study that Roland Tanck and I carried out on the stress experienced by college students. We found that many of the students were experiencing high levels of stress relating to their schoolwork. While college can be a wonderful experience, the experience of these students was adversely affected by this stress. The students who were experiencing higher levels of stress relating to their schoolwork were also experiencing higher levels of anxiety and more frequent bouts of depression than the students who were not experiencing such high levels of stress about their schoolwork. They also reported more stress-related physical complaints such as nausea, weakness, and diarrhea. They often felt defeated; they talked about being lonely and they often felt the need to turn to someone for help in dealing with their problems.

Women students were more likely than the men to internalize the stress, containing the tension within themselves. Stress, for the men, often found its way into their interpersonal relationships. They became irritable and angry and difficult to get along with. Either way, it was not a happy situation; high levels of stress about schoolwork were neither healthy nor helpful.

When we look at the predicament faced by many college students today we begin to see some of the underlying problems. Going to college now can be an enormously expensive undertaking. Getting a four year education from a top flight private college costs a small fortune and even attending one of our many excellent publicly financed state universities can lead to ever mounting debts. If the students are fortunate, they have parents who can underwrite part or most of the costs. However, that help can sometimes put additional pressure on the student. Normal parental expectations for students to do well in college may be intensified. With the kind of investment parents are now making, they may communicate to their children, deliberately or unconsciously, that they expect their children to produce.

Then there are the usual problems faced by college students which can add to this pressure to succeed. Many of these students are on their own for the first time. They often grope with problems of self-identity, career choice, redefining their relationships with parents, and entering into new and often serious romantic relationships and sexual entanglements.

There are stress points in the college year — midterms, final exams, dates at which term papers are due — which raise tension levels to particularly high levels. Even without these days of reckoning, the workload throughout the academic year can be heavy. In medical and law school the workload can be grueling.

If you are a student experiencing high levels of stress, how do you handle it? How do you bring the level of tension down to manageable levels? To a level in which you can do your best work without experiencing undue distress? As students themselves report, friendship is likely to be the first line of defense and often the best. One of the wonderful things about a college or university is that you find many people like yourself, people of your age who are experiencing many of the same things that you are experiencing. You don't have to explain very much to such friends. They know what you are talking about. Having a beer together at the student hangout or taking a walk together around or near the campus are wonderful ways to unwind. Terrific bonding can take place and mutual support can arise very naturally. College students usually find that talking to a friend who cares is an excellent way to dampen down stress.

Probably the easiest way to make friends is to begin one's college career by living in a dormitory. You get to know a lot of people quickly. Then, you'll probably make more friends in the classroom, in student hangouts, at student activities, and by joining student organizations. There are many opportunities to meet people.

When you are of college age, exercise is another obvious choice to reduce stress. If you are 18 or 19 — or an elder statesman of 21 or 22 — you're getting into your physical prime. You're not likely to suffer from poor wind and stiff joints; your muscles are rippling and ready for use. What better time to throw a football around, hit a tennis ball back and forth, swim across the pool, or jog through the campus?

Getting organized is an important step in dealing with college stress. Managing the time ahead of you is important. When the semester begins, think about what you have to do for your courses and do some preliminary planning. My colleague, Roland Tanck, who counseled college students for many years, stressed the need for students to allow sufficient time for study and review. Good planning can reduce the need to cram when examinations approach, and leave you with the time to do a credible job on term papers.

How good are your study habits? If they fall short of what you would like, there are probably things you can try to improve them. Generally speaking it's better to distribute your reading assignments over the day or days than read for hours and hours consecutively. Research on learning and memory suggests that students probably won't remember as much if they put in hour after hour of reading. And it will probably help you to remember if you frequently close the text and try paraphrasing in your own words what you have just read. If you really didn't understand or absorb what you read, you'll know that quickly.

If talking with friends, exercise, and good planning do not do the trick and you are still feeling too much stress, as a matriculated student you have an important resource available to you — the student counseling center. In a university, the counseling center will probably be staffed by trained psychologists and psychology graduate students. These people are usually very familiar with the problems of students and may be able to help you in many ways. They will probably have suggestions that can help improve your study habits. They can give vocational aptitude tests that may help you in formulating your career choice. And, perhaps most importantly, the counselors can probably help you cope better with the stress that is undermining your college experience.

If you suffer from test anxiety — feeling panicky and coming unraveled during a test — the counseling center may be able to help you deal with this problem. Some of the techniques we mentioned that behavior therapists use — systematic desensitization and implosion therapy can be useful in reducing test anxiety. And there are some old verities about taking tests which are worth keeping in mind when you are about to take an exam, such as taking an initial quick look at the scope of the test so you can budget your time wisely and answering the easy questions first, getting them out of the way so you can give your undivided attention to the difficult ones.

I would like to pass on an observation about test anxiety from a very experienced college mathematics teacher. She told me that some students become worried while taking a test when they see other students leaving early. The students surmised that the test had been very easy for the other students, while they themselves were having a difficult time, and this raised their anxiety level even more. The teacher has observed over the years that many students leave early, not because they have answered the questions, but because they can't answer them!

Let's turn to a third area from our checklist: stress on the job. As we stated earlier, stress on the job is a big issue in America. Surveys indicate that a large number of Americans are experiencing stress at the workplace. If we look at the problem in historical terms, we can see that job stress is nothing new; there has probably always been stress related to jobs. In nineteenth century America, for example, long working hours, unsafe working conditions and low pay created considerable stress and discontent. The discontent led to strikes which were sometimes brutally put down by local law enforcement and federal troops. With a constant supply of new immigrant labor, few effective laws about working conditions or effective unions, the owners could have their way and they usually did — and sometimes acted shamelessly. Young children worked 15 hour days in coal mines. If you want to learn about difficult, stressful working conditions, read about sweatshops at the turn of the century. You will find it an eye-opener.

In the twentieth century, things got better, albeit slowly. Workplaces became healthier and safer; workers organized and bargained for pensions and health insurance. Laws were passed ending child labor and protecting the American working man and woman from unsafe conditions. But as we indicated in our first chapter, stress in the workplace has not gone away. Not by any means. In recent years it may have gotten worse!

Economists can make very sophisticated analyses of business conditions and so can many of our business leaders. But no one yet has figured out a way to abolish the business cycle. Periods of prosperity are followed by recession, economic expansion by economic contraction. The knowledge that in our free market economy, business activity will eventually slow down and that an employee could be laid off— that an employee might be on the receiving end of a pink slip — can never be fully ignored. This recognition is a basic source of insecurity for many employees. It is not so much a problem when the economy is expanding, but when it is cooling, uncertainty increases.

Not only can one's job disappear from downturns in the economy, it may disappear because of the advances of technology. If the job is straightforward, involving actions and decisions for which there are clear cut rules, it is becoming increasingly likely that a computer programmer can design software that can do the job. And a computer does not require health benefits and a pension. Goodbye job!

Here is another cheerful thought. If there are no immediate plans to replace an employee with a computer, management, which is usually interested in reducing costs, may consider as an interim measure outsourcing your job to some part of the world where people will work for much lower wages.

There was a time when a young employee could expect to work for many years in the same company — perhaps until retirement. This is much less likely to happen today. An employee can probably expect to change jobs every few years. Dislocations become part of life. New places to live, new people to work with, new tasks to learn. It can all be very unsettling.

With the recognition that workers performing certain types of jobs may not be needed over the long haul, companies may be less likely to make the investments in training and compensation for these workers that they would make for long term career employees. Nor is it likely that employees will feel much loyalty to a company that they perceive has little commitment to them. Perceptions of employment situations can become pragmatic. The sentiment may be, "I'll stay here while I work on my resume for the next job."

You can glimpse the cultural changes in the way we look at jobs in books written about the American workplace. In the early years of the 20th Century, a series of books by Horatio Alger was extremely popular. The heroes in these books succeeded in the workplace by a combination of pluck, ingenuity, honesty, and hard work. In the 1960s a smash Broadway musical, *How to Get Ahead in Business Without Really Trying*, eschewed the virtues of the Horatio Alger novels in favor of more devious methods of advancement. And if you want to see how far the wheel has turned in regard to prospering in the American workplace, read Scott Adams' delightfully humorous and often cynical book *The Dilbert Principle*.[1] Hard work, honesty, and pluck? Forget it.

The sources of stress in yesterday's workplace — low pay, very long hours, and unsafe conditions — have given way to new stresses: life in a confining cubicle, staring at a screen and wondering if your job will disappear. While these contemporary sources of stress are not as hazardous as the ones experienced by our forbears, they are no great shakes, either.

How do you deal with stress relating to your job? This is not an easy question. My first rule of thumb (and this may not be possible for you) is not to make the job your entire life. If things go wrong on a job that is totally consuming, you won't have much left. I am aware that the pressure to work longer and longer hours is a reality in many jobs and if your principal goal in life is to get rich, you can easily find yourself climbing on a circular wheel that turns and turns endlessly. But if you can avoid becoming a workaholic and fashion a meaningful life outside the job, you should find yourself less stressed out. And if you can possibly manage it, try not to bring the job home with you.

Family, friends, and diverting activities outside the workplace would be the first line of defense to cope with job stress. A pleasant home life and fun-filled weekends can help a lot.

My second rule of thumb is for people who have the kind of job that is likely to disappear—be automated into oblivion by a computer or outsourced to Timbuktu. If you feel vulnerable this way, don't wait until the last minute to begin thinking about retraining for a job that has a future. Consider jobs in which there is a high premium on interpersonal skills or in which complex judgments based on knowledge and experience must be made. Because it is very difficult to program computers to do these things, such jobs are likely to remain viable for the foreseeable future and are not likely to be shipped to some remote corner of the world.

Many companies have stress management programs. If there is such a program at your job, look into it and see what it offers. Some companies have exercise facilities for the employees. If such facilities are available, use them whenever you can. If you have a decent size lunch hour, get into the habit of taking a walk. Exercise can be helpful anywhere. While it may not be possible for you to engage in meditation or muscle relaxation during work hours, consider reserving some time in the evening for such activities. That can help you unwind.

Stress in the workplace often arises from two sources, the work itself and the people you work with. I have had patients tell me, "I really like the people I work with, but the work is boring and meaningless." I have also had patients tell me, "I like what I'm doing but some of the people in the office are just awful." I would like to focus on the latter situation.

If you are in close proximity to co-workers with whom you have problems, it's something like being in a bad marriage. In some ways it can be even worse. You may be around the people you have difficulties with all day long. To repair a troubled marriage, you can try marriage counseling. What do you do at the job?

If the work relationship calls for working together in a cooperative way, there is always hope because the two of you have a common interest in success. It is something like being in a small boat that is taking on water. If it sinks, both of you go down. The suggestions that we have advanced for attentive listening and negotiation may be very useful under these circumstances. If, on the other hand, the relationship is essentially competitive, the chances of these strategies working are probably reduced.

In some work situations, office politics, gossip, and cliques are a way of life. In some ways it's like the schoolyard revisited, and can be just as nasty. You may not like it, but there's probably not much you can do about it. If you are inclined, you can play these games yourself as a matter of self defense. If you are not inclined to do this, you may have to simply accept the fact that you may be a target from time to time, ignore it and go about your work. It's not a perfect world out there.

There is extensive research to support the idea that the attitude you bring to the job can make a difference in both your satisfaction with the job and the level of stress you will experience at the workplace.[2] People who tend to be positive about life, about themselves and about others, and who like to become engaged in activities tend to experience fewer problems and less stress in the workplace. They have fewer role conflicts and experience fewer daily hassles. People with more negative attitudes, who tend to view themselves and others unfavorably and the environment as hostile, are more prone to experience job stress. They are more likely to have conflicts and hassles. The high level of job stress that may come with negative attitudes can affect the person's overall stress levels and increase the chances of emotional exhaustion.

It is not easy to change one's basic attitudes, but it is worth considering, in a manner analogous to the way in which cognitive therapy proceeds, whether some of these negative perceptions are fully accurate. If your attitudes about the job are negative, ask yourself, is it possible that you are overgeneralizing? Are you painting the work situation with an overly broad brush? Are you overlooking aspects of your job that are, in fact, satisfying, and co-workers that you like? A more balanced view of the job might lessen the stress that you feel eminating from the workplace.

Most people need a job. They not only need a paycheck, they like the structure in life that a job provides. Unless one is near retirement age, it is usually better to have someplace to go during the day and something meaningful to do than to stay home all day. If there are specific issues in the workplace that are causing stress, it would clearly be beneficial if changes could be instituted that would reduce the stress. It is, of course, one thing to identify changes that would be desirable and another to make these changes. How nice it would be if you were the boss and you made up the rules and were running things. Then, you would be in a better position to make the adjustments needed to reduce stress levels. But chances are that you're not the boss; someone else makes up the rules and is running things. And, as a consequence, if you find the job stressful, your options to lower the stress levels you are experiencing are probably limited. You may find yourself in one of those very difficult conflicts we have alluded to where no options appear to be very good. You need the job, but the stress is really getting to you.

Could you approach your boss about the situation, or would that cause you more difficulties than you have now? Is there a stress management program at work? Is it worth consulting? Would there be repercussions if you did? In contemplating actions to reduce stress levels on the job, one has to consider the options that are available and the possible consequences of using them. Here are some questions to consider. Are there steps that could be taken at the workplace that might ease the stress that is engendered there? Are there mechanisms in place for you to do this? Would taking these steps cause more problems for you than the benefits from such steps would be worth?

In some workplaces there may be risks in speaking up, in sticking your neck out. How big a risk depends on the culture of the workplace. If the workplace is one in which conformity is rewarded, where the employees are not expected to make waves, where the culture is to go along to get along, it could be a considerable risk to venture suggestions about changing the way things are done at work. If, on the other hand, the culture at the workplace puts a premium on innovation, then such suggestions might be welcomed. It is a judgment call.

These could be difficult, troubling questions requiring a lot of thought. If you conclude that pushing for changes on the job would be impractical or counterproductive, and you decide you need to stay with the job, then you may have to look outside the job for relief of stress. By all means do what you can outside the job to add to the meaning and satisfaction in your life.

In these three examples, romantic relationships, the classroom, and the workplace we have tried to show how the ideas that were presented in previous chapters concerning stress are applicable to the everyday problems of life. I think that you can see that the strategies that may be most effective in one area of living — e.g., romantic relationships — may not be the best for other areas such as the classroom or the job. When you try to reduce stress in a given area of your life, you will need to select options that are not only appropriate to the situation, but also with which you are personally comfortable. You are a unique individual with a unique personality with your own strengths and weaknesses, and your comfort level with what you try to do is of paramount importance.

I have always felt it is a good idea not to get locked into one way of doing things. If you do something that isn't working and do it repetitively, it's like knocking your head against a stone wall. This book offers a variety of ideas on how to cope with stress. If what you are doing doesn't work, try something else. The results may surprise you.

Most of the commonsense suggestions advanced in the book, such as talking things over with a good friend, exercise, and diversion, are unlikely to have adverse effects if carried out in moderation. However one can exercise to the point of exhaustion, wear out one's friends, or watch TV until one becomes a couch potato. Moderation is a good rule of thumb for dealing with problems of stress. We have presented a cafeteria of ideas and suggestions. Select those which make the best sense for you, then use them judiciously. We hope you find the ideas useful.

# *Chapter Notes*

## *Chapter 1*

1. A brief report of our findings may be found in the Health Section of *The Washington Post*, October 2, 1985.

2. The study of stress in Swedish schoolchildren was carried out by Lindahl et al.

3. See McGuire.

4. The study on job stress in Canada was reported by Marchand and his colleagues.

5. The research on job stress in England was reported by Ferrie and her colleagues.

6. See Daw.

7. See Barnett et al.

8. See Robbins, Meyersburg and Tanck. See, in particular, Table 1.

9. The quotations from Gold and Friedman's West Point study are from pages 149 and 151.

10. A very detailed account of life at West Point about 160 years ago, including the stress experience, may be found in John Waugh's book, *The Class of 1846: From West Point to Appomattox: Stonewall Jackson, George McClellan, and Their Brothers.*

11. The research carried out in Germany on the effects of noise level was reported by H. Ising and R. Michalak.

12. See Meyerhoff et al.

13. The study of stress in couples was reported by Kiecolt-Glaser et al. (1996).

14. See Cannon's book *The Wisdom of the Body.*

15. For an overview of Selye's contributions and a history of early research on stress, see Mason.

16. See Dickerson et al. Data for the return to normal levels of cortisol after exposure to stressors are presented on page 379.

17. Meta-analysis is a statistical technique now in wide use that allows researchers to examine the results of many different studies using different methods and samples to obtain an estimate of the overall effect.

18. See Taylor et al. (2000a). For a review of research on gender differences, see Luckow et al.

19. See Shin et al. (1999).

20. See Davidson et al. The quotation is from page 895.

21. See Albright et al.

22. For a discussion of the role of the amygdala in emotions, see Davidson et al., McEwen, and Albright et al.

23. For a recent study of amygdala activity of PTSD patients, see Shin et al. (2005).

24. See Segerstrom and Miller, page 610.

25. Ibid.

26. Ibid., page 618.

27. Ibid., page 614.

28. See A. Baum et al. *Research on Three Mile Island* is reviewed in O'Leary, page 367.

29. The study of immune system functioning of caretakers of patients with Alzheimer's disease was reported by Kiecolt-Glaser et al. (1987).

30. The study of the effects of unemployment on immune system functioning was carried out by Arnetz et al.

31. See O'Leary, page 368.

32. See Robbins, Meyersburg, and Tanck.

33. See Robbins and Tanck (1982).

34. See Kasl et al.

35. See S. Cohen et al.

36. Ibid., page 221.

37. The *Merck Manual for General Medicine*, 1989, Volume 1, page 559–560.

38. The study of patients with irritable bowel syndrome was reported by Charles Murray et al.

39. See Youell and McCullough.

40. The type A personality was described by Friedman and Rosenman.

41. For a review of studies relating hostility and cardiovascular disease, see Miller et al.

42. See the two papers by Walton et al. The authors noted the beneficial effects of transcendental meditation on cardiac measures.

43. See Blumenthal et al.

44. The article appearing in *Parade* was written by Meyer.

45. See L. Robbins, *Going Bridal.*

46. Another horrific example of the psychological effects of extreme stress was the experience of people imprisoned in concentration camps. In a review of studies of the victims, Julius Segal noted that the inmates experienced anxiety, startle reactions, chronic depression, insomnia, and nightmares.

## *Chapter 2*

1. For a description of the health benefits model, see Rosenstock.

2. See Skinner et al. A compilation of rationally based coping inventories is presented in Appendix C. Coping inventories based on factor analysis are presented in Appendix B.

3. Lazarus has written extensively about coping and stress and many citations could be offered for his work. For one of his early works, see *Psychological Stress and the Coping Process.*

4. See Tennan et al.

5. Weisz et al., page 330.

6. For the original factor analysis, see Robbins and Tanck (1978).

7. Our data concerning the use of social support by college students is presented in Robbins and Tanck (1995).

8. The study of prostate cancer support groups was reported by Steginga et al.

9. The study of Internet support groups was reported by L. Baum. Seeking social support via the Internet is not a risk-free venture. Writing in the *Washington Post*, Yoki Noguchi noted that some people who maintain blogs on the Internet are using them in a way that resembles group therapy, chronicling their personal experiences and problems and waiting for comments and reactions from the vast array of Internet users. In posting their experiences, they may find support from a virtual community of unknown people. The problem is that some of the comments may be hostile rather than supportive and blogging becomes a wide-open situation without the checks used to protect participants in group therapy.

10. See Karen Horney's book, *The Neurotic Personality in Our Time.*

11. Data linking escape-avoidance as a coping technique and eating disorders is presented in a paper by Ghaderi and Scott. Additional studies linking escape-avoidance coping and eating disorders are referenced in the paper. See, for example, the studies by Neckowitz and Morrison and Troop et al.

12. See Folkman and Lazarus.

13. See Revenson and Felton.

14. Ibid. The quotations are on page 347.

15. The study relating appraisal of pain to coping behaviors was carried out by Dysvik et al.

16. A discussion of various approaches that have been used to assess coping behaviors in children may be found in the paper by L. Peterson.

17. See Kato and Pederson.

18. Ibid., page 154.

19. See L. Peterson, page 380.

20. See Marco, page 756.

21. See Lazarus (2000).

22. Coyne and Racioppo's attack on coping research appeared in the June 2000 issue of the *American Psychologist* along with a reply by Lazarus. The quotation is from page 659.

23. For an illustrative study using the electronic monitoring technique, see Csikszentmihalyi and Larson.

24. See, for example, Stone and Shifman's 1994 paper.

25. The study in the Netherlands assessing the effects of teaching coping skills was reported by Kole-Snijders et al.

## Chapter 3

1. In discussing their findings from a study dealing with attachment and stress, Constance Hammen and her colleagues noted, "Individual vulnerability in the interpersonal realm, as indicated by fears of abandonment and desire to merge with another, and insecurity about one's ability to maintain the caring of others, is highly likely to predict maladjustment and symptomatic reaction to negative interpersonal events." See Hammen et al., page 441.

2. For a study of the tendency to idealize partners in a romantic relationship, see S. Murray et al. See also Joiner, et al.

3. Lyubomirsky et al., page 1041.

4. For a discussion of research using the white bear procedure, see Wenzlaff & Wegner.

5. See Purdon.

6. The ideas advanced here are drawn in part from the theory of and research on cognitive therapy.

7. See Brown et al.

8. These findings were reported by Zuroff et al.

9. See Horney.

10. The study of stress and drinking was carried out by Mohr et al.

11. For a review of research relating smoking and stress, see Kassel et al. A discussion of smoker expectations is presented on page 270.

12. See Nesbitt, page 137.

13. See Kassel, in particular page 281.

14. Ibid., page 275.

15. See Robbins, *Marijuana: A Short Course: Update for the Eighties*. The quotations are on page 29.

16. See Robbins (1972), in particular Table 1.

17. The study carried out in Finland using body mass index was reported by Kouvonen et al.

18. This research was carried out by Grunberg and Straub.

19. These data are cited in Robbins, *Anorexia and Bulimia*, page 66.

20. The studies are summarized in a paper by Greeno & Wing.

21. For a historical account of changing concepts of beauty in America, see Banner, *American Beauty*.

22. See Anderson.

23. Ibid., page 139.

24. Ibid., page 140.

## Chapter 4

1. See Nabetani and Tokunaga.

2. See Aldana et al.

3. See Salmon.

4. McAuley and his colleagues observed that when the subjects stopped exercising, the psychological benefits began to decline. See McAuley et al.

5. The student's comment was cited in Robbins and Tanck (1995), page 776.

6. The study of the effects of social support carried out in a German hospital was reported by Heinz Krohne and Kerstin Slangen.

7. Taylor and her colleagues reviewed research on the physiological benefits of social support. The quotation is from the article by Taylor et al. (2000a), page 419.

8. Ibid., page 418.

9. Ibid.

10. Ibid.

11. See Krause et al.

12. See Green et al.

13. See Barker et al. (2005).

14. Ibid. Barker (2005) presented a review of studies showing the beneficial effects of pets.

15. See Allen et al.

16. See Nagengast et al.

17. The effects of watching fish swim in an aquarium were reported by Barker et al. (2003). The study of birds as companions was reported by Jesser et al.

18. See Hanser and Mandel.

19. The effects of listening to music on chronic cardiac patients were reported by J. M. White.

20. See Hanser and Mandel, page 18.

21. Ibid.

22. Ibid.

23. Koenig and his colleagues at Duke University have contributed a number of studies relating religious beliefs and practices to longevity. See, for example, Koenig et al. (1999).

24. For data indicating that church attendance was associated with less depression, see Koenig et al. (1998), table 4, page 518.

25. See Pargement et al.

26. See McIntosh et al.

27. The study of reactions to terrorist bombings in Nairobi, Kenya, and Oklahoma City was reported by S. North et al.

28. See. E. Jacobson's book, *Progressive Relaxation*.

29. See Holmes. In his article, he reviews some of the early research on the effects of meditation.

30. Ibid., page 6.

31. Ibid.

32. The study carried out in Spain on stress hormone levels of mediators was reported by J.R. Infante et al. For additional studies showing the effects of meditation on cortisol and catecholamine levels, see the recent review paper by Cahn & Polich (p. 201). The authors concluded, "A considerable body of research supports the idea that meditative training can mitigate the effects of anxiety and stress on psychological and physiological functioning."

33. The study examining the effects of meditation on irritable bowel syndrome was carried out by L. Keefer and E. B. Blanchard.

34. A paper by A. Cohen et al. cites reports of adverse reactions to progressive muscle relaxation.

35. Negative problem-orientation resembles what we often think of as a defeatist attitude. See Robichaud and Dugas.

36. A number of studies have reported positive benefits for patients undergoing medical procedures. The study involving reactions to an endoscopic procedure was reported by Shipley et al.

37. See Nicklaus, *Play Better Golf*, page 45. For a review of studies showing the benefits of mental preparation, see Feltz & Landers.

38. See Taylor et al. (1998).

39. Ibid., page 432.

40. See Peale, *The Power of Positive Thinking*.

41. See Robbins and Tanck (1992), page 151.

42. For research linking optimism to the response to coronary bypass surgery see FitzGerald et al.; to survival time for AIDS patients, Reed et al.; to immune system functioning in law students, Segerstrom et al. (1998); and to children's reactions to the incarceration of their mothers, Hagen et al.

43. See Danner et al.

44. Ibid., page 806.

45. Ibid., page 809.

46. See C. Peterson, page 49.

47. See Taylor et al. (2000b) article, page 107.

48. For a discussion of research concerning humor and stress in patient care, see Christie and Moore.

49. See Berk et al.

50. See Martin, in particular pages 507–508.

51. The study reporting reduced tension after exposure to humor was carried out by Takahashi et al. The study relating humor as a coping mechanism to health was carried out by Carrol & Schmidt. The study of funny people was carried out by Wanzer et al.

52. The survey of nurses was cited by Wanzer et al.

53. The article in the *Journal of the American Medical Association* was written by Levinson et al.

## *Chapter 5*

1. The study of the behavior of judges was reported by Blanck et al.

2. The phrase "thin slices of expressive behavior" was used in an article on social perception written by Ambady and Rosenthal.

3. See Kenny and DePaulo, page 157.

4. Ibid., page 157.

5. See N. Jacobson & Moore.

6. The study of the accuracy of the perceptions of distressed couples was reported by Elwood and Jacobson.

7. See Bradbury and Fincham, page 3.

8. Ibid. See in particular pages 5 and 13.

9. See N. Jacobson and Addis, page 86.

10. The study of the usefulness of premarital counseling in communication skills and conflict management was carried out by Markman et al.

11. See Sternberg and Dobson, in particular the discussion on page 810.

12. See Reese-Weber.

13. The study describing conflict resolution styles in adolescents was reported by Black.

14. See Sternberg and Dobson. The quotation is on page 796.

15. For discussions of gender differences in negotiations, see Kray et al. and Thompson et al.

## Chapter 6

1. For a discussion of the developmental aspects of defense mechanisms, see Cramer and Kelly.

2. Anna Freud's book on defense mechanisms is entitled *The Ego and the Mechanisms of Defense*.

3. See Byrne.

4. Our data relating Byrne's scale to measures of dream content, dream recall, and dream associations appeared in Robbins and Tanck (1970).

5. See Bond et al. (1983) and (2004).

6. See, for example, Perry and Kardos.

7. The study relating to defense mechanisms to depression was carried out by DeFife and Hilsenroth.

8. See Cramer and Kelly.

9. Ibid.

10. For further discussion of and research on bracing for possible loss, see Shepperd et al.

11. See Mezulis et al. The paper presents a review of studies which show the robustness of the tendency toward a positive spin.

12. For a discussion of various types of rationalizations, see Symond's book *The Dynamics of Human Adjustment*.

13. The rationalization about smoking was reported by Irwin et al.

## Chapter 7

1. For technical descriptions and diagnostic criteria for the various anxiety disorders, see the American Psychiatric Association's *Diagnostic and Statistical Manual of Mental Disorders* (fourth edition).

2. The study of nightmares experienced by San Francisco Bay area students after a major earthquake was reported by Wood et al.

3. An estimate of the likelihood that an episode of acute stress disorder will be followed by post-traumatic stress disorder was provided in a study carried out in Australia. Researchers followed people admitted to a major trauma hospital for motor vehicle accidents. The average length of hospitalization for the accident victims exceeded a week. After a clinical assessment, 13 percent of the patients included in the study were diagnosed as suffering from acute stress disorder and another 21 percent as having some signs of the disorder. Six months later, about three out of four of the patients who were initially diagnosed as having acute stress disorder were subsequently diagnosed as having post-traumatic stress disorder. Acute stress disorder poses a significant risk factor for the subsequent development of post-traumatic stress disorder. See Harvey and Bryant.

4. Surveys estimating the number of people who have experienced traumatic events are cited in Ozer et al., page 54.

5. Ibid. Lifetime prevalence estimates for post-traumatic stress disorder are given on page 54.

6. The case study of the woman experiencing panic attacks was reported by A. Cohen. See page 97.

7. See Clark et al. (1997), page 203.

8. Ibid.

9. Ibid.

## Chapter 8

1. See Phenobarbital.

2. See Meprobamate.

3. See Sullivan's article in *The Washington Post*.

4. See Diazepam.

5. See Alprazolam. The study of alprazolam treatment of panic disorder patients was reported by Ballenger et al.

6. For the reports of overdoses of benzodiazepines, see Mantooth.

## Chapter 9

1. The case of the boy with the phobic reaction to blood was reported by Ollendick and Gruen.

2. The case of school phobia was reported by Smith and Sharpe.

3. For a description of the development of virtual reality techniques for the treatment of phobia see Winerman.

4. See Dittmann. The prevalence data for social phobia are given on page 93.

5. Ibid. Dittmann presents a discussion of Heimberg's approach to treating social phobia. See also Heimberg, et al.

6. See Clark et al. (1999).

7. Ibid., page 584.

## Chapter 10

1. The study in which gender identity was altered by hypnosis was reported by Noble and McConkey. The quotation is on page 69. The phrase "streams of consciousness" was adopted from an article by Kirsch & Lynn.

2. For a review of studies showing the effectiveness of hypnosis in the control of pain, see Patterson and Jensen.

3. For a discussion of the use of hypnosis in the treatment of asthma, see Bowers and Kelly. For a study using hypnosis to decrease phobic reactions, see Horowitz.

4. The study of hypnosis in patients undergoing plastic surgery was reported by Faymonville et al.

5. The study combining cognitive-behavior therapy with hypnosis was reported by Bryant et al.

6. See Field et al. and Moyer et al. for reviews of the beneficial effects of massage therapy.

7. For the FDA alert about Kava, see *Consumer Advisory*.

8. The story in *The Washington Post* was written by Gillis.

## Chapter 11

1. The study of self-efficacy as a moderating influence on the effect of stress on headaches was reported by Marlowe.

2. The study of stress in college students at the University of Florida was reported by Largo-Wight et al.

3. See Rotter.

4. The study relating locus of control of reinforcement to the response to noise stress was carried out by Bollini et al.

5. The research on heart failure patients was reported by Draycup et al.

6. The study of children in transition from elementary to junior high school was reported by Robinson et al.

## Chapter 12

1. See Adams, *The Dilbert Principle: A Cubicle's Eye View of Bosses, Meetings, Management Fads, and Other Workplace Afflictions.*

2. For a review of research examining the relationship of emotion and job attitudes, see Thorsen et al.

# Bibliography

Adams, S. *(1996). The Dilbert Principle: A Cubicle's Eye View of Bosses, Meetings, Management Fads, and Other Workplace Afflictions.* New York: Harper Business.

Albright, T. D., Kandel, E. R., and Posner, M. I. (2000). Cognitive neuroscience. *Current Opinion in Neurobiology*, 10, 612–624.

Aldana, S. G., Sutton, L. D., Jacobson, B. H., and Quirk, M. G. (1996). Relationships between leisure time physical activity and perceived stress. *Perceptual and Motor Skills*, 82, 315–321.

Allen, K., Blascovich, J., and Mendes, W. B. (2002). Cardiovascular reactivity and the presence of pets, friends and spouses: The truth about cats and dogs. *Psychosomatic Medicine*, 64, 727–739.

Alprazolam. http://www.nlm.nih.gov/medlineplus/druginfo/medmasster/a6840001.html

Ambady, N., and Rosenthal, R. (1992). Thin slices of expressive behavior as predictors of interpersonal consequences: a meta-analysis. *Psychological Bulletin*, 111, 256–274. American Psychiatric Association (1994). *Diagnostic and Statistical Manual of Mental Disorders.* (Fourth edition). Washington, D.C.

Anderson, C. J. (2003). The psychology of doing nothing: Forms of decision avoidance result from reason and emotion. *Psychological Bulletin*, 129, 139–167.

Arnetz, B. B., Wasserman, J., Petrini, B., Brenner, S. O., Levi, L., Eneroth, P., Salovara, H., Hjelm, R., Salovara, L., Theorell, T., and Petterson, I. L. (1987). Immune functioning in unemployed women. *Psychosomatic Medicine*, 49, 3–12.

Ballenger, J. C., Burrous, G. D., Dupont, R. L., Jr., Lesser, I. M., Noyes, R., Jr., Pecknold, J. C., Rifkin, A., and Swinson, R. (1988). Alprazolam in panic disorder and agoraphobia: Results from a multicenter trial: I. Efficacy in short-term treatment. *Archives of General Psychiatry*, 45, 413–422.

Banner, L. W. (1993). *American Beauty*. New York: Knopf.

Barker, S. B., Rasmussen, K. G., and Best, A. M. (2003). Effect of aquariums on electroconvulsive therapy patients. *Anthrozoos*, 16, 229–240.

Barker, S. B., Knisley, J. S., McCain, N. L., and Best, A. M. (2005). Measuring stress and immune response in healthcare professionals following interaction with a therapy dog: A pilot study. *Psychological Reports*, 96, 713–929.

Barnett, R. C., Steptoe, A., and Gareis, K. C. (2005). Marital-role quality and stress-related psychobiological indicators. *Annals of Behavioral Medicine*, 30, 36–43.

Baum, A., Schaeffer, M. A., Lake, C. R., Fleming, R., and Collins, D. L. (1985). Psychological and endocrinological correlates of chronic stress at Three Mile Island.

In R. Williams (Ed.). *Perspective on Behavioral Medicine* (vol. 2, pp. 201–217). San Diego: Academic Press.

Baum, L. S. (2004). Internet parent support groups for primary caregivers of a child with special health care needs. *Pediatric Nursing*, 30, 381–388.

Berk, L. S., Tan, S. A., Fry, W. F., Napier, B. J., Lee, J. W., and Hubbard, R. W. (1989). Neuroendocrine changes during mirthful laughter. *American Journal of the Medical Sciences*, 298, 390–396.

Black, K. A. (2000). Gender differences and adolescence behavior during conflict resolution tasks with best friends. *Adolescence*, 35, 499–512.

Blanck, P. D., Rosenthal, R., and Cordell, L. A. (1985). The appearance of justice: Judges' verbal and nonverbal behavior in criminal jury trials. *Stanford Law Review*, 38, 89–164.

Blumenthal, J. A., Sherwood, A., Babyak, M. A., Watkins, L. L., Waugh, R., Georgiades, A., Bacon, S. L., Hayano, J., Coleman, E. R., and Hinderliter, A. (2005). Effects of exercise and stress management training on markers of cardiovascular risk with ischemic heart disease: A randomized controlled trial. *Journal of the American Medical Association*, 293, 1626–1634.

Bollini, A. M., Walker, E. F., Hamann, S., and Kestler, L. (2004). The influence of perceived control and locus of control on the cortisol and subjective responses to stress. *Biological Psychology*, 67, 245–260.

Bond, M. (2004). Empirical studies of defense style: relationships with psychopathology and change. *Harvard Review of Psychiatry*, 12, 263–278.

_____, Gardner, S. T., Christian, J., and Sigal, J. J. (1983). Empirical study of self-rated defense styles. *Archives of General Psychiatry*, 40, 333–338.

Bowers, K. S., and Kelly, P. (1979). Stress, disease, psychotherapy, and hypnosis. *Journal of Abnormal Psychology*, 88, 490–505.

Bradbury, T. N., and Fincham, F. D. (1990). Attributions in marriage: Review and critique. *Psychological Bulletin*, 107, 3–33.

Brown, G. P., Hammen, C. L., Craske, M. G., and Wickens, T. D. (1995). Dimensions of dysfunctional attitudes as vulnerability to depressive symptoms. *Journal of Abnormal Psychology*, 104, 431–435.

Bryant, R. A., Moulds, M. L., Guthrie, R. M., and Nixon, R. D. (2005). The additive benefit of hypnotic and cognitive-behavioral therapy in treating acute stress disorder. *Journal of Consulting and Clinical Psychology*, 73, 334–340.

Byrne, D., (1961). The Repression-Sensitization scale: Rationale, reliability, and validity. *Journal of Personality*, 29, 334–349.

Cahn, B. R., and Polich, J. (2006). Meditation states and traits: EEG, ERP, and neuroimaging studies. *Psychological Bulletin*, 132, 180–211.

Cannon, W. B. (1932). *The Wisdom of the Body*. New York: Norton.

Carroll, J. L., and Schmidt, J. L., Jr. (1992). Correlation between humorous coping style and health. *Psychological Reports*, 70, 402.

Christie, W., and Moore, C. (2005). The impact of humor on patients with cancer. *Clinical Journal of Oncology Nursing*, 9, 211–218.

Clark, D. M., Salkovskis, P. M., Lars-Goran, O., Breitholtz, E., Koehler, K. A., Westling, B. E., Jeavons, A., and Gelder, M. (1997). Misinterpretation of body sensations in panic disorder. *Journal of Consulting and Clinical Psychology*, 65, 203–213.

_____, Salkovskis, P. M., Hackmann, A., Wells, A., Ludgate, J., and Gelder, M. (1999). Brief cognitive therapy for panic disorder: A randomized controlled trial. *Journal of Consulting and Clinical Psychology*, 67, 583–589.

Cohen, A. S., Barlow, D. H., and Blanchard, E. B. (1985). Psychophysiology of relaxation-associated panic attacks. *Journal of Abnormal Psychology*, 94, 96–101.

Cohen, S., Frank, E., Doyle, W. J., Skoner, D. P., Rabin, B. S., and Gwaltney, J. M., Jr. (1998). Types of stressors that increase susceptibility to the common cold in healthy adults. *Health Psychology*, 17, 214–223.

*Consumer advisory*. (2002). Kava-containing dietary supplements may be associated with severe liver injury. U. S. Food and Drug Administration, March 25.

Coyne, J. C., and Racioppo, M. W. (2000). Never the twain shall meet? Closing the gap between coping research and clinical intervention research. *American Psychologist*, 55, 655–664.

Cramer, P., and Kelly, F. D. (2004). Defense mechanisms in adolescent conduct disorder and adjustment reactions. *Journal of Nervous* and *Mental Disease*, 192, 139–145.

Csikszentmihaly, M., and Larson, R. (1984). *Being Adolescent: Conflict and Growth in the Teenage Years*. New York: Basic Books.

Danner, D. D., Snowdon, D. A., and Friesen, W. V. (2001). Positive emotions in early life and longevity: Findings from the nun study. *Journal of Personality and Social Psychology*, 80, 804–813.

Davidson, R. J., Jackson, D. C., and Kalin, N. H. (2000). Emotion, plasticity, context, and regulation: Perspectives from affective neuroscience. *Psychological Bulletin*, 126, 890–909.

Daw, J. (2001). Road rage, air rage, and now 'desk rage.' *Monitor on Psychology*, 32, July-August, 52.

Defife, J. A., and Hilsenroth, M. J. (2005). Clinical utility of The Defensive Functioning Scale in the assessment of depression. *Journal of Nervous and Mental Disease*, 193, 176–182.

Diazepam. http://www.nlm.nih.gov/medlineplus/druginfo/medmaster/a682047.html

Dickerson, S. S., and Kemeny, M. E. (2004). Acute stressors and cortisol responses: A theoretical integration and synthesis of laboratory research. *Psychological Bulletin*, 130, 355–391.

Dittmann, M. (2005). Stemming social phobias. *Monitor on Psychology*, 36, 92–94.

Draycup, K., Westlake, C., Erickson, V. S., Moser, D. K., Caldwell, M. L., and Hamilton, M. A. (2003). Perceived control reduces emotional stress in patients with heart failure *Journal of Heart and Lung Transplant*, 22, 90–93.

Dysvik, E., Natvig, G. K., Eikeland, O.-J., and Lindstrom, T. C. (2005). Coping with chronic pain. *International Journal* of *Nursing Studies*, 42, 297–305.

Elwood, R. W., and Jacobson, N. S. (1982). Spouses' agreement in reporting their behavioral interactions: A clinical replication. *Journal of Consulting and Clinical Psychology*, 50, 783–784.

Faymonville, M. E., Mambourg, P. H., Joris, J., Vrijens, B., Fissette, J., Albert, A., and Lamy, M. (1997). Psychological approaches during conscious sedation. Hypnotic versus stress reducing strategies: A prospective randomized study. *Pain*, 73, 361–367.

Feltz, D. L., and Landers, D. M. (1983). The effects of mental practice on motor skill learning and performance: A meta-analysis. *Journal of Sports Psychology*, 5, 25–57.

Ferrie, J. E., Shipley, M. J., Newman, K., Stansfeld, S. A., Marmot, M. (2005). Self-reported job insecurity and health and the Whitehall II study: Potential explanations of the relationship. *Social Science and Medicine*, 60, 1593–1602.

Field, T., Hernandez-Reif, M., Diego, M., Schanberg, S., and Kuhn, C. (2005) Cortisol decreases and serotonin and dopamine increase following massage therapy. *International Journal of Neuroscience*, 115, 1397–1413.

Fitzgerald, T. E., Tennen, H., Affleck, G., and Pransky, G. S. (1993). The relative importance of dispositional optimism and control appraisals in quality of life after coronary bypass surgery. *Journal of Behavioral Medicine*, 16, 25–43.

Folkman, S., and Lazarus, R. S. (1988). *Ways of Coping Questionnaire*. Palo Alto, Calif.: Consulting Psychologists Press.

Freud, A. (1946). *The Ego and the Mechanisms of Defense*. New York: International Universities Press.

Friedman, M., and. Rosenman, R. (1974). *Type A Behavior and Your Heart*, New York: Knopf.

Ghaderi, A., and Scott, B. (2000). Coping in dieting and eating disorders: A population-based study. *Journal of Nervous and Mental Disease*, 188, 273–279.

Gold, M. A., and Friedman, S. B. (2000). Cadet basic training: An ethnographic study of stress and coping. *Military Medicine*, 165, 147–152.

Green, B. L., Grace, M. C., and Gleser, G. C. (1985). Identifying survivors at risk: Long-term impairment following the Beverly Hills Supper Club fire. *Journal of Consulting and Clinical Psychology*, 53, 672–678.

Greeno, C. G., and Wing, R. R. (1994). Stress-induced eating. *Psychological Bulletin*, 115, 444–464.

Grunberg, N. E., and Straub, R. O. (1992). The role of gender and taste class and the effects of stress on eating. *Health Psychology*, 11, 97–100.

Hagen, K. A., Myers, B. J., and Mackintosh, V. H. (2005). Hope, social support, and behavioral problems in at-risk children. *American Journal of Orthopsychiatry*, 75, 211–219.

Hammen, C. L., Burge, D., Daley, S. E., Davila, J., Paley, B., and Rudolph, K. D. (1995). Interpersonal attachment cognitions and prediction of symptomatic responses to interpersonal stress. *Journal of Abnormal Psychology* 104, 436–443.

Hanser, S. B., and Mandel, S. E. (2005). The effects of music therapy in cardiac health care. *Cardiology in Review*, 13, 18–23.

Harvey, A. G., and Bryant, R. A. (1998). The relation between acute stress disorder and posttraumatic stress disorder: A prospective evaluation of motor vehicle accident survivors. *Journal of Consulting and Clinical Psychology*, 66, 507–512.

Heimberg, R. G., Liebowitz, M. R., Hope, D. A., and Schneier, F. R. (Eds.) (1995). *Social Phobia: Diagnosis, Assessment and Treatment*. New York: Guilford.

Holmes, D. S. (1984). Meditation and somatic arousal reduction: A review of the experimental evidence. *American Psychologist*, 39, 1–10.

Horney, K. (1937). *The Neurotic Personality of Our Time*. New York: Norton.

Horowitz, S. L. (1970). Strategies within hypnosis for reducing phobic behavior. *Journal of Abnormal Psychology*, 75, 104–112.

Infante, J. R., Torres-Avisbal, M., Pinel, P., Vallejo, J. A., Peran, F., Gonzalez, F., Contreras, P., Pacheco, C., Roldan, A., and Latre, J. M. (2001). Catecholamine levels in practitioners of the transcendental meditation technique. *Physiological Behavior*, 72, 141–146.

Irwin, L. G., Johnson, J. L., and Bottorff, J. L. (2005). Mothers who smoke: Confessions and justifications. *Health Care of Women, International*, 26, 577–590.

Ising, H., and Michalak, R. (2004). Stress effects of noise in a field experiment in comparison to reactions to short term noise exposure in the laboratory. *Noise Health*, 6, 1–7.

Jacobson, E. (1938). *Progressive Relaxation*. Chicago: University of Chicago Press.

Jacobson, N. S., and Moore, D. (1981). Spouses as observers of the events in their relationship. *Journal of Consulting and Clinical Psychology*, 49, 269–277.

_____, and Addis, M. E. (1993). Research on couples and couples therapy: What do we know? Where are we going? *Journal of Consulting and Clinical Psychology*, 61, 85–93.

Jessen, J., Cardiello, F., and Baum, M. M. (1996). Avian companionship in the alleviation of depression, loneliness, and low morale of older adults in skilled rehabilitation units. *Psychological Reports*, 78, 339–348.

Joiner, T. E., Katz, J., and Lew, A. (1999). Harbingers of depressotypic reassurance seeking: Negative life events, increased anxiety, and decreased self-esteem. *Personality and Social Psychology Bulletin*, 25, 630–637.

Kasl, S., Gore, S., and Cobb, S. (1975). The experience of losing a job: Reported changes in health, symptoms and illness behavior. *Psychosomatic Medicine*, 37, 106–122.

Kassel, J. D., Stroud, L. R., and Paronis, C. A. (2003). Smoking, stress, and negative affect: Correlation, causation, and context across stages of smoking. *Psychological Bulletin*, 129, 270–304.

Kato, K., and Pederson, N. L. (2005). Personality and coping: A study of twins reared apart and twins reared together. *Behavior Genetics*, 35, 147–158.

Keefer, L., and Blanchard, E. B. (2001). The effects of relaxation response meditation on the symptoms of irritable bowel syndrome: Results of a controlled treatment study. *Behavior Research and Therapy*, 39, 801–811.

Kenny, D. A., and DePaulo, B. M. (1993). Do people know how others view them? An empirical and theoretical account. *Psychological Bulletin*, 114, 145–161.

Kiecolt-Glaser, J. K., Glaser, R., Shuttleworth, E. C., Dyer, C. S., Ogrocki, P., and Speicher, S. E. (1987). Chronic stress and immunity in family caregivers of Alzheimer's disease. *Psychosomatic Medicine*, 49, 523–535.

_____, Newton, T., Cacioppo, J. T., MacCallum, R. C., Glaser, R., and Malarkey, W. B. (1996). Marital conflict and endocrine function: Are men really more physiologically affected than women? *Journal of Consulting and Clinical Psychology*, 64, 324–332.

Kirsch, I., and Lynn, S. J. (1998). Dissociation theories of hypnosis. *Psychological Bulletin*, 123, 100–115.

Koenig, H. G., Pargament, K. I., and Nielsen, J. (1998). Religious coping and health status in medically ill hospitalized older adults. *Journal of Nervous and Mental Disease*, 186, 513–521.

_____, Hays, J. C., Larson, D. B., George, L. K., Cohen, H. J., McCullough, M. E., Meader, K. G. and Blazer, D. G. (1999). Does religious attendance prolong survival? A six-year follow-up study of 3,968 older adults. *Journal of Gerontology*, 54 A, M370-M 376.

Kole-Snijders, A. M. J., Vlaeyen, J. W. S., Goossens, M. E. J. B, Rutten-van Molken M. P. M. H., Heuts, P. H. T. G., Van Breukelen, G., and van Eek, H. (1999). Chronic low back pain: What does cognitive coping skills training add to operant behavioral treatment? Results of a randomized clinical trial. *Journal of Consulting and Clinical Psychology*, 67, 931–944.

Kouvonen, A., Kivimaki, M., Cox, S. J., Cox, T., and Vahtera, J. (2005). Relationship between work stress and body mass index among 45,810 female and male employees. *Psychosomatic Medicine*, 67, 577–583.

Krause, N. (2004). Stressors in highly valued roles, meaning in life, and the physical health status of older adults. *Journal of Gerontology B: Psychological Sciences, Social Sciences*, 59B , 5287–5297.

Kray, L. J., Thompson, L., and Galinsky, A. (2001). Battle of the sexes: Gender stereotype confirmation and reactance in negotiations. *Journal of Personality and Social Psychology*, 80, 942–958.

Krohne, H. W., and Slangen, K. E. (2005). Influence of social support on adaptation to surgery. *Health Psychology*, 24, 101–105.

Largo-Wight, E., Peterson, M. P., and Chen, W. W. (2005). Perceived problem solving, stress, and health among college students. *American Journal of Health Behavior*, 29, 360–370.

Lazarus, R. S. (1966). *Psychological Stress and the Coping Process*. New York: McGraw-Hill.

_____. (2000). Toward better research on stress and coping. *American Psychologist*, 55, 665–673.

Levinson, W., Roter, D., Mullooly, J., Dull, V., and Frankel, R. (1997). Physician-patient communication: The relationship with malpractice claims among primary care physicians and surgeons. *Journal of the American Medical Association*, 277, 533–559.

Lindahl, M., Tores, T., and Lindblad, F. (2005). Test performance and self-esteem in relation to experienced stress in Swedish six and ninth graders — saliva cortisol levels and psychological reactions to demands. *Acta Pediatrica*, 94, 489–495.

Luckow, A., Reifman, A., and McIntosh, D.N. (1998). Gender differences in coping: A meta-analysis. Poster session presented at the 106th annual convention of the American Psychological Association. San Francisco, CA.

Lyubomirsky, S., Tucker, K. L., Caldwell, N. D., and Berg, K. (1999). Why ruminators are poor problem solvers: Clues from the phenomenology of dysphoric rumination. *Journal of Personality and Social Psychology*, 77, 1041–1060.

McAuley, E., Blissmer, B., Katula, J., Duncan, T. E., and Mihalko, S. L. (2000). Physical activity, self-esteem, and self-efficacy relationships in older adults: A randomized controlled trial. *Annals of Behavioral Medicine*, 22, 131–139.

McEwen, B. S. (2005). Glucose corticoids, depression, and mood disorders: Structural remodeling in the brain. *Metabolism*, 54 (5 Supplement 1) 20–23.

McGuire, P. A. (1999). Workers' stress, health reaching critical point. *APA Monitor*, 30, 1.

McIntosh, D. N., Silver, R. C., and Wortman, C. B. (1993). Religion's role in adjustment to a negative life event: Coping with the loss of a child. *Journal of Personality and Social Psychology*, 65, 812–821.

Mantooth, R. (2005, November 23, updated). Toxicity, Benzodiazepine. http://www.emedicine.com/emerg/topic58.htm.

Marchand, A., Demers, A., and Durand, P. (2005). Does work really cause distress? The contributions of occupational structure and work organization to the experience of psychological distress. *Social Science and Medicine*, 61, 1–14.

Marco, C. A., Neale, J. M., Schwartz, J. E., Shiffman, S., and Stone, A. A. (1999). Coping with daily events and short-term mood changes: An unexpected failure to observe the effects of coping. *Journal of Consulting and Clinical Psychology*, 67, 755–764.

Markman, H. J., Renick, M. J., Floyd, F. J., Stanley, S. M., and Clements, M. (1993). Preventing marital distress through communication and conflict management training: A 4- and 5-year follow-up. *Journal of Consulting and Clinical Psychology*, 61, 70–77.

Marlowe, N. (1998). Self-efficacy moderates the impact of stressful events on headache. *Headache*, 38, 662–67.

Martin, R. A. (2001). Humor, laughter, and physical health: Methodological issues and research findings. *Psychological Bulletin*, 127, 504–519.

Mason, J. W. (1975). A historical view of the stress field. Parts 1 and 2. *Journal of Human Stress*. March issue.

Meprobamate. Http://www.nlm.nih.gov/medlineplus/druginfo/uspdi/2023458.html.

The Merck Manual. Volume 1. General Medicine 15th edition (1987). Rahway, New York: Merck and Company.

Meyer, M. (2000). There's help for social phobia. *Parade*, December 17, 10.

Meyerhoff, J. L., Norris, W., Saviolakis, G. A., Wollert, T., Burge, B., Atkins, V., and Spielberger, C. (2004). Evaluating performance of law enforcement personnel during a stressful training scenario. *Annals of the New York Academy of Sciences*, 1032, 250–253.

Mezulis, A. H., Abramson, L. Y., Hyde, J. S., and Hankin, B. L. (2004). Is there a universal positivity bias in attributions? A meta-analytic review of individual, developmental, and cultural differences in the sell-serving attributional bias. *Psychological Bulletin*, 130, 711–747.

Miller, T. Q., Smith, T. W., Turner, C. W., Guijarro, M. L., and Hullet, A. J. (1996). A meta-analytic review of research on hostility and physical health. *Psychological Bulletin,* 119, 322–348.

Mohr, C. D., Armeli, S., Tennen, H., Carney, M. A., Afflect, G., and Hromi, A. (2001). Daily interpersonal experiences, context, and alcohol consumption: Crying in your beer and toasting good times. *Journal of Personality and Social Psychology*, 80, 489–500. Moyer, C. A., Rounds, J., and Hannum, J. W. (2004). A Meta-analysis of massage therapy research. *Psychological Bulletin*, 130, 3–18.

Moyer, C., Rounds, J., & Hannum, J.W. (2004). A meta-analysis of massage therapy research. *Psychological Bulletin*, 130, 3–18.

Murray, C. D. R., Flynn, J., Ratcliffe, L., Jacyna, M. R., Kamm, M. A., and Emmanuel, A. V. (2004). Effect of acute physical and psychological stress on gut autonomic innervation in irritable bowel syndrome. *Gastroenterology*, 127, 1695–1703.

Murray, S. L., Holmes, J. G., and Griffin, D. W. (1996). The benefits of positive illusions: idealizations and the construction of satisfaction in close relationships. *Journal of Personality and Social Psychology*, 70, 79–98.

Nabetani, T., and Tokunaga, M. ( 2001). The effect of short-term (10- and 15-min) running at self-selected intensity on mood alteration. *Journal of Physiological Anthropology and Applied Human Sciences,* 20, 231–239.

Nagengast, S. L., Baun, M., Megel, M. M., and Leibowitz, J. M. (1997). The effect of the presence of a companion animal on physiological arousal and behavioral distress in children during a physical examination. *Journal of Pediatric Nursing*, 12, 323–330.

Neckowitz, P., and Morrison, T. L. (1991). Interactional coping strategies of normal-weight bulimic women in intimate and non-intimate stressful situations. *Psychological Reports*, 69, 1167–1175.

Nesbitt, P. D. (1973). Smoking, physiological arousal, and emotional response. *Journal of Personality and Social Psychology*, 25, 137–144.

Nicklaus, J. (1976). *Play Better Golf.* New York: King Features.

Noble, J., and McConkey, K. M. (1995). Hypnotic sex change: Creating and challenging a delusion in the laboratory. *Journal of Abnormal Psychology*, 104, 69–74.

Noguchi, Y. (1995). Cyber-catharsis: Bloggers use web sites as therapy. *Washington Post,* October 12, A-1.

North, C. S., Pfefferbaum, B., Narayanan, P., Thielman, S., McCoy, G., Dumont, C., Kawasaki, A., Ryosho, N., and Spitznagel, E. L. (2005). Comparison of post-disaster psychiatric disorders after terrorist bombings in Nairobi and Oklahoma City. *British Journal of Psychiatry*, 186, 487–493.

O'Leary, A. (1990). Stress, emotion, and human immune functioning. *Psychological Bulletin*, 108, 363–382.

Ollendick, T. H., and Gruen, G. E. (1972). Treatment of a bodily injury phobia with implosive therapy. *Journal of Consulting and Clinical Psychology*, 38, 389–393.

Ozer, E. J., Best, S. R., Lipsey, T. L., and Weiss, D. S. (2003). Predictors of posttraumatic stress disorder and symptoms in adults: A meta-analysis. *Psychological Bulletin*, 129, 52–73.

Pargament, K. I., Koenig, H. G., Tarakeshwar, N., and Hahn, J. (2000). Negative religious coping as a predictor of mortality among medically ill elderly patients: A two year longitudinal study. Paper presented at the annual meeting of the American Psychological Association, Washington, D.C.

Patterson, D. R., and Jensen, M. P. (2003). Hypnosis and clinical pain. *Psychological Bulletin*, 129, 495–521.

Peale, N. V. (1952). *The Power of Positive Thinking.* New York: Prentice-Hall.

Perry, J., and Kardos, M. (1995). A review of research using the defense mechanisms rating scales. In H. Conte and R. Plutchik (Eds.), *Ego Defenses: Theory and Measurement* (pp 283–299). New York: Wiley.

Peterson, C. (2000). The future of optimism. *American Psychologist*, 55, 44–55.

Peterson, L. (1989). Coping by children undergoing stressful medical procedures: Some conceptual, methodological, and therapeutic issues. *Journal of Consulting and Clinical Psychology*, 57, 380–387.

Phenobarbital. Medline Plus. National Library of Medicine. Http://www.nlm.nih.gov/medlineplus/druginfo.

Purdon, C. (1999). Thought suppression and psychopathology. *Behavior Research and Therapy*, 37, 1029–1054.

Reed, G. M., Kemeny, M. E., Taylor S. E., Wang, H-Y. J., and Visscher, B. R. (1994). "Realistic acceptance" as a predictor of decreased survival time in gay men with AIDS. *Health Psychology*, 13, 299–307.

Reese-Weber, M. (2000). Middle and late adolescents' conflict resolution skills with siblings: Associations with interparental and parent-adolescent conflict resolution. *Journal of Youth and Adolescence*, 29, 697–711.

Revenson, T. A., and Felton, B. J. (1989). Disability and coping as predictors of psychological adjustment to rheumatoid arthritis. *Journal of Consulting and Clinical Psychology*, 57, 344–348.

Robbins, L. (2004). *Going Bridal: How to Get Married without Losing Your Mind.* New York: Contemporary.

Robbins, P. R., and Tanck, R. H. (1970). The Repression-Sensitization scale, dreams, and dream associations. *Journal of Clinical Psychology*, 26, 219–221.

_____, Meyersberg, H. A., and Tanck, R. H. (1974). Interpersonal stress and physical complaints. *Journal of Personality Assessment*, 38, 578–585.

_____, and Tanck, R. H. (1978). A factor analysis of coping behaviors. *Journal of Clinical Psychology*, 34, 379–380.

_____ (1982). Further research using a psychological diary technique to investigate psychosomatic relationships. *Journal of Clinical Psychology*, 38, 356–359.

_____ (1983). *Marijuana: A short course: Update for the '80s. Second edition.* Brookline Village, MA: Branden Press.

_____ (1984). Sex differences in problems related to depression. *Sex Roles*, 11, 703–707.

_____ and Tanck, R. H. (1985, October 2). There are ways to fight college anxiety and stress. *Washington Post.* Health Section.

_____ and Tanck, R. H. (1992). Stress, coping techniques and depressed affect: Explorations within a normal sample. *Psychological Reports,* 70, 147–152.

_____ and Tanck, R. H. (1995). University students' preferred choices for social support. *Journal of Social Psychology,* 135, 775–776.

_____ (1998). *Anorexia and Bulimia.* Springfield, N. J.: Enslow.

Robichaud, M., and Dugas, M. J. (2005). Negative problem orientation (Part II): Construct validity and specificity to worry. *Behavior Research and Therapy,* 43, 403–412.

Robinson, N. S., Garber, J., and Hilsman, R. (1995). Cognitions and stress: Direct and moderating effects on depressive verses externalizing symptoms during the junior high school transition. *Journal of Abnormal Psychology,* 104, 453–463.

Rosenstock, I. M. (1966). Why people use health services. *Milbank Memorial Fund Quarterly,* 44, 94–127.

Rotter, J. (1966). Generalized expectancies for internal verses external control of reinforcement. *Psychological Monographs,* 80, (1, Whole Number 609).

Salmon, P. (2001). Effects of physical exercise on anxiety, depression, and sensitivity to stress: A unifying theory. *Clinical Psychology Review,* 21, 33–61.

Segal, J. (1973). Long-term psychological and physical effects of the POW experience: A review of the literature. Report No. 74–2. Naval Health Research Center, San Diego, CA.

Segerstrom, S. C., Taylor, S. E., Kemeny, M. E., and Fahey, J. L. (1998). Optimism is associated with mood, coping, and immune changes in response to stress. *Journal of Personality and Social Psychology,* 74, 1646–1655.

Segerstrom, S. C., Miller, G. E. (2004). Psychological stress and the human immune system: A meta-analytic study of 30 years of inquiry. *Psychological Bulletin,* 130, 601–630.

Shepperd, J. A., Findley-Klein, C., Kwavnick, K. D., Walker, D., and Perez, S. (2000). Bracing for loss. *Journal of Personality and Social Psychology,* 78, 620–634.

Shin, L. M., McNally, R. J., Kosslyn, S. M., Thompson, W. L., Rauch, S. L., Alpert, N. M., Metzger, L. J., Lasko, N. B., Orr, S. P., and Pitman, R. K. (1999). Regional cerebral blood flow during script-driven imagery in childhood sexual abuse-related PTSD, a PET investigation. *American Journal of Psychiatry,* 156, 575–584.

_____, Wright, C. I., Cannistraro, P. A., Wedig, M. M., McMullin, K., Martis, B., Macklin, M. L., Lasko, N. B., Cavanagh, S. R., Krangel, T. S., Orr, S. P., Pitman, R.K., Whalen, P. J., and Rauch, S. L. (2005). A functional magnetic resonance imaging study of amygdala and medial prefrontal cortex responses to overtly presented fearful faces in posttraumatic stress disorder. *Archives of General Psychiatry,* 62, 273–281.

Shipley, R. H., Butt, J. H., Horwitz, B., and Farbry, J. E. (1978). Preparation for a stressful medical procedure: Effect of amount of stimulus pre-exposure and coping style. *Journal of Consulting and Clinical Psychology,* 46, 499–507.

Skinner, E. A., Edge, K., Altman, J., and Sherwood, H. (2003). Searching for the structure of coping: A review and critique of category systems for classifying ways of coping. *Psychological Bulletin,* 129, 216–269.

Smith, R. E., and Sharpe, T. M. (1970). Treatment of a school phobia with implosive therapy. *Journal of Consulting and Clinical Psychology,* 35, 239–243.

Steginga, S. K., Pinnock, C., Gardner, M., Gardiner, R. A. F., and Dunn, J. (2005). Evaluating peer support for prostate cancer: The prostate cancer peer support inventory. *British Association of Urological Surgeons,* 95, 46–50.

Sternberg, R. J., and Dobson, D. M. (1987). Resolving interpersonal conflicts: An analysis of stylistic consistency. *Journal of Personality and Social Psychology,* 52, 794–812.

Stone, A. A., and Shiffman, S. S. (1994). Ecological momentary assessment (EMA) in behavioral medicine. *Annals of Behavioral Medicine*, 16, 199–202.

Sullivan, P. (2005). Inventor of Valium, once the most often prescribed drug, dies. *Washington Post*, October 1, 1.

Symonds, P. M. (1946). *The Dynamics of Human Adjustment*. New York: Appleton-Century.

Takahashi, K., Iwase, M., Yamashita, K., Tatsumoto, Y., Ue, H., and Kuratsune, H. (2001). The elevation of natural killer cell activity induced by laughter in a crossover designed study. *International Journal of Molecular Medicine*, 8, 645–650.

Taylor, S. E., Pham, L. B., Rivkin, I. D., and Armor, D. A. (1998). Harnessing the imagination: Mental simulation, self-regulation and coping. *American Psychologist*, 53, 429–439.

Taylor, S. E., Klein, L. C., Lewis, B. P., Gruenwald, T. L., Gurung, R. A. R., and Updegraff, J. A. (2000a). Biobehavioral responses to stress in females: Tend-and-befriend, not fight-or-flight. *Psychological Review*, 107, 411–429.

Taylor, S. E., Kemeny, M. E., Reed, G. M., Bower, J. E., and Gruenewald, T. L. (2000b). Psychological resources, positive illusions and health. *American Psychologist*, 55, 99- 109.

Tennen, H., Affleck, G., Armeli, S., and Carney, M. A. (2000). A daily process approach to coping: Linking theory, research, and practice. *American Psychologist*, 55, 626–636.

Thompson, L. (1990). Negotiation behavior and outcomes: Empirical evidence and theoretical issues. *Psychological Bulletin*, 108, 515–532.

Thoresen, C. J., Kaplan, S. A., Barsky, A. P., deChermont, K., and Warren, C. R. (2003). The affective underpinnings of job perceptions and attitudes: A meta-analytic review and integration. *Psychological Bulletin*, 129, 914–945.

Troop, N. A., Holbrey, A., Trowler, R., and Treasure, J. L. (1994). Ways of coping with women with eating disorders. *Journal of Nervous and Mental Disease*, 182, 535–540.

Walton, K. G., Schneider, R. H., Nidich, S. I., Salerno, J. W., Nordstrom, C. K., and Mertz, C. N. B. ( 2002). Psychosocial stress and cardiovascular disease. Part 2: Effectiveness of the transcendental meditation program in treatment and prevention. *Behavioral Medicine*, 28, 106–123

_____, Schneider, R. H., Salerno, J. W., and Nidich, S. I. (2005). Psychosocial stress and cardiovascular diseases. Part 3: Clinical and policy implications of research on the transcendental meditation program. *Behavioral Medicine*, 30, 173–183.

Wanzer, M., Booth-Butterfield, M., Booth-Butterfield, S. (2005). "If we didn't use humor, we'd cry": Humorous coping communications in health care settings. *Journal of Health Communication*, 10, 105–125.

Waugh, J. C. (1994). *The Class of 1846: From West Point to Appomattox: Stonewall Jackson, George McClellan, and Their Brothers*. New York: Warner.

Weisz, J. R., McCabe, M. A., and Dennig, M. D. (1994). Primary and secondary control among children undergoing medical procedures: Adjustment as a function of coping style. *Journal of Consulting and Clinical Psychology*, 62, 324–332.

Wenzlaff, R. M., and Wegner, D. M. (2000). Thought suppression. *Annual Review of Psychology*, 51, 59–91.

White, J. M. (1999). Effects of relaxing music on cardiac autonomic balance and anxiety after acute myocardial infarction. *American Journal of Critical Care*, 8, 220–227.

Winerman, L. (2005). A virtual cure. *Monitor on Psychology*, 36, 87–89.

Wood, J. M., Bootzin, R. R., Rosenhan, D., Nolen-Hoeksema, S., and Jourden, F. (1992). Effects of the 1989 San Francisco earthquake on frequency and content of nightmares. *Journal of Abnormal Psychology,* 101, 219–224.

Youell, K. J., and McCullough, J. P. (1975). Behavioral treatment of mucous colitis. *Journal of Consulting and Clinical Psychology,* 43, 740–745.

Zuroff, D. C., Blatt, S. J., Sotsky, S. M., Krupnick, J. L., Martin, D. J., Sanislow, III, C. A., and Simmons, S. (2000). Relation of therapeutic alliance and perfectionism to outcome in brief outpatient therapy of depression. *Journal of Consulting and Clinical Psychology,* 68, 114–124.

# Index